READING UNRULY

SYMPLOKĒ STUDIES IN CONTEMPORARY THEORY

Series Editor: Jeffrey R. Di Leo

Reading Unruly

INTERPRETATION *and*
its ETHICAL DEMANDS

ZAHI ZALLOUA

University of Nebraska Press / Lincoln and London

© 2014 by the Board of Regents
of the University of Nebraska

Acknowledgments for the use of copyrighted material appear on page x, which constitutes an extension of the copyright page.

All rights reserved
Manufactured in the United
States of America

Library of Congress Cataloging-in-Publication Data

Zalloua, Zahi Anbra, 1971–
Reading Unruly: Interpretation and Its
Ethical Demands / Zahi Zalloua.
pages cm.—(Symplokē Studies
in Contemporary Theory)
Includes bibliographical references and index.
ISBN 978-0-8032-4627-0 (pbk.: alk. paper)—ISBN 978-0-8032-5468-8 (epub)—ISBN 978-0-8032-5470-1 (mobi)—ISBN 978-0-8032-5465-7 (pdf) 1. French literature—History and criticism—Theory, etc. 2. Literature and morals. 3. Disorderly conduct in literature. 4. Aesthetics in literature. 5. Ethics in literature. I. Title.
PQ142.Z35 2014
840.9'355—dc23
2013041119

Set in Arno by Laura Wellington.

To Nicole Simek

Contents

Acknowledgments
ix

Introduction:
An Ethics of the Unruly
1

1. Montaigne:
The Accidental Theorist
21

2. Diderot's *Rameau's Nephew*:
Allegory and the
Mind-and-Body Problem
43

3. Translating *Modernité*: Narrative,
Violence, and Aesthetics in
Baudelaire's *Spleen of Paris*
65

4. Living with Nausea:
Sartre and Roquentin
87

5. Intoxicating Meaning: Alain
Robbe-Grillet's *Jealousy*
111

6. Fidelity to Sexual Difference:
Marguerite Duras's *The Ravishing
of Lol Stein*
129

Conclusion: Unruly Theory
149

Notes
155

Works Cited
185

Index
201

Acknowledgments

Reading Unruly is the product of many voices. I am deeply indebted to my colleagues as well as to my students at Whitman College. Teaching supplemented my theorizing about the unruly in ways that I could have never anticipated. And for this, I am truly grateful. At Whitman, I have especially benefited from exchanges with Paul Apostolidis, Shampa Biswas, Aaron Bobrow-Strain, Bill Bogard, Dana Burgess, Chetna Chopra, Theresa DiPasquale, Scott Elliot, Rebecca Hanrahan, Tim Kaufman-Osborn, Gaurav Majumdar, Bruce Magnusson, Jeanne Morefield, Suzanne Morrissey, Jason Pribilsky, Matt Reynolds, Lynn Sharp, Bob Tobin, Jon Walters, and Melissa Wilcox.

Outside Whitman, I am grateful to my brother Mounir, whose encouragement and confidence in my work never wavered. Bits and pieces of this book were initially presented at conferences and seminars. For their insightful and kind comments, I want to thank Katie Chenoweth, Larry Kritzman, Kathleen Perry Long, Sophia A. McClennen, Uppinder Mehan, Hassan Melehy, Christian Moraru, Paul Allen Miller, Brian O'Keeffe, Richard Regosin, François Rigolot, and Tom Trezise. A special thanks to Jim Phelan and the participants of the 2008 NEH seminar "Narrative Theory," where I first articulated my reading of Baudelaire, and to Ann Hartle and her seminar "Montaigne and the Origins of Modern Philosophy," funded by the Institute for the History of Philosophy.

My sincere thanks to the series editor Jeffrey R. Di Leo for his commitment to this project as well as to Kristen Elias Rowley and the staff of the University of Nebraska Press for their attentiveness to my manuscript. My deepest gratitude goes to Nicole Simek, whose generous eye for the unruly made this book possible.

ACKNOWLEDGMENTS

Portions of my book appeared in a different form, and I am grateful for the permission to reproduce these sections: the introduction in "Fidelity to the Unruly," originally published in *SubStance* 38, no. 3 (2009): 3–17, © 2009 by the Board of Regents of the University of Wisconsin System, reproduced courtesy of the University of Wisconsin Press; chapter 1 in "Montaigne and the Levinasian Other," *L'Esprit Créateur* 46, no. 1 (2006): 86–95, reprinted by permission of the Johns Hopkins University Press; chapter 2 in "The Mind and Body Problem in *Le Neveu de Rameau*," *Symposium* 56, no. 4 (2003): 196–209; chapter 3 in "Baudelaire and the Translation of Modernity," *Romance Notes* 48, no. 1 (2007): 67–78; chapter 4 in "Sartre's *La Nausée*: Roquentin and the Question of Identity," *Romance Quarterly* 49, no. 4 (2002): 249–59; chapter 5 in "Alain Robbe-Grillet's *La Jalousie*: Realism and the Ethics of Reading," *Journal of Narrative Theory* 38, no. 1 (2008): 13–36; and chapter 6 in "Reading Duras's *Le Ravissement de Lol V. Stein* like a Feminist," *Women in French Studies* 10 (2002): 228–42.

READING UNRULY

Introduction

AN ETHICS OF THE UNRULY

> There is ethics — that is to say, an injunction which
> cannot be grounded in ontology — in so far as there is a
> crack in the ontological edifice of the universe: at its most
> elementary, ethics designates fidelity to this crack.
>
> SLAVOJ ŽIŽEK

The late twentieth century witnessed unprecedented attention to ethics in literary studies. This burgeoning academic interest proved strong enough to earn the label "Ethical Turn," a term that points to an undeniable shift in the concerns of interpretive communities but risks homogenizing the unruly voices responsible for such a change.[1] A genealogy of the turn quickly reveals its contested origins, its fraught beginnings, and its uncertain duration. Is/was the "Ethical Turn" a mere moment in the cyclical history of interpretive turns, situated between the "Linguistic Turn" and the nascent "Aesthetic Turn," with the "Political Turn" eagerly waiting in the hermeneutic queue?[2] While debates over the function of literary criticism surely date back to the very inception of literature, Frank Kermode detects among contemporary critics an unparalleled hostility to both the ethical value of criticism (which, in the past, "was extremely important; it could be taught; it was an influence for civilization and even for personal amendment"[3]) and the aesthetic value of literature in its own right.[4] It might be tempting to see the "turn to ethics" as a kind of exorcism of the post-68 mentality that gave us the slogan of "the death of the author" and the rise of symptomatic readings.[5] The turn to ethics would be, in this respect, tantamount to a return to the so-called older dispensation. By contrast, Wayne C. Booth resists such a nostalgic and potentially reactionary move in his 1988 *The Company We Keep: An Ethics of Fiction*, and adopts a broader and less exclusionary definition of ethics, not only taking stock of a new ethical sensibility sweeping literary studies but also, and perhaps more importantly, reading it back into its most trenchant opponents:

> I'm thinking here not only of the various new overtly ethical and political challenges to "formalism": by feminist critics asking embarrassing questions about a male-dominated literary canon and what it has done to the "consciousness" of both men and women; by black critics pursuing Paul Moses's kind of question about racism in American classics; by neo-Marxists exploring class biases in European literary traditions; by religious critics attacking modern literature for its "nihilism" or "atheism." I am thinking more of the way in which even those critics who work hard to purge themselves of all but the most abstract formal interests turn out to have an ethical program in mind — a belief that a given way of reading, or a given kind of genuine literature, is what will do us most good.[6]

The following study takes seriously the invitation to adopt a more inclusive approach to ethics (one that brings contesting viewpoints together under the umbrella of ethical criticism) but remains wary of defining an ethics of reading as a commitment to the "most good," a term at once disarming for its obviousness (who, among ethical critics, doubts that a literary ethical sensibility is beneficial?) and alarming for its vagueness (what is meant by beneficial or good?). *Reading Unruly: Interpretation and Its Ethical Demands* advocates an ethics of interpretation that foregrounds fidelity to literature's unruliness, that is, its resistance to hermeneutic mastery, its ungovernable character. Such an ethics deviates from the paradigmatic model of Neo-Aristotelian tradition, according to which the reader's ethical task requires the faithful reconstruction of the beliefs, values, and norms that the author desires to communicate.[7] While this tradition emphasizes questions of exemplarity — the belief that literature teaches us through examples and counterexamples — *Reading Unruly* conceives of fidelity as related less to the interpretation of an artwork's content or message than to the reader's receptivity and responsiveness to it.

Attesting faithfully to the unruly, and to the "singularity of literature," to borrow Derek Attridge's suggestive formulation, means vigilantly resisting literature's conflation with moral philosophy. Disentangling a literary work's ethical concern from its universalist aspiration is perhaps the most distinctive feature of this mode of ethical criticism. An ethics of reading articulated in these terms owes much to literary theorists such as Roland Barthes and Maurice Blanchot, who constantly underscored literature's recalcitrance, as well as to Jacques Derrida and Emmanuel Levinas, whose philosophical work brought about a shift in hermeneutic climate and reorientation of ethics toward responsiveness.[8] *Reading Unruly* puts these disparate lines of thought into relation with one another in the goal not of harmonizing their contradictions but of exploring their productive tensions in an effort to think the future of an ethics/aesthetics of difference and its multiple challenges.

What is in contention in debates over the place of alterity and universalism in ethical criticism is the paradigmatic status of the face-to-face encounter as a fruitful model, or at the very least a source of inspiration, for thinking differently the relation to the literary. Analogously related to the self's exposure to the other, characterized in Levinasian terms by excess and opacity, the reader's relation to the work, on this model, takes the form of an "interpellation."[9] In the act of reading, the reader confronts a "double bind," two competing and conflicting injunctions. The first is to thematize or make sense of the work's aesthetic otherness — that is, to adhere to the rules of literary discourse, the protocols of commentary. The second, however, is to attend to the work's inventiveness — its seductive refractoriness — to recognize that the attempt to give meaning and the appeal to contextual markers (cultural, historical, or authorial) might very well elucidate aspects of a literary work but can never exhaust that meaning nor fully meet or answer its ethical demands. Needless to say, the movement between these two injunctions is shot through with hesitation. "To find oneself reading an inventive work," as Attridge puts it, "is to find oneself subject to certain obligations — to respect its otherness, to respond to its singularity, to avoid reducing it to the familiar and the utilitarian even while attempting to comprehend by relating it to these."[10]

The double bind reminds the reader of his or her status as an interpreter. In rejecting consumption as a preferred model of reading, the responsive reader that emerges from a Levinasian-inspired ethics resembles Barthes's producer of text, a reader who actively engages "writerly" (or *scriptible*) fiction by becoming a willing collaborator in the production of its meaning(s) — by becoming an *inventive reader*, so to speak.[11] Breaking with the consumerist model of reading, Barthes calls for the radicalization of the "work of commentary," so that the task of the reader no longer consists in slavishly following the "classic text," nor in repeating it (via a faithful commentary), but in *"manhandl[ing]* the text, *interrupt[ing]* it,"[12] demystifying its apparent "naturalness" by revealing its "constructedness" (its ideological staging of meaning as something transparent and self-evident). More recently, Slavoj Žižek has advanced a similar agonistic model of interpretation, deploying the shock of short-circuiting as a metaphor for critical reading:

> A short circuit occurs when there is a faulty connection in the network — faulty, of course, from the standpoint of the network's smooth functioning. Is not the shock of short-circuiting, therefore, one of the best metaphors for critical reading? Is not one of the most effective critical procedures to cross wires that do not usually touch: to take a major classic (text, author, notion), and read it in a short-circuiting way, through the lens of a "minor" author, text, or conceptual apparatus . . . ? If the minor reference is well chosen, such a procedure can lead to insights which completely shatter and undermine our common perceptions.[13]

The Žižekian reader performs a symptomatic reading — a more radicalized version of Ricoeur's "hermeneutics of suspicion" — challenging the text's surface meaning in order to disclose its blind spots or "unthought."[14] Toward that end, the literary text (or any text) is no longer to be conceived in isolation, only in terms of its own discourse. Appeals to other fields of study (psychoanalysis, anthropology, philosophy, sociology, etc.) are particularly welcome, since their otherness plays a crucial role in "short-circuiting" the source text.

Žižek's daring electrician and Barthes's manhandler of text are both endowed with a strong sense of agency — an agency necessary, in this model, to the execution and performance of productive readings. Yet such a model poses a number of problems: What or who really gets short-circuited here? Do these models not conflate the text as such and dominant interpretations of the text (interpretations legitimized by a given interpretive community)? Is agency clearly on the side of the reader? Or is it on the side of the inventive works — unruly texts that short-circuit the dogmatic or doctrinal reader?[15]

In *The Pleasure of the Text*, Barthes can be seen as exploring the latter alternative, tying unruliness more closely to literary texts themselves, and more specifically, to the different kinds of pleasures that they solicit from their readers. For Barthes, the experience of *plaisir* (pleasure) results from a "*comfortable* practice of reading,"[16] a communicable knowledge about the reader's societal values, whereas the experience of *jouissance* (a sexualized sense of pleasure [from the verb *jouir*, meaning "to come"] that evokes, at once, joy and dismay) "imposes a state of loss"[17] by jolting the reader out of docility and complacency, out of his or her sense of communal belonging. Yet Barthes himself refuses a strict opposition between the two. He maintains that the text of pleasure (what he had previously characterized as the "readerly" or classic text), or more generally, any experience of aesthetics, holds the potential for unruliness, because the idea of pleasure itself — or rather the insistence on pleasure — "can embarrass the text's return to morality, to truth: to the morality of truth: it is an oblique, a drag anchor, so to speak, without which the theory of the text would revert to a centered system, a philosophy of meaning."[18] The reader's taste for pleasure, then, produces cognitive friction, blocking the most blatant forms of instrumentalization and commodification: literature's reduction to either scientific-like knowledge or pure didacticism. At the same time, however, pleasure and the processes of normalization are not, strictly speaking, at odds with one another:

> Now the subject who keeps the two texts in his field and in his hands the reins of pleasure and bliss is an anachronic subject, for he simultaneously and contradictorily participates in the profound hedonism of all culture (which permeates him quietly under cover of an *art de vivre* shared by the old books) and in the destruction of that culture: he enjoys the consistency of his selfhood (that is his pleasure) and seeks its loss (that is his bliss). He is a subject split twice over, doubly perverse.[19]

Hedonism both perpetuates the principle of identity and calls for its dissolution; it sustains and interrupts the subject's self-sufficiency or *conatus essendi*, the desire to persist in being. For the reader, then, hedonism offers the possibility for both socialization (yet another instantiation, albeit a more "pleasurable" one, of the process of subjectivization[20]) and emancipation (the possibility of "get[ting] free from oneself" [*se déprendre de soi-même*]," as Foucault puts it).[21] While the concept of the text of *jouissance* qualifies the model of the reader as producer, it does not really break its general mold; behind the orgasmic experience of self-dissolution lies a narcissistic reader, freely desiring and indulging in eroticized fantasies.[22] Unlike the writerly, which might be said to please the reader by submitting to his or her phantasms, the unruly, as I have been describing it, interpellates; it solicits from the reader an ethical response. Unruly works call upon the reader not only to produce and delight in potentially endless interpretations but also to hesitate, to sustain their singularity, and to resist the narcissistic assumption that they exist purely for oneself.[23] To put it differently, answerability necessitates an alternative mode of reading, one that moves beyond the dualistic, stale model of a passive/active consumption.

In *The Writing of the Disaster*, Maurice Blanchot ostensibly gestures toward such a reading:

> There is an active, productive way of reading which produces text and reader and thus transports us. There is a passive kind of reading which betrays the text while appearing to submit to it, by giving the illusion that the text exists objectively, fully, sovereignly: as one whole. Finally, *there is the reading that is no longer passive, but is passivity's reading. It is without pleasure, without joy; it escapes both comprehension and desire*. It is like the nocturnal vigil, that "inspiring" insomnia when, all having been said, "Saying" [*le Dire*] is heard, and the testimony of the last witness is pronounced.[24]

Blanchot's last type of reading — "passivity's reading" — undercuts any instrumental relation to the text. His analysis invites us to reevaluate the one-dimensional model of reading as consumption but also to question the reader's autonomy and agency (actualized in the pleasurable practice of interpretation, that is, an interpretation without hesitation) and the communicative dimension of reading and writing, since the "Saying" of the text is ultimately incommensurable with anything said or spoken; it expresses no meaning. Recalling Levinas's philosophy of the other, this uncanny model of reading compels us to reconfigure what it means to *care* — to develop a genuine openness to textual otherness that is at odds with the ideal of self-care as self-mastery.[25] In *Totality and Infinity*, Levinas locates the ethical moment in the face-to-face encounter with the other, which he describes as a primordial moment of cognitive frustration — since the other's face "exceed[s] *the idea of the other in me*" — that brings into question the autonomy, spontaneity, and self-sufficiency of the self.[26] The face of the other interrupts the self's habitual economy, its tendency to reduce otherness to the order of the Same. Like Levinas, Blanchot foregrounds the exposure to otherness in his experience of literature, making it analogous to the Levinasian encounter with the face of the other.[27] Unruliness, in this inflection, is more or less synonymous with pure difference, the anarchic and the non-thematizable. Though appealing in its alternative approach to literary criticism (criticism as a determination of textual meaning or an appreciation of a work's formal features), the emphasis on radical alterity, on that which is putatively beyond or even prior to discursivity, threatens to transform the literary work into an unspeakable, unknowable, and unassayable mystical Text.[28]

So is Levinasian otherness truly a viable model for an ethics of the unruly? Alain Badiou has taken issue with Levinas's dominant, cult-like status in ethical circles, and with his having almost single-handedly framed all of ethical discourse in terms of an "ethics of difference" (a category under which he lumps together, not unproblematically, multiculturalism, postcolonialism, and poststructuralism).[29] Badiou scrutinizes, in particular, Levinas's contention that the other is radically other: "The other always resembles me too much for the hypothesis of an originary exposure of his alterity to be *necessarily* true."[30] For Levinas, he argues, the source of the other's radical otherness or transcendent alterity must originate elsewhere, in an absolute Other, which can, ultimately, only be God: "There can be no ethics without God the ineffable" (22). When one tries to secularize Levinas's ethics of difference, by bracketing the divine, as it were, the result is simply a "decomposed religion," worth no more than "dog's dinner [*de la bouillie pour les chats*]" (23). Such an ethics of difference treats all others as others abstractly and formally, but in practice distinguishes between others who resemble oneself and those who do not. As Badiou puts it, "This celebrated 'other' is acceptable only if he is a *good* other.... That is to say: I respect differences, but only, of course, in so far as that which differs also respects, just as I do, the said differences" (24). *Pace* Levinas, Badiou makes the recognition of the Same central to the ethical act, and ties ethics to truth, "the coming-to-be of that which is not yet" (27):

> The whole ethical predication based upon recognition of the other should be purely and simply abandoned. For the real question — and it is an extraordinarily difficult one — is much more that of *recognizing the Same*.... The Same, in effect, is not what is (i.e. the infinite multiplicity of differences) but what *comes to be*. I have already named that in regard to which only the advent of the Same occurs: it is a *truth*. Only a truth is, as such, *indifferent to differences*. (25, 27)[31]

Truth takes the form of a commitment, a response to the demand of what Badiou calls an "event": it is "the real process of fidelity to an event" (42).[32]

Receptivity and response to the event are inextricably linked for Badiou. In an ethical framework that is uncannily reminiscent of Levinas's, Badiou's notion of "event," which he associates with the Lacanian Real (52), can be described as a situated experience of the unruly: the disorganizing and deroutinizing alterity of the event reveals a "void" in the order of being (the Symbolic order), involving an interpellation (the becoming-subject of the event) and an unending task of responsibility (the ethical subject's subsequent "fidelity" to this "crack in the ontological edifice of the universe," to recall Žižek's language quoted in the epigraph).[33] "To be really faithful to the event," writes Badiou, "I must completely rework my ordinary way of living my situation" (41–42). While the truth-event is open to all, Badiou insists on its irreducible singularity and the incommunicability of its meaning: "What arises from a truth-process... cannot be communicated.... To enter into the composition of a subject of truth can only be something that happens to you. Confirmation of the point is provided by the concrete circumstances in which someone is seized by a fidelity" (47). Žižek perceives an ironic affinity between Badiou and Levinas on this point: "Does Badiou, *the* anti-Levinas, with this topic of the respect for the unnameable, not come dangerously close precisely to the Levinasian notion of the respect for Otherness?"[34]

Whereas Žižek sees in Badiou unfortunate lapses into Levinasianism, I propose to read Badiou against the grain, to read Badiou *with* Levinas, and to pursue an alternative basis for their *rapprochement*, one that passes through Derrida's encounter with Levinas before returning to the demands of fidelity. In "Violence and Metaphysics," an earlier, and more generous, engagement with Levinas's thought (one that predates Badiou's by three decades), Derrida similarly called into question Levinas's ethics of difference, disputing "the *dream* of a purely *heterological* thought," "a *pure* thought of *pure* difference."[35] Yet Derrida does not dismiss Levinas's radical project. Quite the contrary: while scrupulously exposing Levinas's dependence on a philosophical discourse that he claims to have left behind, Derrida nevertheless argues that the question is not one of choosing between "the opening and the totality,"[36] infinity and sameness. Refusing either/or logic, Derrida prefers to hesitate between the two in response to the challenge of Levinasian philosophy. Adopting instead a logic of both/and, Derrida works through and against Levinas's philosophy, insisting on the *relationality* of the other. Though there is always something surprising about the other, something "wholly other [*tout autre*],"[37] a pure or unmediated encounter with the other remains something of a *phantasm*. And to be sure, we find Derrida, at times, all too enthralled by this *phantasm* of a "pure ethics":

Pure ethics, if there is any, begins with the respectable dignity of the other as absolute *unlike*, recognized as nonrecognizable, indeed as unrecognizable, beyond all knowledge, all cognition and all recognition: far from being the beginning of pure ethics, the neighbor as like or as resembling, as looking like, spells the end or the ruin of such an ethics, if there is any.[38]

Yet we must pay sufficient attention to Derrida's self-puncturing moments of doubt, such as the one above, where Derrida entertains thoughts of a pure ethics while qualifying such remarks with the repetition of the words "if there is any" — drawing attention, as it were, to the phantasmatic character of a "pure ethics." Relationality rather than absolute separation conditions my relation to the other. Abraham's asymmetrical relation to God exemplifies what Derrida paradoxically characterizes as a "relation without relation," a "*rapport sans rapport.*"[39] "What can be said about Abraham's relation to God can be said about my relation without relation to *every other (one) as every (bit) other* [*tout autre comme tout autre*], in particular my relation to my neighbor or my loved ones who are as inaccessible to me, as secret and transcendent as Jahweh."[40] Perplexingly entailing both a relation and a nonrelation to the other, this relationless relation joins *and* disjoins. It answers the aporetic demands made upon me by the other: to be understood without being reduced to an object of comprehension, to never dissolve the "without" of the "relation without relation" that interrupts any traditional, static subject-object relation of knowledge and that respects (by sustaining through discourse) the enigmaticity and irreducibility of the other. Derrida's ethics (of the relationless relation), as Gayatri Spivak incisively notes, is "not a problem of knowledge but a call of relationship (without relationship, as limit case)."[41] Denoting more than an epistemological impasse, ethics is an exposure to the demands of the other, that is, an invitation for interpretation.

In his later philosophical masterwork, *Otherwise than Being*, Levinas implicitly responds to the concerns Derrida expressed in "Violence and Metaphysics," moving away from the face-to-face encounter as the paradigmatic ethical scene to the question of language and the possibility of ethical figuring. Levinas comes to realize that the ethical can signify *within* the realm of representation, that the language of ontology does not preclude nor exhaust what Levinas calls the "ethical Saying" (in this respect, Blanchot's evocation of the "Saying" in *The Writing of the Disaster* might register a different meaning). Contrasting Saying (*le Dire*) with the Said (*le Dit*) — "the birth place of ontology"[42] — Levinas argues that saying "is not a modality of cognition" (48) nor an "exchange of information" (92). Reminiscent of the "phatic" function of language in its insistence on intersubjectivity — the contact between speaker and addressee without the transfer of information — Saying expresses nothing but the desire to communicate.[43] Levinas is aware, however, of the paradox that as soon as one utters something, once meaning happens, one enters into the domain of the Said. Yet he does not stop there. Refusing the false choice between Saying and the Said, between pure alterity and comprehension, respect and violence, Levinas advocates a kind of skepticism, an "endless critique" (44) or "an incessant unsaying of the said [*un incessant dédit du Dit*]" (181). The unruliness of the Saying, then, invariably passes through the scene of language; its anarchic character is not obliterated (domesticated) but preserved and rearticulated through the activities of interpretation and rereading.[44]

In a similar vein, Derrida urges us to go beyond the stagnant, predictable debate over sameness and difference, pointing out that relating ethically to otherness or alterity should not lead to either a cannibalistic (purely assimilative) or a noncannibalistic (purely indigestible) mode of contact: "The moral question is . . . not, nor has it ever been: should one eat or not eat . . . but since *one must* eat in any case . . . *how* for goodness sake should one *eat well* [*bien manger*]?"[45] Reframing the terms of the ethical debate, Derrida insists that fidelity to the other will always bring with it a sense of betrayal, since fidelity *as such* does not lie in refusing the Said in order to dwell only in the idyllic time of the Saying, but in the ethical exigency to unsay and resay the Said — to perpetually "eat better."[46]

Extrapolating from Derrida's comments, I would argue that the notion of eating well serves as a more fitting metaphor for ethical criticism, an ethically preferable hermeneutic mode through which to assess the inventive work. First of all, it helps move beyond the early reception of Levinas in literary studies, which always risked moral sentimentalism by reducing the disruptive Levinasian encounter with the other to a series of predictable, familiar, and easily translatable pathetic scenes. Second, and perhaps more importantly, the notion of eating well gestures to an understanding of and engagement with the aesthetic unruly that take the form of a *response*.[47] Creatively hesitating between incommensurable demands (to interpret but not to translate back into familiar terms), the ethical reader is invited to cultivate an appreciation for the unruly, to curb his or her desire for hermeneutic mastery (a desire that finds its origins in the Symbolic Order and the voracious appetite for consumption that it propagates) without simultaneously renouncing meaning or the interpretive endeavor.[48] Doing justice to the unruly both acknowledges and endlessly works to counter this desire to master, comprehend, or pin down a work's meaning.[49] Reading itself becomes a desire for more, a transgressive desire not to arrest but to prolong the act of interpretation. As such, interpretation, then, can be described as "imperfect" in the etymological sense of incomplete, "foreign to the category of completion," as Blanchot notes in his musings on "fragmentary speech" in *The Infinite Conversation*.[50]

Reading unruly is obviously also a learned behavior ("how we read" matters as much as "what we read"[51]), and does not constitute in any way a more "natural" ethico-aesthetic disposition toward literature (what a timeless ethics of reading presupposes). To fail to see reading as a historically and culturally specific practice is to fall prey to ideology. In seeing works as unruly we must not ignore the reconstructive or belated quality of such a recognition.[52] Moreover, unruliness as such is not located *in* the text, ready to be deciphered by its faithful reader; it is not an immanent or formal property of the literary work, connoting, for instance, its essential ambiguity (as in New Criticism). Nor is it adequately understood as an incommunicable sublime or epiphanic moment of a truth event (Badiou's version of the Real).[53] On the latter, Žižek offers a suggestive alternative, redefining the Real in terms of the parallax gap. If parallax is commonly understood as "the apparent displacement of an object (the shift of its position against a background), caused by a change in observational position," for Žižek, the parallax gap signifies far more, enabling him to reconceptualize the interpretive scene itself. As he puts it,

> The philosophical twist to be added [to the standard definition of parallax] . . . is that the observed difference is not simply "subjective," due to the fact that the same object which exists "out there" is seen from two different stances, or points of view. It is rather that . . . subject and object are inherently "mediated," so that an "epistemological" shift in the subject's point of view always reflects an "ontological" shift in the object itself.[54]

Reading Lacan with Hegel, and Hegel with Lacan, Žižek conceives of the dialectic as an ongoing process involving a constant shift in perspective between two points "between which no synthesis or mediation is possible" (4): indeed, the parallax gap reveals that "there is no common language, no shared ground" (5) on or through which such a synthesis or mediation could take place.

The notion of the parallax view has led Žižek to clarify his own understanding of the function of the Real; no longer conceived as that which "always returns to its place," the Lacanian Real is now better understood as the gap between appearances, something — or rather a "nonsubstantial" thing — that is triangulated or retroactively reconstructed through the interpretive work of analysis and critique (26). Žižek explicitly distances the parallax gap from Badiou's notion of the event, accusing Badiou of binary thought, stressing that "there is nothing but the order of Being" (167), that the event *as such* is constitutive of the order of Being.

Recalling Derrida's now infamous — but often misunderstood — "there is nothing outside of the text [*il n'y pas de hors-texte*],"[55] we can agree with Žižek that, analogously, there is no outside the order of Being if by "no outside the order of Being," one means that the event is profoundly relational, even if (or because) it is a strain on relationality. That is, in the exposure to the event, one, strictly speaking, does not have *a relation* to Being nor *a nonrelation* to Being. Parallactic thinking, in its constant oscillation between incommensurable perspectives, fosters a Derridean mode of interpretation that helps to sustain the "without" of the "relation without relation," that is, the double bind of the ethical relation.[56] The double bind of ethical criticism can thus be reread dialectically in terms of the parallax gap:[57] the two injunctions informing our exposure to the aesthetic object (*both* not to compromise *and* to compromise on the singularity of the aesthetic work) *share no common language*. The "Real" of the literary work, so to speak, resides in this parallax gap.

Taking seriously Badiou's ethical call to "persevere in the interruption" (47) thus requires a more robust understanding of the unruliness of the event and of the ethical demands it imposes on its faithful subjects. Unruliness, indistinguishable from the *experience* of unruliness, does not exist outside interpretive communities, but is generated by them and contributes as well to their "engine of change,"[58] compelling unsatisfied readers to think with and beyond their existing protocols of interpretation and current norms of readability. What is at the heart of this dissatisfaction is an unruly will to know/enjoy, a curiosity that the event of reading does not so much create ex nihilo as accentuate and enable. It is a type of curiosity that disrupts the economy of the Same, the reduction of the new to the familiar. It is a "passion for knowledge," as Foucault aptly put it, that does not seek "to assimilate what it is proper for one to know" but results in the "straying afield" of oneself, effectively disrupting the sovereignty and centrality of the knowing self.[59] In this respect, curiosity would lead not only to a sense of empowerment (*I* want to know) but also to one of vulnerability and heteronomy (the object of knowledge is irreducible to me). Curiosity, and the kind of knowledge (or truth, in Badiou's terms) it generates, introduces a critical distance between the reader and his or her interpretive community: to be a curious reader is to remain always open to the event of reading, to the surprising and "incalculable novelty" of its truth.[60] Curiosity, then, functions as an antidote to interpretive conformism, opening the possibility, even if momentarily, for "no longer being, doing, or thinking what we are, do, or think."[61] With curiosity also comes a sense of care, an eye for the unruly:

> Curiosity . . . evokes "care" [*souci*]; it evokes the care [*soin*] one takes of what exists and what might exist; a sharpened sense of reality, but one that is never immobilized before it; a readiness to find what surrounds us strange and odd; a certain determination to throw off familiar ways of thought and to look at the same things in a different way; a passion for seizing what is happening now and what is disappearing; a lack of respect for the traditional hierarchies of what is important and fundamental.[62]

A readiness to find in literary works strangeness and unfamiliarity, or what we might describe as an unruly care for the unruly, is a sine qua non for experiencing aesthetic *jouissance*.

Like the just judge — whose legal judgment, as Derrida points out, does not simply consist of "applying the law" like "a calculating machine"[63] but requires that each decision be the result of an *invention*[64] — the curious reader/the subject of aesthetic pleasure confronts, and returns to, each book as a singularity, answering its interpellation as reader-judge, its call for "an absolutely unique interpretation."[65] *Ethical exigency is not a hermeneutic necessity*; ethics emerges precisely in the absence of interpretive certainty.[66] Yet, to be clear, what an inventive work elicits from its reader is not a dismissal of all prior commentaries (an attempt to read a work in a historical vacuum), but a recognition of the reader's infinite responsibility as an interpretive subject. And to borrow from Badiou's example of Saint Paul, who, as a faithful subject of the event of Christ's resurrection, enacts his fidelity to its truth by preaching the Word ("there is no longer Jew nor Greek") to all, readers of literature can be said to perform their fidelity to the event of reading, which coincides with the coming-into-being of the inventive work as such, not in isolation (the original, quasi-private scene of reading — the dyadic encounter of reader and work) but in the public, shared act of interpretation.[67]

What motivates a reader to respond to an inventive work—to justify his or her reading to others—is undoubtedly multiple. The works I have selected all figure among the most frequently reprinted, studied, and commented works in French literature. This choice might be said both to stem from and to reinforce existing literary canons, leaving unquestioned their ideological complicity in the production of "cultural capital." As Pierre Bourdieu has aptly demonstrated, canon watch, the dutiful patrolling of the "magical division" separating high from low art, and the "cultural consecration" afforded by it,[68] performs, intentionally or unintentionally, "a social function of legitimating social differences."[69] It is true that the literary—and in some cases the philosophical—worth of the selected works is (currently) beyond dispute. Literary critics and humanities professors must therefore be cognizant that the promotion and teaching of such canonical works frequently serve, again consciously or unconsciously, as "strategies of distinction,"[70] inculcating in students, or readers more generally, not only a love for high culture but also a sense of cultural superiority. Yet to give attention only to this, to warn solely against an investment in and a perpetuation of the literary canon, would be to miss a fundamental point of the book. Unruly works make demands on *all* readers: from neophytes to the most seasoned interpreters of literature, from students to professors to critics.[71] Refusing both their idolatry and instrumentalization, unruly works stubbornly insist that their readers constantly question and reevaluate their readerly habitus or hermeneutic *parti pris*.[72] In this respect, affirming the canonical status of these works in any straightforward manner—either by making them an unchanging "sure and safe repository of the values of Western culture"[73] (what hegemonic cultural norms of distinction presuppose and promote), or, as we shall see more closely, by seeing them simply as representative of a particular period or movement—would be antithetical to our project, since it would function only to further their monumentalization, to contain and domesticate their un-ruly and profoundly inventive force, disciplining and curtailing, by extension, their readers' curiosity.[74]

This book constitutes a series of case studies, responses to the challenges of thinking the ethical in/as aesthetics. The selected works demonstrate the multiplicity of the unruly, the differing ways in which unruliness manifests itself across genres and in relation to varying and rivaling horizons of interpretation marking different historical periods. In this sense, my choice represents only a sample of the many texts who share an ability to provoke an ethical response through their inventiveness, an ability to render the familiar unfamiliar — and, conversely, the unfamiliar familiar. My choice is not random, however, in that I focus on works that point up the way in which a shared intellectual history cannot fully account for or exhaust a particular text's unique figuration of the ethical double bind: the need both to understand and respect the singularity of a literary work. Each unruly work stages the ethical scene in unique and subtle ways, inciting us to engage in the act of interpretation, to prolong the moment of meaning-making. Moreover, this incitement is itself felt differently; texts that foster readerly identification, that seemingly welcome explication, exert the force of the double bind in ways that remain distinct from, but equally important as, the techniques deployed by those works that explicitly frustrate interpretation through their modernist, non-mimetic or deliberately opaque form.

Chapter 1 takes up the conjunctions and frictions between philosophy, theory, and the literary through an examination of Michel de Montaigne's sixteenth-century *Essays*. As a work of accidental theory, the *Essays* inaugurate a new type of philosophy: an unruly philosophy and a philosophy of the unruly made possible through the essay form itself. Exceeding any strict generic definition, the essay operates as a mode of reading that emerges from, and helps to sustain, Montaigne's desire to *think differently*, to read *otherwise than being*. As a mode of inquiry, essayistic thinking privileges a productive skepticism that affords a different way of apprehending alterity — his own and that of others. The essay unavoidably imposes form on Montaigne's "unruly fantasies" but a form that relentlessly refuses its own homogenization, illustrating but also performing the elusive, fluctuating, and imperfect character of the self that frustrates metaphysical permanence, ontological stability, or any sense of completion. Focusing on Montaigne's essaying of the self in its relation to the other, this chapter explores the *Essays* as and through parallax, the dialectical triangulation that the work itself both performs and demands of its readers.

Chapter 2 further interrogates the demands that an artwork makes of its readers by turning to the concept of the "book as friend" in Denis Diderot's eighteenth-century fictional dialogue, *Rameau's Nephew*. Diderot's dialogue between author-narrator-philosopher (referred to as "Moi," or "Me") and his interlocutor, the morally depraved nephew ("Lui," or "Him"), ostensibly stages an allegory of the mind-and-body problem, a self-critical philosophical debate between Cartesian idealism (the philosopher's disembodied mind) and eighteenth-century materialism (the nephew's hungry body). Yet this

Enlightenment dialogue reveals itself to be less concerned with arriving at a moral lesson than first expected. Presenting its readers an unstable, distorted, and maddening moral universe, *Rameau's Nephew* invites but also frustrates readerly desire for friendship, the desire to identify (with) the storyteller's *ethos*. To whom is the dialogue most hospitable? The reader's sympathy *hesitates* between the philosopher — the defender of moral values (and status quo) — and the cynical, lazy, and seemingly "mad" nephew, philosophy's excluded other. Accommodating a series of divergent readings without ever fully endorsing any, *Rameau's Nephew* effectively short-circuits its own philosophical subtext, and thwarts its own allegorical mechanisms. Reading Diderot's dialogue in light of the mind-and-body problem, then, does not so much privilege a philosophical approach to the artwork (as yet another eighteenth-century interpretation of the Cartesian problematic) as foreground the work's unruliness, its heteroclite and dislocating character: its status as both a familiar product of Enlightenment philosophy and something foreign to it.

If the unruliness of *Rameau's Nephew* resides in its elusive authorial voice and refusal to serve as an illustration of either Enlightenment discourse or its counterdiscourse, Charles Baudelaire's nineteenth-century writings make the unruly an aesthetic category of sorts. With Baudelaire's neologism *modernité* — "the transient, the fleeting, the contingent; it is one half of art, the other being the eternal and the immutable"[75] — the unruly undergoes a radical transvaluation, becoming coterminous with the aesthetic experience: to be modern is to be unruly. Chapter 3 investigates Baudelaire's theorization and practice of *modernité* (translatable both as modernity and modernism), his engagement with translation as a means for challenging understandings about poetry and reality and, more urgently, for thinking differently about the experience and framing of modern life. The visual arts, especially painting and caricature, provided Baudelaire with valuable insights into *modernité* that he sought, in turn, to translate into poetic language. For Baudelaire, visual art did not simply help mediate his perception of modern life; it also pointed to the violence and limits of translatability, serving as a parallax, elucidating the gap between modern life and its aestheticized image. In his later prose poems, collected in *The Spleen of Paris*, Baudelaire committed himself to elucidating this ideological gap for his reading public. Through his playful, self-critical, and inventive use of irony, Baudelaire contested the modernist belief in the "autonomy of aesthetics," exposing its dubious separation of art and its material source (implicating himself in the process), while simultaneously disrupting his audience's relentless thirst for interpretive pleasure and moral guidance.

Chapter 4 follows the developing and vexed relationship between author and reader in Jean-Paul Sartre's 1938 novel *Nausea*. From its very inception *Nausea* has been intimately linked to Sartrean philosophy. The novel has been said to highlight, through Roquentin's drama, something timeless about the existential condition, the absurdity of life, and the ultimate meaninglessness of the world (Sartre had conceived of the novel as a "factum on Contingency"). Critics writing in the aftermath of the "death of the author" have begun to complicate the relationship between *Nausea* and its author, refusing to submit it to an "author function" — that is, to make it "fit" into the larger, coherent "thought" of Sartre. Yet refusing to read *Nausea* from within a hermeneutic horizon determined by existential phenomenology need not result in a disavowal of the artwork's existentialist qualities. A responsive and responsible encounter with *Nausea* cannot simply jettison an engagement with its author, nor can it simply submit to Sartre's authorial authority, to either his early philosophy or his later self-critical assessment of *Nausea* in his autobiography *The Words*. This chapter instead reads *Nausea* as Sartre's unruly progeny. Confirming and "countersigning" Sartre — reading his novel with an eye for narrative moments that both reiterate and displace Sartrean understanding[76] — opens up the possibility for a different encounter with the work, one that makes *Nausea* less readable but more inventive, one that is less strictly faithful to its ideas but more responsive to its provocations.

The *nouveau roman* (New Novel) is the focus of chapters 5 and 6. Alain Robbe-Grillet's novel *Jealousy*, in many ways, can be said to illustrate Robbe-Grillet's modernist, if not postmodernist, bias against meaning, realism, and narration, captured by his observation that "to tell a story has become strictly impossible."[77] Offering these remarks in his influential manifesto *For a New Novel*, Robbe-Grillet made clear his intention to renovate both the novel form and the critical reading practices used in approaching the genre as a whole. Robbe-Grillet's radical contestation did not, however, simply provide readers with a new interpretive paradigm; the question of how one can or should interpret *Jealousy*'s formal strategies, its explicit rebuke of hermeneutic containment and cognitive mastery, still remains open. The question of how to respond to the Saying of *Jealousy* — a question of readerly responsibility that the novel itself allegorizes or stages in several key scenes — is not just an intellectual or epistemological challenge but also an ethical one. Finally, chapter 6 considers the gendering of unruliness in Marguerite Duras's *The Ravishing of Lol Stein*, a novel that radically rewrites the male fantasy narrative about female trauma or madness, questioning the role of gendered experience in the interpretive process. Attending to the intersubjective demands of the novel, its figuration of the ethical within and through language, this chapter highlights the work's inventiveness for feminism: the ways it elicits and frustrates familiar, utilitarian, or overdetermined responses to sexual difference. More specifically, the chapter reframes the terms of the debate surrounding *The Ravishing of Lol Stein*, asking to what extent a faithful feminist reading depends on the reader's ability to share Lol's "experience," and to what extent the complexity of the male narrator's writing of Lol — that is, his writing of her ravishing and the ravishing of his writing — resists or exceeds any straightforward identification with the female character or with the "feminine" more generally.

The analyses that follow do not aim, of course, to exhaust an understanding of unruliness. Nor do they offer a hermeneutic key for unlocking the unruliness of any other text. Quite the opposite, the book offers itself as an apprenticeship in the unruly. There is no theory of the unruly; the unruly cannot be determined in advance. It can only be grasped, or better yet, encountered through examples. The study also takes to heart Montaigne's observation that "every example is lame [*tout exemple cloche*],"[78] that every model (every prior example or precedent) is always to some degree deficient in explaining or accounting for the meaning of the specific case at hand. Montaigne's self-critical assessment — his implicit refusal to present himself as exemplary, a model for imitation — could be paired with Derrida's hyperbolic ethical utterance "*tout autre est tout autre*."[79] Derrida's phrase contains within it a double meaning; it can be translated as either "every other is completely other" or "every other is every other." But again, it is not a question of simply choosing between the two meanings. The sentence's aporetic character demands a parallactic reading. Likewise, each unruly work is radically singular, and yet each work shares the identity of singularity, of unruliness. Conceptualizing the relation to the unruly as a "relation without relation" renders problematic the choice between pure otherness or pure sameness, and serves to block or forestall the (illusory) hermeneutic security that the copula "is" (the unruly work *is*. . .) might provide. Each case study can be said to exemplify the unruly, while simultaneously resisting the imposition of the constraining logic of exemplarity (where an account of the unruly is made to *stand for* other instances or, more precisely, readings of the unruly). Such a formulation of the (non)exemplarity of case studies foregrounds an understanding of the literary as an inappropriable alterity — with the ethical imperative to sustain this alterity through the work of interpretation. Recognizing the lameness of every reading thus goes hand in hand with recognizing the singularity of the work interpreted. Such a recognition does not result in paralysis or starvation (in a denial of the reader's will to know/interpret), nor in aesthetic and epistemological relativism (an uncritical reiteration of the truism that "all readings are misreadings"), but in the testing of readings and the fragile promise of eating well.

I

Montaigne

THE ACCIDENTAL THEORIST

> Theory... has no vested interests inasmuch as it never lays claim to an absolute system, a non-ideological formulation of itself and its "truths"; indeed, always itself complicit in the being of current language, it has only the never-finished task and vocation of undermining philosophy as such, of unraveling affirmative statements and propositions of all kinds.
>
> FREDRIC JAMESON

After reflecting on the limits of man's cognitive powers in a key passage from the "Apology for Raymond Sebond," Michel de Montaigne turns his attention to himself, taking stock of his own practice and its potential effects on future generations:

> *Having found by experience* that where one man had failed, another has succeeded, and that what was unknown to one century the following century has made clear, and that the sciences and arts are not cast in a mold, but are formed and shaped little by little, by repeated handling and polishing, as the bears lick their cubs into shape at leisure, I do not leave off *sounding and testing* what my powers cannot discover; and by handling again and kneading this *new matter*, stirring it and heating it, I open up to whoever follows me some facility to enjoy it more at his ease, and make it more supple and manageable for him.

> *Ayant essayé par experience* que ce à quoy l'un s'estoit failly, l'autre y est arrivé, et ce qui estoit incogneu à un siecle, le siecle suyvant l'a esclaircy, et que les sciences et les arts ne se jettent pas en moule, ains se forment et figurent peu à peu en les maniant et pollissant à plusieurs fois, comme les ours façonnent leurs petits en les lechant à loisir: ce que ma force ne peut descouvrir, je ne laisse pas de le *sonder et essayer*; et, en retastant et pétrissant cette *nouvelle matiere*, la remuant et l'eschaufant, j'ouvre à celuy qui me suit quelque facilité pour en jouir plus à son ayse, et le luy rends plus souple et plus maniable.[1]

As the product of "experience" and "essaying," Montaigne's "new matter" denotes at once his self and his book. It represents his contribution to the existing and ever expanding body of human knowledge, his own response to the Delphic injunction to "know thyself," as well as the material product of his intellectual labor. Montaigne's "new matter" — which reminds us of his address to the reader ("I am the matter of my book" ["je suis moy-mesme la matiere de mon livre"]) — will then be passed on to his *readers to come*, "whoever follows [him]." This process is not absent of authorial anxieties, however. Not unlike a child who leaves home to go out into the world, the printed book of the *Essays* attains a degree of autonomy and eventually comes to lie outside the hermeneutic control of its father. Montaigne already hints at an uncanny dissymmetry between himself and his book (his child of the mind):

> Even in my own writings I do not always find again the sense of my first thought; I do not know what I meant to say. (II, 12, 425–26b)

> [My book] may know a good many things that I no longer know and hold from me what I have not retained and what, just like a *stranger*, I should have to borrow from it if I came to need it. *If I am wiser than it, it is richer than I*. (II, 8, 293c, emphasis added)

> En mes escris memes, je ne retrouve pas tousjours l'air de ma premiere imagination: je ne scay ce que j'ay voulu dire. (566)

> [Mon livre] peut sçavoir assez de choses que je ne sçay plus, et tenir de moy ce que je n'ay point retenu et qu'il faudroit que, tout ainsi qu'un *estranger*, j'empruntasse de luy, si besoin m'en venoit. *Il est plus riche que moy, si je suis plus sage que luy*. (401–2)

Montaigne's book is *his*, yet it is also like a *stranger* to him: *it is him and not him*.

It is not surprising, then, that Montaigne expressed concern about his reception. This chapter considers several questions first posed by the essayist himself. Would the *Essays* be read as an "inventive work," as a work that elicits creative responses from its readers? Would the audience heed the author's call to be read and understood ("I am hungry to make myself known" [III, 5, 643b] ["Je suis affamé de me faire connoistre" (847)])? And more importantly, would they do justice to the singularity of his work — "the only book in the world of its kind" [II, 8, 278c] ["le seul livre au monde de son espece" (385)], as Montaigne describes it? Everything hinges on the readers' refusal to impose an unequivocal meaning (what would amount to casting his *matter* in a rigid mold). Or to put it in more positive terms: it all depends on readers' openness to the author's essayistic process, on their recognition of and contribution to Montaigne's Pygmalion-like project of bringing his philosophical work to life.[2]

The Essay: Between History and Philosophy

It is now a commonplace to acknowledge the "newness" and singularity of Montaigne's work in crediting him as the father of the essay, this extraordinary hybrid genre that has appealed so well to readers' hunger for both substance and style. With the creation of the unruly essay, Montaigne did not simply make famous a particular style of writing but also inaugurated a mode of thinking intimately tied to the values of irresolution, wonder, and surprise. Contingency rather than necessity guides the unfolding of Montaigne's writing: "My conceptions and my judgment move only by groping, staggering, stumbling, and blundering" (I, 26, 107a) ["Mes conceptions et mon jugement ne marche qu'à tastons, chancelant, bronchant et chopant" (146)]. Though they constantly probe the "inner springs" (II, 17, 481a) ["les resorts" (634)] of his mind, Montaigne's meditations yield no concrete foundational knowledge. Purposive inquiry is met at every turn with textual resistance; indeed, an irreducible gap between intention and outcome structures the writings of the *Essays* — "I do not find myself in the place where I look; and I find myself more by chance encounter than by searching my judgment" (I, 10, 26–27c) ["Je ne me trouve pas où je me cherche; et me trouve plus par rencontre que par l'inquisition de mon jugement" (40)] — prefiguring, as it were, Lacan's anti-Cartesian claim, "I think where I am not, therefore I am where I do not think."[3]

Philosophers and critical theorists have long recognized the disruptive potential of the essay form, especially as practiced by Montaigne. Once described by Theodor Adorno as "the critical force *par excellence*," the essay "gently defies the ideals of *clara et distincta perceptio* and of absolute certainty."[4] Michel Foucault also recognizes the essay's contestative impulse and its distrust of authoritative discourses. The essay — "the living substance of philosophy" — does not legitimate "what is already known" but rather desires to know "to what extent it might be possible to think differently."[5] Liberating in an oblique, rather than straightforward way, the essay works to expand thought and to create new ways of thinking: it unavoidably imposes form on thought but a kind of form that relentlessly refuses its own homogenization as it tries to think both beyond its own cognitive limits and against the dogmatic "image of thought"[6] of any given historical period. As a mode of philosophical discourse, essayistic thinking clearly exceeds a strict formalistic definition of the essay. More than an approach to written thought, the essay is a mode of reading reflecting a desire to know "to what extent it might be possible" to *read differently*.

Yet as Montaignian critics with an eye for history continue to remind us, the late sixteenth-century writer was working with a somewhat different, historically specific concept, that of "essays." In fact, we are arguably being unfaithful to his use of the term when we refer to each *chapter* of the *Essays* as *an essay*. "Publications *à l'essai*," or trial publications, as George Hoffmann points out, "did not so much constitute a genre as foster a provisional status for their writers."[7] Hoffmann's observation does not just clarify the historical origins of a contemporary term, however. It hints at the larger fault lines distinguishing prevalent approaches to the *Essays*, and the essayistic process, within the field of Montaigne scholarship. In his 2007 book, *How to Read Montaigne*, Terence Cave explores such lines, explicitly addressing the hermeneutic pitfalls facing any reader of the *Essays*. For Cave, the interpretive dilemma turns on the split consciousness that an author like Montaigne demands of his audience.

> A... fundamental question is whether we are to read the *Essais* primarily as a product of late Renaissance humanism, steeped in the cultural habits of that period, or as already a remarkably modern work. The answer is that it is both, and that any viable reading will need to see both aspects, shuttling between them as between the duck and the rabbit in the famous

trick picture that Wittgenstein discusses in the *Philosophical Investigations* (a drawing that can be seen as the head of either a duck or a rabbit but not both at the same time).[8]

Reading Montaigne, according to Cave, does not simply entail choosing between a historically sensitive reading of Montaigne's *Essays* or adopting a contemporary theoretical lens when interpreting his work. A "viable reading" must acknowledge both. The duck/rabbit metaphor adds a further layer of complexity, since a harmonious account of the two is, strictly speaking, impossible: you cannot see both the duck and the rabbit at the same time. Yet Cave does qualify somewhat his observation, affirming the ideality of its simultaneous representation: "*Ideally*, one would present the duck and the rabbit as a *single creature*, but that isn't possible in the linear mode of expository prose."[9] It is unclear whether Cave means that it isn't possible to visually capture the *Essays* as a "singular creature" given the confinement of the series (*How to Read*) under which the monograph appears. More likely, Cave is alluding here to the general problem of commentary and its inevitable betrayal of any text that it seeks to elucidate.

While the argument that we must not conflate the historical Montaigne and our modern version of him is quite appealing, the hermeneutic value of the duck/rabbit metaphor — especially when its aporetic structure is, *ideally*, surmountable — requires more scrutiny. Cave's argument echoes and updates in certain respects earlier debates about the limits of historicism. As François Rigolot put it in an intervention on this subject, the charge of anachronism should not give the accuser a false sense of hermeneutic security, since any critic must avoid not only anachronism (the "aberrant projection of the present onto the past") but also catachronism (the "equally aberrant illusion that one can capture the past without regard for the present that is conditioning that capture").[10] Anachronism is indeed constitutive of any reading of a historically distant author, so to read Montaigne today is to read him anachronistically.[11]

Montaigne himself did not seem disturbed by this interpretive reality; he readily acknowledged this practice, even praising its effects:

> An able reader often discovers in other men's writings perfections beyond those that the author put in or perceived, and lends them richer meanings and aspects. (I, 24, 93a)

> Un suffisant lecteur descouvre souvant és escrits d'autruy des perfections autres que celles que l'autheur y a mises et apperceuës, et y preste des sens et des visages plus riches. (127)[12]

Montaigne recognized, that is, that a work's meaning inevitably exceeds authorial intention and control. For Montaigne, then, anachronism (along with one's awareness of it) was not an obstacle but a condition for creative interpretation, interpretation that would generously add to the semantic richness of the text rather than reifying it as a pure object of analysis devoid of any readerly participation.[13]

Imperfection's Parallax

Might it not be more productive to see the reconstructive historical perspective and the contemporary theoretical perspective on Montaigne in terms of the parallax view? Reading the *Essays* parallactically would affirm the aporia of reading the *historical* Montaigne through our *modern* lens, an aporia that the duck/rabbit metaphor articulates but ultimately fails to sustain. A parallax view on the *Essays* begins with shifting the terms of the debate, calling into question the contemporary interpretive scene, a scene dominated if not overdetermined by categories like the historical versus the modern (or in Cave's example, the duck versus the rabbit — or its happy synthesis in a magical "single creature"). A parallactic mode of reading, in this respect, would resemble and be faithful to the *illogical logic* of the essay: it would carefully attend to the ways the essayist produces an array of incommensurable perspectives (there is no metalanguage of the *Essays*), sampling a wide range of semiotic codes, while acknowledging that readers will invariably offer their own perspectives on the *Essays*' inexhaustible mix.[14]

This way of framing the parallax view also enables us to entertain more than two perspectives on Montaigne (Montaigne as a man of the Renaissance *and* Montaigne as our contemporary), opening a space for a multiplicity of alternatives. In some ways, it recognizes that these perspectives were already multiple, split from within: a contextualist approach may privilege the personal life of Montaigne (the *Essays* as autobiography) or it may accentuate the historical events of the period (the wars of religion, the New World conquest, etc.). Likewise, a contemporary perspective may borrow from the language of psychoanalysis, deconstruction, or feminism, to name a few. Again, the interpretive challenge lies not in any attempt to harmonize these perspectives, to naturalize their differences, but to embrace (and responsively contribute to) their frictions and incommensurabilities.

To return to Hoffmann's observation that "publications *à l'essai* did not so much constitute a genre as foster a provisional status for their writers," I would propose that the problematic of imperfection itself — a major concern of the *Essays* — exceeds its original context. The notion itself needs to be rethought parallactically. Lacking the perfection of some authors — who did not hesitate to produce final versions of their work, published as discourses, for example — Montaigne keenly recognizes his ontological *unrootedness*, which in turn compels the act of essaying: "If my mind could gain a firm footing," Montaigne famously pondered in "Of Repentance," "I would not make essays, I would make decisions; but it is always in apprenticeship and on trial" (III, 2, 611b) ["Si mon ame pouvoit prendre pied, je ne m'essaierois pas, je me resoudrois: elle est tousjours en apprentissage et en espreuve" (805)]. Adding to the essay's semantic richness and complexity is its transmutation into a verb. This move arguably shifts our attention from the question of the essay (the essay as a genre and the vexed issue of its historicity) to the meaning of essaying (the essay as a hermeneutic practice).

In the liminal chapter "Of Idleness," Montaigne presents himself first and foremost as an interpreter of his own unruliness. It is Montaigne's ideas or *fantaisies* that evoke defiance and frustration. By describing them as "chimeras and fantastic monsters" (I, 8, 21a) ["chimeres et monstres fantasques" (33)], Montaigne from the start recognizes his subject matter's profound indocility, its challenge to hermeneutic mastery. In a late addition to "Of the Power of the Imagination," Montaigne also evokes the theme of unruliness when talking of his sexual organ:

> People are right to notice the unruly liberty of this member, obtruding so importunately when we have no use for it, and failing so importunately when we have the most use for it, and struggling for mastery so imperiously with our will, refusing with so much pride and obstinacy our solicitations, both mental and manual. (I, 20, 72c)

> On a raison de remarquer l'indocile liberté de ce membre, s'ingerant si importunement, lors que nous n'en avons que faire, et defaillant si importunement, lors que nous en avons le plus affaire, et contestant de l'authorité si imperieusement avec nostre volonté, refusant avec tant de fierté et d'obstination noz solicitations et mentales et manuelles. (102).

Ironically imputing agency to his "unruly member," Montaigne rejects the ideal of *perfectio* (man's identification with the divine), expressing his skepticism about the mind's ability to achieve any semblance of classic self-mastery. Here Montaigne, through his emphasis on the arbitrariness of sexual desire, demystifies the concept of the will valorized by prior Renaissance humanists such as Pico della Mirandola.[15] In his *Oration on the Dignity of Man* (1486), the Italian philosopher argued that God made man neither mortal nor immortal, giving him instead the freedom and power to be his own sculptor and creator.[16] With this ontological makeup of the self, Pico all but created the Renaissance myth of the self-made man — a subject capable of freely cultivating his soul and elevating himself to God-like stature. This optimistic humanist ideal finds its radical counterpart in Montaigne, who, in the closing pages of the *Essays*, depicts the violence inherent in the project of perfecting the self when *perfectio hominis* becomes coterminous with the eradication of one's libidinal desires and corporeality: "That is madness: instead of *changing* into angels [in order to be closer to the *divinitas* of God], they *change* into beasts [a regression to the realm of *animalitas*]; instead of raising themselves, they lower themselves" (III, 13, 856b, emphasis added) ["C'est folie: au lieu de *se transformer* en anges, ils *se transforment* en bestes; au lieu de se hausser, ils s'abattent" (1115)]. With this *conduplicatio*, the repetition of the verb "se transformer," Montaigne emphasizes the role of agency, thus pointing out that those who seek to perfect themselves are to a large extent *responsible* for their condition in their practices of self-care, practices that ironically might be better described, following Nietzsche, as symptomatic of an *"incuria sui,"* a *carelessness of the self*.[17] The essayist, for his part, declines such a transcendental pull to go outside oneself (857b/1115), joyfully affirming his temporality, or as he puts it, his "temporal greatness," (III, 7, 700c) ["grandeur temporelle" (917)].

Indeed, the essay form thrives in the absence of permanence. Not conducive to conceptuality — to the formation of concepts for the purpose of hermeneutic mastery — the essay produces monsters, engendering unruly images in the perplexed mind of its author, making it (the essay) and him (Montaigne) unlikely models of and for perfection. The author's original desire to impose a discursive order on his formless thoughts, "hoping in time to make [his] mind ashamed of itself" (I, 8, 21a) ["esperant avec le temps luy en faire honte à luy mesmes" (33)], proves unsuccessful, as evidenced by his reference to them in a later essay as "grotesques and monstrous bodies" (I, 28, 135a) ["crotesques et corps monstrueux" (183)]. Such a failure to conform to the ideal of *stasis*, an ideal revered by the Senecan sage, has led critics to reconceptualize the author's understanding of perfection (and imperfection) in terms of his investment in skepticism. In his article "*Epoche* as Perfection: Montaigne's View of Ancient Skepticism," José R. Maia Neto carefully examines Montaigne's description of skepticism in the "Apology for Raymond Sebond," demonstrating how the essayist conceives of this ancient school as having reached "the utmost height of human nature" (371a) ["la hauteur extreme de l'humaine nature" (502)]. Understanding perfection in the Aristotelian sense of accomplishment, Neto argues that the skeptic notion of *epoche*, the suspension of judgment ("'I hold back, I do not budge'" (374a) ["je soutiens, je ne bouge" [505]), enables individuals to be who they are (it acknowledges the limited character of their nature) and thus provides, for Montaigne, the best means of attaining happiness. According to Neto, Socrates — the father of ancient skepticism — becomes the object of genuine *imitatio* for Montaigne, since the former embodies the disruptive and dialogical thrust —

> The leader of his dialogues, Socrates, is always asking questions and stirring up discussion, never concluding, never satisfying; and says he has no other knowledge than that of opposing. (II, 12, 377c)

> Le conducteur de ses dialogismes, Socrates, va tousjours demandant et esmouvant la dispute, jamais l'arrestant, jamais satisfaisant, et dict n'avoir autre science que la science de s'opposer. (509)

— that the latter's essayistic style will seek to duplicate at the textual level.[18]

Conversely, Emmanuel Faye, in his impressive volume *Philosophie et perfection de l'homme: De la Renaissance à Descartes*, relegates this central passage from the "Apology" to a footnote, choosing instead to focus on "the moral wisdom of Socrates,"[19] on a Socrates who embodies the ethos of philosophy, "this confidence in the natural capacities and faculties of man, in his aptitude to fulfill his potential on his own, in the goal of achieving his own perfection."[20] Sharing the Socratic ideal of wisdom, Montaigne defines humanity in moral rather than theological terms, grounding it in conscience rather than devotion.[21] On Faye's account, Montaigne's perfection does not lie in his skeptical *epoche* but in his valorization of human dignity, in his quest for knowledge. Faye reminds us that the essayist, far from being critical of philosophy, recommends to his ideal tutor that philosophy become the primary subject matter for the pupil: "For philosophy, which, as the molder of judgment and conduct, will be his principal lesson, has this privilege of being everywhere at home" (I, 26, 121–22a) ["Car la philosophie, qui, comme formatrice des jugements et des meurs, sera sa principale leçon, a ce privilege de se mesler par tout" (164)]. Montaigne's *Essays* and *fantasies* are indeed presented by their own author as "purely human and philosophical, with no admixture of theology" (I, 56, 234b) ["purement humains et philosophiques, sans meslange de Theologie" (322)].

These words take center stage as well in Tzvetan Todorov's study *Le Jardin imparfait: La pensée humaniste en France*, inaugurating, as it were, a new humanism that will find its full realization in the Enlightenment:

> The term *humanist* has several meanings, but we can say in a first approximation that it refers to the doctrines according to which man is the point of departure and the point of reference for human actions.... The term *humanist* figures, perhaps for the first time in French, in a passage by Montaigne in which he uses it to characterize his own practice, in contrast to that of theologians. Though he grants the theologians their right to respect, and certainly to existence, he prefers to separate the two domains and reserve a new field for the "humanists," which consists of strictly human activities or "fantasies," of "pure human" writings.[22]

Contrary to Faye, Todorov does not perceive any commitment to *perfectio hominis* in Montaigne's *Essays*. Quite the opposite, it is imperfection, synonymous here with critical skepticism, that plays a structural role in the author's work. Todorov borrows the title of his volume from Montaigne: "(a) Je veux qu'on agisse, (c) et qu'on allonge les offices de la vie tant qu'on peut, (a) et que la mort me treuve plantant mes choux, mais nonchalant d'elle, et encore plus de mon jardin imparfait" (I, 20, 89). The English title of Todorov's book is *Imperfect Garden*, which cannot fully convey the semantic richness of the French word. The term has posed a problem for Montaigne's English translators, as the following versions show:

> I would have a man to be doing, and to prolong his lives offices, as much as lieth in him, and let death carelesse of her dart, but more of my unperfect garden.[23]

> I want us to be doing things, prolonging life's duties as much as we can; I want Death to find me planting my cabbages, neither worrying about it nor the unfinished gardening.[24]

> I want a man to act, and to prolong the functions of life as long as he can; and I want death to find me planting my cabbages, but careless of death, and still more of my unfinished garden.²⁵

Of the three translations, Florio's now archaic *unperfect* retains *imparfait*'s double meaning of *imperfect* and *incomplete*. A recent translation into modern French substitutes *inachevé* (unfinished) for *imparfait* in order to capture one sense of the word lost to modern ears, but thereby excludes the other.²⁶ It is not, of course, a question of choosing between the two: Montaigne is surely playing with the epithet's double meaning. As with Neto and Faye, Todorov opts for a "philosophical" interpretation of *imparfait*, limiting, in turn, the word's semantic slipperiness. Such a content-oriented reading fails to appreciate fully the performative dimension of the *Essays*. To do justice to any problematic addressed in the *Essays*, Montaigne's reader must take seriously the unruly form of the essay.

Resolutely dwelling in his *jardin imparfait*, in the world of perpetual flux, Montaigne is the anti-Parmenides par excellence, refusing the unity of being and thinking. In contradistinction to the metaphysical view that being and thinking coincide, Montaigne embraces a subject matter that is, in Levinasian parlance, *otherwise than being*. Its pursuit is an endless task: "There is no end to our researches; our end is in the other world" (III, 13, 817b) ["Il n'y a point de fin en nos inquisitions; nostre fin est en l'autre monde" (1068)]. At this point, one is tempted to see Montaigne as a philosopher of *becoming*:

> I cannot keep my subject still. It goes along befuddled and staggering, with a natural drunkenness. I take it in this condition, just as it is at the moment I give my attention to it. I do not portray being: I portray passing.... If my mind could gain a firm footing, I would not make essays, I would make decisions; but it is always in apprenticeship and on trial. (III, 2, 610–11b)

> Je ne puis asseurer mon object. Il va trouble et chancelant, d'une yvresse naturelle. Je le prens en ce poinct, comme il est, en l'instant que je m'amuse à luy. Je ne peints pas l'estre. Je peints le passage.... Si mon ame pouvoit prendre pied, je ne m'essaierois pas, je me resoudrois: elle est tousjours en apprentissage et en espreuve. (805)

Contrary to the didactic humanist *leçons* that preceded them, the *Essays* do not easily lend themselves to hermeneutic consumption; they only afford tentative and contestable self-knowledge.

This might make Montaigne the essayist more of an anti-philosopher to the extent that perfection is not simply recognized as an impossibility — imperfection is not, as the classic philosopher would have it, what one has to settle for in light of the unreachable plenitude of Being. Imperfection as such undergoes a process of transvaluation in the *Essays*. Like Nietzsche, who critically reappraised the world of appearance — conceiving of it outside the static Platonic opposition of appearance and reality ("We have abolished the real world: what world is left? The apparent world perhaps? . . . But no! With the real world we have also abolished the apparent world!"[27]) — Montaigne alters the received meaning of imperfection, and more importantly, compels us to question the desirability of perfection, short-circuiting the Platonist system of thought.

Throughout the *Essays*, Montaigne expresses an unwillingness to mask his imperfections, preferring instead that his self-portrait be that of an imperfect, incomplete, and ever-changing face:

> However that may be, I mean to say, and whatever these absurdities may be, I have had no intention of concealing them, any more than I would a bald and graying portrait of myself, in which the painter had drawn not a perfect face, but mine. (I, 26, 108a)

> Quoy qu'il en soit, veux-je dire, et quelles que soyent ces inepties, je n'ay pas deliberé de les cacher, non plus qu'un mien pourtraict chauve et grisonnant, où le peintre auroit mis, non un visage parfaict, mais le mien. (148)

Montaigne's acknowledgment of his own "imperfect face" not only contributes to the problematization of a definitive answer to the question of identity (who he *is*) but also informs his interpretation of others (who the other *is*). But what does the face of the other look like? Hospitality toward alterity, as Lawrence Kritzman rightly observes, "requires the ability to transcend the self-contained world of narcissism."[28] Montaigne thematizes most clearly his ethics of alterity in the beginning of his essay "Of Cato the Younger," where he admits his aversion to a relation to the other that neutralizes and assimilates the other's difference:

> [a] I do not share that common error of judging another by myself. I easily believe that another man may have qualities different from mine. . . . [c] I more easily admit difference than resemblance between us. . . . *I consider*

him simply in himself, without relations to others; I mold him to his own model. (I, 37, 169, emphasis added)

[a] Je n'ay point cette erreur commune de juger d'un autre selon que je suis. J'en croy aysément des choses diverses à moy. Je ... [c] reçoy plus facilement la différence que la ressemblance en nous. Je ... *le considere simplement en luy-mesme, sans relation, l'estoffant sur son propre modelle.* (I, 37, 229)

We cannot solely rely, of course, on Montaigne's stated predilection to receive alterity. We must always keep Montaigne's desire in mind while also separating this desire from his textual performances. What Montaigne expresses in the above passage is a paradoxical ethical relation to the other. Montaigne's hermeneutics of difference is paradoxical to the extent that his ethical relation to the other — to any other — is, strictly speaking, "without relation." His hermeneutic model posits an object of knowledge without, at the same time, acknowledging the voracious subject of knowledge. Yet not unlike his hunger to make himself known to others, Montaigne's hunger for others is conditioned by an aporetic logic of its own. It expresses a double desire: first, a desire to know the other; second, a desire to sustain a *relation of non-adequation*, in which the other is irreducible to my cognitive powers. Montaigne's generous impulse[29] to engage with the otherness of past, present, and future minds captures the former desire (to know the other), whereas the dream of a pure ethics attests to the latter desire (to keep the other at an ethical distance beyond his narcissistic grasp).

What enables Montaigne to manage the incommensurability of these desires is the essay itself. Resistant to synthesis, the essay foregrounds hesitation as a hermeneutic stance and practice; it illustrates and enacts a new mode of thought. Montaigne may have only dreamed of a new language of skepticism, as his observation on the ancient skeptics suggests:

I can see why the Pyrrhonian philosophers cannot express their general conception in any manner of speaking; for they would need a new language. (II, 12, 392b)

Je voy les philosophes Pyrrhoniens qui ne peuvent exprimer leur generale conception en aucune maniere de parler: car il leur faudroit un nouveau langage. (527).

Yet while the conditional "would need" hints at the virtual character or *irreality* of this "new language," the very language of the *Essays* arguably performs a kind of "Pyrrhonian abstinence,"[30] pointing to the reality of such a new language ("a Pyrrhonism in an affirmative form" [376a] ["un Pyrrhonisme soubs une forme resolutive" (507)], in ways that may have exceeded Montaigne's own imagination. The newness of this skeptical language might also figure in Montaigne's scandalous question "What do I know?" (393b) ["Que sçay-je?" (527)].[31] Robert Eaglestone sums up well the ethical force of the interrogative: "Unlike a statement, a question is to be interrupted: a question starts a dialogue. An idea phrased as a question resists closure and begs not only an answer but another question, an interruption."[32]

As we saw, the initial attempts to tame his unruly thoughts, to discipline them via writing, prove wholly unsuccessful, that is, *not* amenable to humanist discourse. Yet this "failure" gives birth to Montaigne the essayist, "a new figure: an unpremeditated and accidental philosopher" (II, 12, 409c) ["Nouvelle figure: un philosophe impremedité et fortuite" (546)].[33] This "new figure" of the "accidental philosopher" might in fact be better described as *an accidental theorist*, if we understand theory as skeptical resistance,[34] as a resistance to philosophy's timeless dream of permanence and plenitude (the desire for unmediated Being, the Platonic *eidos*, the Thing itself, etc.). Indeed, Montaigne's philosopher of choice is not the authoritative Plato championed by Neoplatonists and others[35] but the skeptical Socrates of Plato's dialogues. Montaigne's Socrates "is always asking questions and stirring up discussion, never concluding, never satisfying; and says he has no other knowledge than that of opposing."[36] It is this Socratic negativity that Montaigne the accidental theorist harnesses in the *Essays*. Montaigne, then, may have begun as a traditional philosopher, committed to hermeneutic self-mastery à la Seneca (as expressed in his desire to be "master of [him]self in every direction" [III, 5, 639b] ["maistre de [s]oy, à tout sens" (841)]), only to come full circle, taking Seneca's observation that "anything that can be added to is imperfect" as a condition for productive thinking rather than a prohibition.[37]

Monstrous Reading/Reading the Monstrous

Montaigne's skepticism can perhaps be ascertained most visibly in his resistance to the humanist ideology of his period. One of the chief tropes of humanist discourse is the digestive metaphor, which transforms the Renaissance author into a cultural cannibal.[38] The metaphor structures Joachim Du Bellay's influential *Defense and Illustration of the French Language* (1549), which calls upon the French to emulate the Romans, who enriched themselves by "imitating the best Greek authors, transforming themselves into them, devouring them, and after having fully digested them, converting them into blood and nourishment."[39] Conforming to his humanist horizon of expectations, Montaigne makes ample use of the digestive metaphor: "What good does it do us to have our belly full of meat if it is not digested, if it is not transformed into us, if it does not make us bigger and stronger?" (I, 25, 101a) ["Que nous sert-il d'avoir la panse pleine de viande, si elle ne se digere? si elle ne se transforme en nous? si elle ne nous augmente et fortifie?" (137).[40] This thought is, of course, already present in Montaigne's "To the Reader," where the essayist asserts that he is himself *the matter of his book*. But what are the ethical implications of the digestive metaphor when it is the other who is the object of knowledge? Isn't there an ethical violence intrinsic to the absorption of the other's otherness, to the humanist literary cannibalization of difference? In other words, then, *how does Montaigne eat?*

In an attempt to answer this question, I propose to turn in this final section to Montaigne's representation of conjoined twins in his chapter "Of a Monstrous Child," juxtaposing this depiction of difference with the author's avowed dream of a relationless account of the other, his wish to consider the other *simply in himself, without relations to others; molding him to his own model*. What is at stake here is the possibility of a "purist" ethical stance, the recognition that, to borrow Derrida's formulation, "every other is completely other [*tout autre est tout autre*]." Is Montaigne's *figuration* of the monstrous child an example of the other as *tout autre*? At first glance, in his appeal to rationality ("this universal and natural reason" [II, 30, 539c] ["cette raison universelle et naturelle" (713)]) as a tool to combat and rectify our tendency to err and be astonished by "novelty" (539c) ("la nouvelleté" [713]), Montaigne's representation of the monstrous child might strike the reader more as proto-Cartesian than Levinasian.[41] For Montaigne *the rationalist*, the experience of monstrosity is ultimately a misrecognition, evidence of our inability to transcend our particular perspective, to step outside the workings of custom — to emancipate ourselves from this "violent and treacherous schoolmistress" (I, 23, 77a) ["violente et traistresse maistresse d'escole" (109)]. The child in itself is not monstrous either to God or to nature. Following Augustine, Montaigne writes in his Bordeaux Copy,

> What we call monsters are not so to God, who sees in the immensity of his work the infinity of forms that he has comprised in it.... We call

contrary to nature what happens contrary to custom; nothing is anything but according to nature, whatever it may be. (539c)

> Ce que nous appellons monstres, ne le sont pas à Dieu, qui voit en l'immensité de son ouvrage l'infinité des formes qu'il y a comprinses.... Nous apelons contre nature ce qui advient contre la coustume: rien n'est que selon elle, quel qu'il soit. (713)

To be sure, the use of the term "monstrous" might be necessary (Montaigne, in fact, gives it prominence by placing it in the title of the essay) until we detach ourselves from our (subjective) perspective, elevate ourselves above the insidious workings of custom, and come to view the world from God's standpoint, adopting, in other words, a "view from nowhere."[42] At the very least, Montaigne's reflections on the fictitious nature of monstrosity appear to be hinting at the possibility of an objective apprehension of the child. But by positing the child's objective reality, hasn't Montaigne at the same time reduced the radical other to an object of discourse by transforming him into a theme, an example of Nature?

While Montaigne does seem to gesture toward a purist epistemological stance (a totalized relation to the object of knowledge, a radical reversal of his ethical wish to read the other according *to his own model*), I would argue that Montaigne, unlike Augustine, adopts this ideal epistemic position for rhetorical purposes. As a remedy for our will to allegorize — that is, society's penchant for ideologically transmuting physical deformation into an otherworldly phenomenon — Montaigne posits a divine, unmediated perspective paradoxically in order to demystify common readings of the monstrous child. Such readings interpret the child as an omen, a providential sign ("a favorable prognostic" [539/713a]) within a metaphysical framework: it is sent by God to show the king how to deal with rivaling political factions. If Montaigne is justified in objecting to the instrumentalization and political allegorization of the child,[43] does he go too far in annulling the other's alterity? An answer to this question hinges on the meaning of alterity. Montaigne is not necessarily objecting to a Levinasian understanding of alterity, where "the other bears alterity as an essence,"[44] but to the speculative meaning one imputes to this alterity, to the horizon of meaning under which the child's intelligibility is made manifest. As an alternative to the typically speculative early modern accounts of "monsters," Montaigne offers a remarkably brief physical description of the child, who is joined to a second, headless body,[45] returning him (in the late addition to the essay) to his rightful place within the order of things, among God's diverse creatures. The allegorical reading of the child thus serves as an example of interpretations to avoid; the case of the "imperfect child" (538a) ["enfant imparfait" (713)] illustrates the need to beat down our will to know/mystify, to keep in check our *libido sciendi*, for, as he tells us elsewhere, "I am afraid we have eyes bigger than our stomachs, and more curiosity than capacity" (I, 31, 150a) ["J'ay peur que nous ayons les yeux plus grands que le ventre, et plus de curiosité que nous n'avons de capacité" (203)].

But is a cognitive awareness of the distinction between one's experience of the world (seeing the child as monstrous) and the reality of the world (everything in the world is natural) sufficient to transform or reform our prereflective consciousness of the world? Can we escape so easily from custom? For Montaigne, denaturalizing custom involves a perpetual critique, a constant struggle against the forces that have given us "the laws of conscience" (I, 23, 83c) ["les loix de la conscience" (115)], that have made custom second nature to us: "Habit is a second nature, and no less powerful" (III, 10, 772b) ["L'accoustumance est une seconde nature, et non moins puissante" (1010)]. In this light, Montaigne's more positive imperative to naturalize nature seems naïvely optimistic. To naturalize the strange child would amount to seeing him outside of interpretation, where the other's underlying "natural" sameness — that is, his humanity — would be simultaneously revealed and embraced.

Yet for Montaigne, human nature and more generally the world ("the world is nothing but variety and dissimilarity" [II, 2, 244a] ["le monde n'est que varieté et dissemblance" [339]) are hardly homogenous: "There is more difference between a given man and a given man than between a given animal and a given man" (II, 12, 342a) ["Il se trouve plus de difference de tel homme à tel homme que de tel animal à tel homme" (466)]. Recognizing a shared humanity with the child does not rule out an appreciation of his difference. Moreover, difference does not only pertain to external matters, matters concerning the other. The difference of the other should not blind us to the difference that inhabits all human beings:

> We are all patchwork, and so shapeless and diverse in composition that each bit, each moment, plays its own game. And there is as much difference between us and ourselves as between us and others. (II, 1, 244a)

> Nous sommes tous de lopins, et d'une contexture si informe et diverse, que chaque piece, chaque momant, faict son jeu. Et se trouve autant de difference de nous à nous mesmes, que de nous à autruy. (337)

Montaigne illustrates, if not performs, the unruliness of his own alterity in "Of Cripples," where the cognitive distinction between being and appearance that structures Montaigne's thought in "Of a Monstrous Child" is displaced and rendered virtually ineffective:

> I have seen no more evident monstrosity and miracle in the world than myself. We become habituated to anything strange by use and time; but the more I frequent myself and know myself, the more my deformity astonishes me, and the less I understand myself. (III, 11, 787b)
>
> Je n'ay veu monstre et miracle au monde plus expres que moy-mesme. On s'apprivoise à toute estrangeté par l'usage et le temps; mais plus je me hante et me connois, plus ma difformité m'estonne, moins je m'entens en moy. (1029).[46]

Far from resulting in a privileged access to one's being, or in the affirmation of autonomy, essayistic self-study defamiliarizes and astonishes its faithful practitioner. It discloses reason in its utter weakness or lameness; like a cripple, reason limps. It fails to secure the foundations for self-knowledge; yet in its failure, reason — under the pressure of the essaying process — paradoxically succeeds in revealing to its author his irreducible alterity, his own monstrosity. To be clear, experiencing himself as monstrous here is not a misrecognition (of his "natural" being) but an attestation of his unruly self, or what we could describe as his semiotic monstrosity, a self that is beyond representational or hermeneutic mastery. Indeed, so cognizant of his own foreignness to himself, how can Montaigne assert the transparency and homogeneity of the other?[47] More importantly, Montaigne's untotalizable self-relation obliquely points to an extra-discursivity, to something that escapes the habitual economy of the Same, yet without simultaneously positing a self that is outside the realm of interpretation and becoming.

Counterbalancing the insights of "Of a Monstrous Child" with those of "Of Cripples," then, enables the reader to entertain a parallax view of monstrosity, which reveals a very different and far less Cartesian account of monstrosity than was suggested earlier. While "Of a Monstrous Child" warns against the dangers of astonishment ("the error and astonishment that novelty brings us"

[539c] ["l'erreur et l'estonnement que la nouvelleté nous apporte" [713]), "Of Cripples" presents astonishment as the appropriate response to the author's natural unruliness *and* semiotic monstrosity. As if directly responding to the excesses of the Montaignian self, to the self's internal otherness, Descartes moves to pathologize the experience of "astonishment": "Astonishment is an excess of wonder which can never be anything but bad," he writes in *The Passions of the Soul*.[48] This Cartesian critique of astonishment should not be confused with Montaigne's. If Descartes is primarily concerned with the possibility of epistemological paralysis (the *cogito*'s inability to convert the new — the object of wonder, attractive in its rarity — into an object of knowledge), Montaigne's "Of a Monstrous Child" decries the allergic, exploitative, and totalizing reactions that the newness or singularity of the child's unruly body has provoked.

In "Of Cripples," Montaigne offers an alternative account of astonishment, one that is to be identified not with paralysis but with *care*, that is, an attentiveness to the inexhaustible and heterogeneous nature of his self. Such a care begins with a care for language, expressing his preference for the tentative, the partial:

> It makes me hate probable things when they are planted on me as infallible. I like these words, which soften and moderate the rashness of our propositions: "perhaps," "to some extent," "some," "they say," "I think," and the like. (788b)

> On me faict hayr les choses vray-semblables quand on me les plante pour infaillibles. J'ayme ces mots, qui amollissent et moderent la temerité de nos propositions: A l'avanture, Aucunement, Quelque, On dict, Je pense, et semblables. (1030)

A more nuanced or self-critical response to astonishment is arguably already at work in "Of a Monstrous Child." At first glance, Montaigne might be accused of having replaced one totalized relation for another, affirming at the end of the essay the ontological Said of the child: he is, in the final analysis, natural like us. Does Montaigne fail, then, to respond to the alterity of the child, effacing the differences that ought to have sustained their dissymmetrical relation? How does Montaigne preserve the child as a genuine object of wonder?

It is not by establishing a relation to an absolute alterity that Montaigne extends his care to the other, since reading the other according to *his own model* is, strictly speaking, impossible — or rather, it is only "possible" for God. Knowledge of God is a limit case. In the "Apology for Raymond Sebond," Montaigne also conceives of God as an object of wonder, irreducible to what is *familiar*, an "incomprehensible power" (380a/513).[49] A recognition of God's absolute alterity is what Montaigne, along with Saint Paul, finds "most excusable" in pagan religions (380a/513). Yet Montaigne's relation to others differs from his relation to God in that his quest to know others is problematized rather than relinquished; it is complicated by the essaying process, a constant return to the skeptical question "What do I know?" Montaigne never subjects God to *essaying*. Whereas a respect for the alterity of God stems in large part from one's faith in Him (God cannot be known directly nor by "our analogies and conjectures" [380a/512]), Montaigne's respect for the other's alterity is of a different ethical order; it derives from his self-exploration, from his awareness that the other is as elusive as the author's unruly self.

In "Of a Monstrous Child," the child's alterity (the *tout autre* of the child) is affirmed in relational rather than in absolute terms. Montaigne's ethical sensibility can be formulated in terms of a double movement, a movement intrinsic to the endless act of eating well — the perpetual unsaying and resaying of the ontological Said. The essayist demystifies monstrosity by affirming a shared humanity with the child. In neutralizing the child's *cultural* alterity — his source of instrumentalization, exploitation, and dehumanization — Montaigne cannibalizes or assimilates the monstrous other, transforming him into a comprehensible object of knowledge. Yet this process of cannibalization also reflects an interplay between mastery and opacity. The alterity of the child is not affirmed in abstraction but experienced as a rupture, a textual disturbance *relative to* his readers' expectations. This recognition/reinscription of difference, performed through a problematization of pre-given schemata and categories, is further displayed by Montaigne's staging of the incommensurability of his situated (historical) reader's contingent position and the ideal (ahistorical) epistemological view from nowhere (that of God or Nature). By offering his readers two subject positions that they cannot simply adopt or reject, Montaigne attests to the perplexities involved in representing the other. This rhetorical strategy, especially if read comparatively with the essayist's self-avowed semiotic monstrosity in "Of Cripples," preserves the irreducibility and mystery of the other, which in turn helps to sustain a relation of non-adequation (a "relation without relation") with the child, and guarantees that the "monstrous" other will continue to shock and to produce astonishment in the beholder. But unlike the version condemned by Montaigne in "Of a Monstrous Child," this astonishment is a precondition for ethics or *eating well*, arising from the beholder's generosity and openness to alterity, from a sensibility, that is, to the diversity and unruliness of nature.

II

Diderot's *Rameau's Nephew*

ALLEGORY AND THE MIND-AND-BODY PROBLEM

>The essence of language is friendship and hospitality.
>EMMANUEL LEVINAS

>Philosophy is not a dialogue. Name me a single example of a successful philosophical dialogue that wasn't a dreadful misunderstanding.
>SLAVOJ ŽIŽEK

The dialogue invites friendship. Its protean form makes it most hospitable to difference, yet an unruly difference always risks pushing to the limit an interlocutor's or reader's good will. *Rameau's Nephew*, Denis Diderot's fictional dialogue between "himself" (*Moi*, the narrator, the Enlightenment philosopher) and the historical figure Jean-François Rameau (*Lui*), the eccentric nephew of the famous French composer, infuriatingly tests the boundaries of friendship — the *book as friend* — and hospitality. Published posthumously in 1805 in German translation by Goethe, *Rameau's Nephew* can be seen as Diderot's belated intervention into what is recognized today as the mind-and-body problem.[1] This infamous problem originates in the revolutionary enterprise undertaken by Descartes in the *Discourse on Method* and *Meditations*. In search of epistemological certainty, and responding in no small part to Montaignian skepticism, Descartes maintained that beliefs must be infallible if they are to serve as a reliable source of human knowledge. Accordingly, he subjected all his previous beliefs to a hyperbolic doubt. His radical method led him to hypothesize the existence of an "evil genius," causing him to question all knowledge of the external world — including knowledge of his own existence. In the face of unbearable skepticism, Descartes discovered an indubitable and self-evident truth, namely that he exists, since he cannot doubt and not exist simultaneously. But what is the nature of this "I" that necessarily exists? Descartes inquired into its ontological status and realized soon after that the "I" (that necessarily exists) corresponds only to a thinking "I" (*cogito*) and not to a corporeal "I."

Even though Descartes ultimately justified the existence of the physical world by arguing that a benevolent God would not deceive us — that is, he "reassured" us that our clear and distinct ideas do actually correspond to the external world — our knowledge of the material world (including that of our body) remained immediately uncertain to us. As a result, Descartes established an epistemological hierarchy, one that privileges the mind along with its mental states over the physical body. By affirming the primacy of the mind (*res cogitans*), Descartes implicitly devalorized the body, treating it as a different and distinct substance (*res extensa*), giving rise to what has come to be known as Cartesian dualism. Thinkers after Descartes, particularly those unconvinced by his theistic appeal, sought to overcome the dualistic picture of the self by radically rethinking the uneasy relationship between the mind (the psychic) and the body (the physical).[2]

Given this context, *Rameau's Nephew* can be read as Diderot's allegory of the mind-and-body problem: the nephew's unruly body confronts the philosophe's rational mind. Commonly understood as a trope in which one thing is taken to stand for another, allegory, and allegorical readings, have long commanded respect for their purportedly greater (spiritual) value. François Rabelais, in his prologue to *Gargantua* (1534), famously drew attention to the hermeneutics of allegory (speaking-otherwise), urging his audience to interpret allegorically, for only this kind of reading would go beyond the work's comic surface and guarantee access to a truer or "higher meaning" (*altior sensus*), to his work's "nourishing marrow."[3] Yet allegorical reading easily satisfies a reader's hunger for meaning or deeper truths. As such, it is profoundly antithetical to the experience of literature as unruly. Accordingly, to read *Rameau's Nephew* as a straightforward allegory of the Cartesian problematic — arguing that the dialogue is *about* the mind-and-body problem — threatens more specifically to domesticate the literary work by reducing it to something all too philosophically familiar. The will to allegorize partakes of the economy of the Same, violently translating the particular into the general, the new into the already known. To refuse allegory altogether, however, is to deny the philosophical dialogue's playful dramatization of the mind-and-body problem, its pleasurable interrogation of and engagement with this universalizing mode of reading.[4] In short, it is to deny the inventive ways in which the dialogue itself elicits *and* stymies the reader's desire for allegory, for intimacy and/as comprehension. This chapter asks how one might read both *with* allegory and *against* its hegemonic tendencies, in order to respond more fruitfully, more ethically, to the interpretive challenges posed by Diderot's *Rameau's Nephew*, and to its call for dialogic friendship.[5]

The Narrator and His Other

In the preamble of *Rameau's Nephew*, Diderot's narrator carefully sets up his encounter with the nephew, starting first with an account of himself, a self captured in its habitual mode of being: "No matter what the weather, rain or shine, it's my habit every evening at about five o'clock to take a walk around the Palais Royal" ["Qu'il fasse beau, qu'il fasse laid, c'est mon habitude d'aller sur les cinq heures du soir me promener au Palais-Royal"].[6] This peripatetic narrator quickly reveals his taste for *self*-dialogue:

> I talk to myself about politics, love, taste, or philosophy.... I let my mind rove wantonly. I give it free rein to follow any idea, wise or mad. (8)

> Je m'entretiens avec moi-même de politique, d'amour, de goût ou de philosophie. J'abandonne mon esprit à tout son libertinage. Je le laisse maître de suivre la première idée sage ou folle qui se présente. (585)

Like Montaigne, the narrator describes himself as fully enthralled by his thoughts, willingly *essaying* whatever comes to his mind. In "Of Idleness," Montaigne depicts his *fantaisies* as defiant and frustrating, comparing his mind to a "runaway horse" and its thoughts to "chimeras and fantastic monsters" (21). Unlike Montaigne, however, Diderot's narrator merely *yearns* for self-loss, merely dreams of an unruly mind. The repetition of the first person — "*I* talk to myself... *I* let... *I* give..." — affirms the reality of self-mastery, reinforcing rather than troubling the agency behind the fantasy of unruliness. His narcissistic mode of self-care ultimately leads him to sexualize his mind's cherished activity: "my ideas are my trollops" (8) ["Mes pensées, ce sont mes catins" (585)].

Moving to an account of his encounter with the nephew at the Café de la Régence in the gardens of the Palais Royal, the narrator frames our introduction to the nephew with the verb *aborder* ("to accost"), which is repeated twice: "One day I was there after dinner . . . when *I was accosted* by one of the oddest characters in this country" (8, emphasis added) ["Un après-dîner, j'étais là . . . lorsque je fus abordé par un des plus bizzares personnages de ce pays" (585)] and *"He accosts me"* (10) ["Il m'aborde" (587)]. The repetition of *aborder* stresses that this encounter was first and foremost an interruption. But what is it about the nephew that makes him an unsettling figure, "one of the oddest characters in this country" (8) ["un des plus bizarres personnages de ce pays" (585)]? The nephew's strange mixture of "decency and depravity" (8) ["l'honnête et [le] déshonnête" (585–86)] might be an obvious reason. His moral self thwarts any clear and distinct normative judgments. Yet the narrator moves rather rapidly over this point, choosing instead to dwell on the nephew's physical oddity:

> He has no greater opposite than himself. Sometimes he is thin and wan like a patient in the last stages of consumption; you could count his teeth through his skin; he looks as if he had been days without food or had just come out of a Trappist monastery. The next month, he is sleek and fat as if he ate regularly at a banker's or had shut himself up in a Bernardine convent. . . . His first care on arising in the morning is to ascertain where he will dine; after dinner he ponders supper. (9)

> Rien ne dissemble plus de lui que lui-même. Quelquefois, il est maigre et hâve, comme un malade au dernier degré de la consomption; on compterait ses dents à travers ses joues. On dirait qu'il a passé plusieurs jours sans manger, ou qu'il sort de la Trappe. Le mois suivant, il est gras et replet, comme s'il n'avait pas quitté la table d'un financier, ou qu'il eût été renfermé dans un couvent de Bernardins. . . . Son premier soin, le matin quand il est levé, est de savoir où il dînera; après dîner, il pense où il ira souper. (586)

His comments underscore two key points. First, *his difference to himself*: the disruptive unpredictability of the nephew's bodily economy makes his body physically discontinuous. Second, *his difference from the narrator*: the nephew appears to the narrator as a different kind of being, more of an *eating* subject than a fellow *thinking* subject; the former's care of the belly jars with the latter's care of the mind. The condition of his belly — is it lacking or full? — literally structures the nephew's everyday existence. The narrator makes explicit his aversion to the likes of the nephew, stating that he has no genuine interest in "such eccentrics" (9) ["ces originaux-là" (586)]. Nor does he have any desire to know them or befriend them, unlike some, who "take them on as regular acquaintances or even friends" (9) ["D'autres en font leurs connaissances familières, même leurs amis" (586)]. Yet the narrator clarifies that he does not foreclose *all* relation to eccentrics: "It is only once a year that I stop and fall in with them" (9) ["Ils m'arrêtent une fois l'an, quand je les rencontre" (586)]. Limiting his exposure to eccentrics to an annual event, the narrator can only admit *conditional* hospitality. What saves or recuperates the nephew is his willingness to speak the truth, to expose the hypocrisy of social norms:

> He shakes and stirs us up, makes us praise or blame, smokes out the truth, discloses the worthy and unmasks the rascals. It is then that the sensible man keeps his ears open and sorts out his company. (10)

> Il secoue, il agite; il fait approuver ou blâmer; il fait sortir la vérité; il fait connaître les gens de bien; il démasque les coquins; c'est alors que l'homme de bon sens écoute, et démêle son monde. (587)

The nephew is thus partially acceptable but if, and only if, he conforms to the narrator's philosophical *ethos*. Any transgression from the privileged role of the social critic (namely, to unmask falsehoods) is likely to be met with disengagement, a nonrelation — an end to *any* hospitality.

The dialogue proper begins with the narrator recounting his actual encounter: "*He accosts me*: Ha ha! So there you are, master Philosopher!" (10, emphasis added) ["*Il m'aborde*... Ah, ah, vous voilà, monsieur le philosophe" (587)]. The shift to the present tense of *aborder* creates a sense of immediacy between *Moi* ("I") and *Lui* ("He"), as they are subsequently designated in the body of Diderot's text.[7] It does not take *Lui* long to express the primacy of his corporeal condition. A witty parasite, *Lui* lives off the wealthy patrons who occasionally take him in, exchanging meals for brief entertainment. It is clear what motivates the nephew to act; it is his intestines that govern his behavior: "Who would want to subject himself to play such a part," he says, "unless it be a poor wretch who finds in it twice or thrice a week the means to quell the tumult of his intestines?" (41) ["Qui est-ce qui peut s'assujettir à un rôle pareil, si ce n'est pas le misérable qui trouve là, deux ou trois fois la semaine, de quoi calmer la tribulation de ses intestins?" (618)].[8] For the nephew, the good life is not attained through contemplation; rather, it comes through the satisfaction of everyday bodily needs:

> The important thing is to keep the bowels moving freely, agreeably, copiously, every night. *O stercus pretiosum!* That is the great end of life in all social conditions. (24)

> Hurrah for ... the wisdom of Solomon: to drink good wines, gorge on choice food, tumble pretty women, sleep in downy beds — outside of that, all is vanity. (35)

> Le point est d'aller aisément, librement, agréablement, copieusement, tous les soirs à la garde-robe; *o stercus pretiosum*! voilà le grand résultat de la vie dans tous les états. (601)

> Vive la sagesse de Salomon. Boire de bon vin, se gorger de mets délicats; se rouler sur de jolies femmes; se reposer dans des lits bien mollets; excepté cela, le reste n'est que vanité. (611)

The obvious incompatibility of the philosophe and the nephew complicates, if not simply rules out, a "serious" philosophical discussion. *Moi* fails to secure the most basic of philosophical concessions from *Lui*, namely that of the importance of self-knowledge: "The devil take me if I know what I am like at bottom" [47] ["Que le diable m'emporte si je sais au fond ce que je suis" (623)]). *Lui*'s disruptive presence, as Stéphane Pujol points out, "is ... completely incongruous in the context of an authentic philosophical dialogue. His exuberant corporality pulls him all too often to the side of the animal."[9] Diderot's text "enacts a carnivalesque disruption of the conventional philosophical dialogue,"[10] and at the center of the subversion of philosophical protocols lies the nephew's belly. In this respect, the nephew's belly stands as a synecdoche for his whole body. Far from denying or silencing the body, the nephew remains absolutely enslaved to his physiological drives. As Aram Vartanian notes: "Nothing is made clearer in the dialogue than LUI's utter, indeed abject, obedience to the demands of his belly ... his stomach is where his brain should be."[11]

All the elements for an allegorical reading are now firmly in place: the nephew's unruly *body* exposes the blind spots of the philosophe's disembodied *mind*. The nephew's hunger comes thus to signify more than one character's discomfort; its larger meaning, as Vartanian argues, can be said to reside in Diderot's radical reworking of Cartesian dualism, his refutation of the metaphysical notion of an immaterial soul in favor of a more dynamic and "humanized" version of materialism, one that foregrounds the psychological and physiological dimensions of matter.[12] Such a reading thus reformulates the Cartesian problematic, deciphering within Diderot's text an unambiguous "philosophical message": considered separately, each of the two characters represents "only a mutilated and grotesque version of man."[13] As such, each figure is strictly speaking a "monster,"[14] a deficient subject who fails to conform mimetically to human reality.

The Nephew's Body Politics

Interpreting monstrosity within a framework of "psycho-physiological dualism" risks, however, eliding the social conditions responsible for the nephew's hunger, the cultural dimension of his alienation, ultimately flattening and depoliticizing the asymmetrical character of the philosophe's relationship to his unruly counterpart. As a servant-jester at his patron's many dinner parties, the nephew must be witty or play the fool on command, and it is quite clear that he finds such work both dehumanizing and humiliating.

> I was their dear Rameau, pretty Rameau, *their* Rameau — the jester, the buffoon, the lazy dog, the saucy rogue, the great greedy boob.... Anyone can do what he pleases with me, about me, in front of me. (19)

> J'étais leur petit Rameau, leur joli Rameau, leur Rameau le fou, l'impertinent, l'ignorant, le paresseux, le gourmand, le bouffon, la grosse bête.... On fait de moi, avec moi, devant moi, tout ce qu'on veut, sans que j'en formalise. (596)

Under the ubiquitous threat of eviction, the nephew must perform an appropriate buffoonery in order not to offend his wealthy patron; the dialogue, in fact, begins with the nephew's account of his recent dismissal from the Bertin-Hus household for "the folly of possessing a little good taste, a little wit, a little sense" (19) ["la sottise d'avoir eu un peu de goût, un peu d'esprit, un peu de raison" (596)]. The nephew's unstable identity can thus be explained, at least in part, by his precarious socioeconomic position.

Moreover, the nephew is by no means oblivious to the "injustice" of his abject condition: "I'm perfectly ready to be abject, but not under duress" (40) ["Je veux bien être abject; mais je veux que ce soit sans contrainte" (616)].

At the philosophe's advice to simply go back and beg for his former position, the nephew insists that a minimal respect for his "dignity" prevents him from voluntarily subjugating his will to the whims of others.[15] At times, he even articulates his social critique at a more global level, voicing his frustration with the existing division between those who eat (the haves) and those who starve (the have-nots):

> The voice of conscience and honor is pretty feeble when the guts cry out. (33)

> But if it is natural to be hungry — *I always come back to hunger, for it's with me an ever-present sensation* — I find that it is no part of good order to be sometimes without food. What a hell of an economy! Some men replete with everything while others, whose stomachs are no less importunate, whose hunger is just as recurrent, have nothing to bite on. (82, emphasis added)

> La voix de la conscience et de l'honneur est bien faible, lorsque les boyaux crient. (610)

> Mais s'il est dans la nature d'avoir appétit; *car c'est toujours à l'appétit que j'en reviens, à la sensation qui m'est toujours présente*; je trouve qu'il n'est pas du bon ordre de n'avoir pas toujours de quoi manger. Que diable d'économie, des hommes qui regorgent de tout, tandis que d'autres qui ont un estomac importun comme eux, une faim renaissante comme eux, et pas de quoi mettre sous la dent. (657)

The mind-and-body problem might thus be better understood as a *symptom* of bourgeois culture: the minds are the haves — those, like the narrator of the preamble, who have the luxury to indulge in narcissistic self-dialogue — and the bodies the have-nots — the dispossessed, marginalized others of society. *Moi*'s appeal to nature's inherent *telos* — "Whatever a man tries, Nature destined him for that" (82) ["A quoi que ce soit que l'homme s'applique la nature l'y destinait" (656)] — not only reflects naïve optimism but also helps to sustain a deeply conservative view of social reality. His explanation takes the form of rationalization of the status quo ("so let's accept things as they are" [16] ["acceptons donc les choses comme elles sont" (593)]). Following Hegel's powerful discussion of the nephew's "distorted consciousness" — a consciousness of the "perversion" and contradictions in the received ideas of the Good and the True[16] — Marxist critics such as Henri Lefebvre have allegorized *Lui*'s rebellious, alienated self as a kind of heroic figure of class struggle.[17]

Despite his moving words, however, *Lui*'s social critique — that there is no transcendental justification for such an economic disparity between members of his society — must be qualified. He is *not* an enlightened humanist, since he undeniably accepts the ideals of his greedy bourgeois society, namely the blind pursuit of money: "Gold is everything; and everything, without gold, is nothing" (73) ["L'or est tout; et le reste, sans or, n'est rien" (648)]. *Lui* even blames himself for his failings, for not fully exploiting the system to his own advantage. Full of "self-contempt" (21, translation modified) ["mépris de soi" (598)], he states: "How many times have I not exclaimed, 'Rameau, ten thousand fine tables are set every day in Paris — a dozen to a score of covers laid there, and not one for you'" (21) ["Combien de fois, je me suis dit: Comment, Rameau, il y a dix mille bonnes tables à Paris, à quinze ou vingt couverts chacune; et de ces couverts-là, il n'y en a pas un pour toi!" (598)]. Most puzzling and troubling, still, for the *philosophe* (as well as for the reader whose sympathy he was beginning to win over) is the nephew's contention that if circumstances were different — if he were rich — he would behave no differently than his wealthy patrons:

> I would act like all beggars on horseback. I'd be the most insolent ruffian ever seen. I'd remember every last thing they made me go through and pay them back with slings and arrows. I love bossing people and I will boss them. I love being praised and they will praise me. (34)

> Je ferais comme tous les gueux revêtus; je serais le plus insolent maroufle qu'on eût encore vu. C'est alors que je me rappellerais tout ce qu'ils m'ont fait souffrir; et je leur rendrais bien les avanies qu'ils m'ont faites. J'aime à commander, et je commanderai. J'aime qu'on me loue et l'on me louera. (610)

With obvious sarcasm, *Moi* observes:

> Knowing what worthy use you would make of wealth, I see how deplorable it is that you are poor. You would certainly be doing honor to human nature, good to your compatriots and credit to yourself. (34)

> Au digne emploi que vous feriez de la richesse, je vois combien c'est grand dommage que vous soyez gueux. Vous vivriez là d'une manière bien honorable pour l'espèce humaine, bien utile à vos concitoyens; bien glorieuse pour vous. (611)

But again what is far more revealing is *Lui*'s response:

You don't seem to know that at this very moment I represent the most important part of Town and Court. The well-to-do of every description have either said or not said to themselves the words I've just confided to you; the fact remains that the life I would lead in their position is precisely theirs. (34)

Vous ne vous doutez pas que dans ce moment je représente la partie la plus importante de la ville et de la cour. Nos opulents dans les états ou se sont dit à eux-mêmes ou ne sont pas dit les même choses que je vous ai confiées; mais le fait est que la vie que je mènerais à leur place est exactement la leur. (611)

The nephew short-circuits the philosophe's idealist discourse ("the world as it ought to be"). *Lui*'s beliefs, which *Moi* finds most detestable, are not in conflict with the existing and available norms, but are in fact those held by the majority of people. They conform to the prevailing *sensus communis* ("the world as it is"), and this reversal makes his interlocutor's position ironically seem both novel and unreasonable.

Lui's "political message" is thus profoundly paradoxical: he is sensitive to the injustices of his social reality, but at the same time he would perpetuate those injustices if his social position were reversed. *Lui*'s subversive stance — his critique of asymmetrical socioeconomic relations of power — is counterbalanced, if not completely neutralized, by his yearning to occupy a privileged position within the system he decries. Again, the ambiguity and paradoxes of *Lui*'s rhetoric reflect his engagement in the world, or more precisely, the social conditions of his labor. Unlike *Moi*, who claims sovereignty — "it is the philosopher who has nothing and asks for nothing" (84, translation modified) ["c'est le philosophe qui n'a rien et qui ne demande rien" (658)], as *Moi* emphatically states — *Lui* fully participates in "the beggar's pantomime" (83) ("la pantomime des gueux" [658]). He takes a position (in *Moi*'s words, "whoever stands in need of another is needy and takes a position" (83) ["quiconque a besoin d'un autre, est indigent et prend une position" (658)]), or rather, assumes his prescribed position within the web of dependency.[18] And while hunger and alienation serve as "evidence" for his physical participation in the system, *Lui*'s contradictions illustrate the subtle conditioning and workings of bourgeois ideology (social power). This ideology pervasively reaches his most intimate thoughts and wishes, for, as Michael Bernstein observes, *Lui* has paradoxically internalized "the most corrupt values and paltry aspirations of the society he mocks."[19] Yet the instability of *Lui*'s character — his erratic *lived* body forming the locus of disruption — makes clear that this process of socialization is neither perfect nor absolute. Although *Lui*'s psyche is not immune to ideology, as *Moi* phantasmatically claims his own to be, *Lui* is never simply a one-dimensional, docile, or disciplined body. On the contrary, Diderot's figure of the nephew emerges for the reader as a divided and conflicted subjectivity who is made to maintain contradictory outlooks.

The Madness of Ethics/An Ethics of Madness

The nephew's maddening contradictions can, of course, only be perceived as such — as contradictory — from within the norms of the *logos*. The *logos* derives its hegemonic force from its capacity to abstract, to transcend material (in its double sense of physical and social) limitations. The philosophe's privileging of the mind is equally predicated on the disavowal of embodiment — the successful silencing of his body — and on the bracketing of his personal point of view in favor of a *view from nowhere*:

> Consider the really interesting side of the problem; forget for a moment the point we occupy in time and space, and project your vision into centuries to come, into the most remote places, and nations yet unborn. Think of the welfare of our species. (16)

> Regardons la chose du côté vraiment intéressant; oublions pour un moment le point que nous occupons dans l'espace et dans la durée; et étendons notre vue sur les siècles à venir, les régions les plus éloignées, et les peuples à naître. Songeons au bien de notre espèce. (593)

Moi's *view from nowhere* suggests that any rational, disinterested subject can occupy this abstract space of the "objective" observer of humanity (a space that lacks historical or cultural specificity), and that abstraction is a *conditio sine qua non* for absolute knowledge.[20] *Moi* and *Lui* maintain incommensurable positions. The nephew mocks the philosophe's dubious detachment from the world that he observes:

> You go and perch on the epicycle of Mercury, and like Réaumur, who classifies the flies into seamstresses, surveyors, and reapers, you classify mankind into carpenters, builders, roofers, dancers, and singers: that's your affair. (82)

Perchez-vous sur l'épicycle de Mercure: et de là, distribuez si cela vous convient, et à l'imitation de Réaumur, lui la classe des mouches en couturières, arpenteuses, faucheuses, vous, l'espèce des hommes, en hommes menuisiers, charpentiers, coureurs, danseurs, chanteurs, c'est votre affaire. (656)

Declining *Moi*'s invitation to entertain the world from the self-detached perspective of *a* mind — "I don't follow all that you are preaching to me. Apparently it's philosophy and I tell you I will have no truck with it" (17) ["Je n'entends pas grand-chose à tout ce que vous me débitez là. C'est apparamment de la philosophie; je vous préviens que je ne m'en mêle pas" (593)] — *Lui* stresses his situatedness in the social world, underscoring the material dimension of his existence: "I am in *this* world and here I stay" (82) ["Je suis dans ce monde et j'y reste" (656–57)].[21]

The refusal of philosophy is not, however, tantamount to the refusal of critique. The nephew's reason is a reason inhabited by its other — unreason or madness. The narrator-*Moi* alludes to *Lui*'s singular critical ethos in the preamble: "The fellow is a compound of elevation and abjectness, of good sense and unreason" (8, translation modified) ["C'est un composé de hauteur et de bassesse, de bon sens et de déraison" (585)]. *Lui*'s mixture of "good sense" and "unreason" can be seen as further echoes of the Cartesian intertext. "Good sense," as Descartes announces in the opening line of the *Discourse*, "is the best distributed thing in the world,"[22] and the proliferation of "unreason" is precisely what the meditating subject must vigilantly keep in check. The drama of unreason reaches its apogee in the third meditation, which confronts hyperbolic doubt and the hypothesis of the "evil genius" *(malin génie)*. If the nephew's "good sense" affirms his proximity to the philosophe, his "unreason" signals not only his difference in the eyes of his interlocutor (who enjoys the stability of the *cogito*), but also the return of the evil genius — the return of the threat of madness. Diderot's recasting of the Cartesian encounter with the evil genius is thus markedly different; it now takes place *after* the advent of the *cogito* and the mind-and-body split.

Diderot's text ironically avoids the vexed question concerning the *experience* of madness that fueled the Foucault-Derrida debate. In "Cogito and the History of Madness," Derrida objected to Foucault's hostility toward philosophy and its domestication of madness. "Everything transpires," writes Derrida, "as if Foucault *knew* what madness means," what madness means in itself. But the project of locating an experience of madness — an extra-discursive understanding of madness — is ultimately a dubious endeavor, since any discoursing about madness necessarily involves reasoning with madness, a "*dissension... interior to logos in general.*"[23] Recalling his critique of Levinas in "Violence and Metaphysics," Derrida warned against Foucault's nostalgic or romantic desire for an "inaccessible primitive purity,"[24] insisting that the exposure to madness (pure alterity for Levinas) must take place *within* philosophy and not *before* or *beyond* it. *Rameau's Nephew* makes clear that a dialogue with unreason or madness must pass through the *logos*, the language of reason.[25] At the same time, Diderot's text also reveals that this journey need not be normalizing or one-sided but can be shot through with unexpected and ironic twists and reversals, even involving unreasonable philosophers *and* all too reasonable mad men.[26]

Diderot's philosophe — unlike Descartes' meditating subject who had finally found refuge from madness in the *cogito* — must now defend the *cogito*'s cognitive grounds and protect himself anew from the menace of madness, from the "mad audacity"[27] of the nephew's skepticism. What makes *Lui*'s skepticism especially maddening is its apparent lack of containment; no matter what *Moi* proposes, *Lui* objects mercilessly.

The nephew brings his doubts to bear on the foundations of reason in his discussion with the philosophe about the education of children. *Lui* cynically dismisses *Moi*'s "progressive" pedagogical ideal, seeing it as a desire to defeminize his daughter, to suppress or eradicate her so-called natural attributes and what would typically be taken as her accidental features:

> HE: What then will you teach her, if you please?
> I: To think straight, if I can — a rare thing among men, and still rarer among women.
> HE: Oh, let her think as wildly as she likes if she is only pretty, lively, and coquettish. (27–28, translation modified)

> LUI: Et que lui apprendrez-vous donc, s'il vous plaît?
> MOI: A raisonner juste, si je puis, chose si peu commune parmi les hommes, et plus rare encore parmi les femmes.
> LUI: Et laissez-la déraisonner, tant qu'elle voudra; pourvu qu'elle soit jolie, amusante et coquette. (604–5)

Lui exposes an unbridgeable gap between theory and practice. The promise of a humanist education, namely, the teaching of timeless subjects — "I put in grammar, mythology, history, geography, a little drawing, and *a great deal of ethics*" (28, emphasis added) ["Je mets de la grammaire, de la fable, de l'histoire, de la géographie, un peu de dessin, et *beaucoup de morale*" (605)] — is an ideological lie. His daughter's humanist education is at best counterproductive (its lessons are outdated), at worst disastrous: "How easy it would be for me to prove to you the futility of all those things in the world as we know it! Did I say futility? I should perhaps say the danger" (28) ["Combien il me serait facile de vous prouver l'inutilité de toutes ces connaissances-là, dans un monde tel que le nôtre; que dis-je, l'inutilité, peut-être le danger" (605)].[28]

It is not difficult to see how the philosophe's own model of self-understanding informs his educational concerns for his daughter. Cultivation of self entails a cultivation of the mind through reason.[29] Unreason and the body are, in turn, both excluded from her pedagogical program. The nephew responds by reorienting the discussion back to the body — to her physical and social body ("pretty, lively, and coquettish") — while downplaying the threat of unreason (the rational mind is the far bigger problem!). To be sure, from a feminist perspective, what the nephew seems to offer is profoundly misogynistic, reducing women to their irrational bodies. Is the nephew countering enlightenment pedagogy (egalitarian philosophy — "the mind has no sex"[30]) with medieval misogyny (the hierarchy of the sexes)? Maybe. But such an interpretation would minimize the nephew's penchant for hyperbole and the infuriating play of irony. Valorizing the daughter's physical appearance, social skill, and fashionable look all work to undermine her abstraction by the philosophe — his symbolic reproduction, in her, of another copy of himself. As we have seen, the body, for the nephew, hardly connotes inferiority. It anchors us in the perpetual flux of human existence. In this respect, the values he attributes to the female body might be better understood as a reflection of eighteenth-century phallogocentric norms of beauty than any claim about the essence of woman.

The nephew rails most vigorously against existing moral codes when these codes are represented by the philosophe as self-evident or universally true:

> Remember that in a subject as variable as manners and morals nothing is absolutely, essentially, universally true or false — unless it be that one must be whatever *self-interest* requires, good or bad, wise or foolish, decent or ridiculous, honest or vicious. (50, emphasis added)

> Souvenez-vous que dans un sujet aussi variable que les mœurs, il n'y a d'absolument, d'essentiellement, de généralement vrai ou faux, sinon qu'il

faut être ce que *l'intérêt* veut qu'on soit; bon ou mauvais; sage ou fou; décent ou ridicule; honnête ou vicieux. (626–27)

As Karlis Racevskis remarks, "[*Lui*'s] rantings have the effect of disclosing the pretentiousness of Reason and its claims to Truth."[31] As an antidote to the hypocrisy of both society and moral idealism, the nephew prefers to anchor his discussion of ethics in the "explanatory" category of self-interest, suggesting an egoistical or even Hobbesian view of human nature; indeed, *Lui* constantly returns man to his vicious animality, dispossessing him of any claims of moral superiority:

> We seem to be jolly, but actually we are all grumpy and fiercely hungry. Wolves are not more voracious nor tigers more cruel. We devour one another like wolves when the snow has long been on the ground. Like tigers we tear apart whatever succeeds. (47)

> Nous paraissons gais; mais au fond nous avons tous de l'humeur et grand appétit. Des loups ne sont pas plus affamés; des tigres ne sont pas plus cruels. Nous dévorons comme des loups, lorsque la terre a été longtemps couverte de neige; nous déchirons comme des tigres, tout ce qui réussit. (623–24)

The nephew's imagery of hungry bodies reminds the philosophe of man's proximity to other animals, while simultaneously exposing and exploding the fantasy of the mind's privilege.

This type of Hobbesian interpretation finds further justification in the nephew's cynical treatment of the philosophe's "well-meaning platitudes"[32] — patriotism, friendship, altruism, social duties — by revealing how these lofty ideals ultimately mask man's inherent self-love or vanity:

> I: What! And fighting for your country?
> HE: Vanity! There are no countries left. All I see from pole to pole is tyrants and slaves.
> I: What of helping your friends?
> HE: Vanity! No one has any friends. And even if one had, should one risk making them ungrateful? Look close and you'll see that's all you get for being helpful. Gratitude is a burden and burdens are to be shuffled off.
> I: To hold a position in society and discharge its duties?

HE: Vanity! What difference whether you hold a position or not, provided you have means, since you only seek a position in order to get wealth. Discharge one's duties — what does that bring you? — jealousy, worries, persecution. Is that the way to get on? Nonsense! Pay court, pay court, know the right people, flatter their tastes and fall in with their whims, serve their vices and second their misdeeds — there's the secret. (35, translation modified)

MOI: Quoi! défendre sa patrie?
LUI: Vanité. Il n'y a plus de patrie. Je ne vois d'un pôle à l'autre que des tyrans et des esclaves.
MOI: Servir des amis?
LUI: Vanité. Est-ce qu'on a des amis? quand on en aurait, faudrait-il en faire des ingrats? regardez-y bien; et vous verrez que c'est presque toujours là ce qu'on recueille des services rendus. La reconnaissance est un fardeau; et tout fardeau est fait pour être secoué.
MOI: Avoir un état dans la société et en remplir les devoirs?
LUI: Vanité. Qu'importe qu'on ait un état, ou non; pourvu qu'on soit riche; puisqu'on ne prend un état que pour le devenir. Remplir ses devoirs, à quoi cela mène-t-il? à la jalousie, au trouble, à la persécution. Est-ce ainsi qu'on s'avance? faire sa cour, morbleu; faire sa cour; voir les grands; étudier leurs goûts; se prêter à leurs fantaisies; servir leurs vices; approuver leurs injustices. Voilà le secret. (611–12)

While the nephew is quite adamant that all of the philosophe's virtues and altruistic ideals are ultimately illusory, pointing back to an egoistical self (a self concerned primarily and exclusively with its own interest rather than with the well-being of others), his counter-ideal of self-interest is devoid of any metaphysical pretension.[33] He does not seek to replace one system with another, moral idealism with natural egoism, for example. Rather, the nephew — in his rhetorical role as evil genius — operates most effectively and most disturbingly as a short circuit in the Enlightenment machinery of knowledge production. In his obsessive return to the question of self-interest, the nephew interrupts the philosophe's logic of abstraction (the subtraction of the body from discourse), the smooth functioning of rationality, jolting his interlocutor, forcing him to take stock of unruly exceptions, of which the nephew is a sublime example: "But, Master Philosopher, it is with universal morality just as with universal grammar: there are exceptions" (31–2) ["Mais, monsieur le philosophe, il y a une conscience générale. Comme il y a une grammaire générale; et puis des exceptions" (608)].

The Sublime Body/Text

The philosophe's narcissistic defenses do seem to protect him from the nephew's rhetorical onslaught, leading critics to conclude that the dialogue ends in a kind of philosophical aporia or stalemate, "leaving the reader wondering what has happened and if anything has changed."[34] Yet if the philosophe succeeds in deflecting the nephew's corrosive verbal energy (something the reader is perhaps less successful in doing), this does not mean that *Moi* is left unaltered by his exposure to *Lui*. Quite the contrary. *Lui*'s impact on *Moi* is not fully registered, however, in the dialogue proper, that is, in the explicit staging of the *dialogical*. Rather, it ironically appears in the third, *monological* voice of the narrator-*Moi* — the narrative voice of the philosophe as he comments on his exchange with the nephew. In such brief moments of separation, the philosophe paints a more nuanced portrait of his counterpart (one that recalls the depiction of the nephew from the preamble): "Neither more nor less detestable than other men, [the nephew] was franker than they, more logical, and thus often profound in his depravity" (74) ["(Le neveu) n'était ni plus ni moins abominable qu'eux; il était seulement plus franc, et plus conséquent; et quelquefois profond dans sa dépravation" (649)].[35] What provokes the most telling of these narrative asides is, however, what *Lui does* more so than what he *says*, since words are not his only means of "communication." Through his pantomimes, which represent the most explicit break with the protocols of philosophical discourse, the nephew's *body* itself speaks, or more precisely, his body *performs*.

Unlike *Moi*'s Cartesian body (a separate substance possessing the attribute of extension), which holds the status of mere machine (automaton), *Lui*'s body emerges as a medium for artistic self-expression, the site of rhapsodic performances. *Lui*'s compulsion to engage in pantomimes further underscores his difference from *Moi*. Whereas *Moi* is autonomous and self-sufficient, *Lui*'s identity appears fundamentally heteronomous and relational, dependent on his "borrowing a multiplicity of alien identities through the dialogue."[36] In a sense, the nephew's pantomimes enact his desire for contact with others, or what Louisa Shea has dubbed his "intellectual promiscuity."[37]

As scenes of excess, *Lui*'s pantomimes engender hesitation in the beholder as well as an unsettling mixture of feelings and responses, a mixture of joy and pain, an opportunity for Barthesian *jouissance* that can be qualified as sublime. The narrator-*Moi* comments:

> My soul divided between opposed motives, I hardly knew whether to burst with laughter or with indignation. I was suffering. (23, translation modified)

> I hardly knew whether I should come or go, laugh or get angry. I stayed, wanting to turn the conversation to some subject that would drive out of my soul the horror that filled it. (62)

> If he left the vocal part, it was to take up the instrumental..., gripping our souls [the souls of *Moi* and the onlookers at the café] and keeping them suspended in the most singular state of being that I have ever experienced. (67)

> L'âme agitée de deux mouvements opposés, je ne savais si je m'abandonnerais à l'envie de rire, ou au transport de l'indignation. Je souffrais. (600)

> Je ne savais, moi, si je devais rester ou fuir, rire ou m'indigner. Je restai, dans le dessein de tourner la conversation sur quelque sujet qui chassât de mon âme l'horreur dont elle était remplie. (637)

> S'il quittait la partie du chant, c'était pour prendre celle des instruments...; s'emparant de nos âmes, et les tenant suspendues dans la situation la plus singulière que j'aie jamais éprouvée. (643)

In a manner that betrays his philosophical bias, the narrator interprets the bewildering move from verbal exchange (*Lui*'s dialogue with *Moi*) to body language (the start of *Lui*'s pantomime) as a process through which *Lui* loses his mind:

> He was getting into a passion and beginning to sing, his voice growing louder as his passion increased. Next he gesticulated, and made faces and twisted his body, and I thought to myself: "*There he goes — losing his mind.*" (66, emphasis added and translation modified)

> Il commençait à entrer en passion, et à chanter tout bas. Il élevait le ton, à mesure qu'il se passionnait davantage; vinrent ensuite, les gestes, les grimaces du visage et les contorsions du corps; et je dis, *Bon; voilà la tête qui se perd*. (642)

The loss of self-control, or the absence of a perceivable authoritative "I" governing the body, translates into a loss of mind, that is, a displacement of the *cogito* — a threat to the unquestioned primacy of the speaking subject (*logos*). The philosophe apprehends the nephew's musical and gestural performance as flirting with madness:

> He noticed nothing, he kept on, in the grip of mental possession, an enthusiasm so close to madness that it seemed doubtful whether he would recover. (67)

> Lui n'apercevait rien; il continuait, saisi d'une aliénation d'esprit, d'un enthousiasme si voisin de la folie qu'il est incertain qu'il en revienne. (642)

The philosophe ends his description of *Lui*'s spectacular rhapsody with the repetition of the expression *perdre la tête*: "He had completely lost his mind" (68, translation modified) ["sa tête était tout à fait perdue" (643)]. From "losing his mind" to "completely lost his mind," *Lui*'s metamorphosis from speaking Mind into performing Body comes to full fruition, dramatizing what the body can do once it escapes the masterful control of the sovereign mind. In this great pantomime, the body as *homme orchestre* undergoes nothing short of a Nietzschean transvaluation. "From an eighteenth-century perspective," as Lynne Huffer points out, "the pantomimes can be 'heard' as the artistic transformation of a madness made mute by the Cartesian exclusion of unreason from the cogito."[38] The saying of *Lui*'s body pierces *Moi*'s narcissistic defenses, compelling him to confess his admiration of and pity for the nephew: "Did I admire? Yes, I did admire. Was I moved to pity? I was moved" (67) ["Admirais-je? Oui, j'admirais! Étais-je touché de pitié? J'étais touché de pitié" (643)].

Yet the narrator also finds himself compelled to qualify his ethico-aesthetic judgment: "But a streak of derision was interwoven with these feelings and denatured them" (67) ["Mais une teinte de ridicule était fondue dans ces sentiments, et les dénaturait" (643)]. Critics for the most part have interpreted this critical supplement to the nephew's more hospitable or favorable assessment in the context of Diderot's own reflections, in *Paradox on the Comedian*, on the actor's need for rational self-mastery and control over his emotions:[39]

> I say: "It is extreme sensibility that makes mediocre actors; it is mediocre sensibility that creates the large number of bad actors; and it's the complete lack of sensibility that prepares sublime actors." The tears of the actor come down from his brain, those of the sensible being rise up from his heart.[40]

The nephew is thus ridiculed for failing to act as a successful actor would, for failing to uphold Diderot's ideal of self-mastery (mind over matter, reason over sensibility). Such a conflation between *Moi* and Diderot, as tempting as it might be, invariably leads to a myopic interpretation of the pantomime, positing self-mastery as an aesthetic ideal without simultaneously subjecting it to the aporetic logic of the dialogue. *Lui*, as we have seen, mockingly flaunts his skepticism about anything related to an idealized version of the self — self-sufficiency (*Lui*'s identity is fully relational as he is firmly inscribed in "the web of dependency"), self-detachment (he does not share *Moi*'s stance of epistemological detachment), and self-knowledge (he lacks a cognitive grasp of the *cogito*). Why would self-mastery be any more desirable? Why should the reader be any less critical of it?

The question of self-mastery is not limited to the nephew's situation, however. It exceeds its original context, ironically turning back on the philosophe. It refers us back to him not only in relation to his aesthetic preferences but also, and more importantly, in relation to his interpretive practices — the ways he reads the dizzying otherness of *Lui*'s pantomimes. Simply stated, the self-mastery of the beholder confronts the disruptive powers of the sublime object. If, in the preamble, the philosophe entertains the idea of madness, or rather, contemplates madness as an idea, as a self-generated thought emanating from his mind ("I let my mind rove wantonly. I give it free rein to follow any idea, wise or mad"), the philosophe of the dialogue proper faces madness as *exteriority*, as a sublime force in need of either rechanneling (turning the conversation to some other topic) or hermeneutic subduing (judging *Lui* as worthy of admiration and pity). What is at stake here is the philosophe's exposure and response to the sublimity of the nephew, to the otherness of (his) unreason. The former option of reorienting their discussion toward more suitable matters proves wholly unsuccessful, while the latter seems more promising. In recognizing the nephew as an object of admiration and pity, the philosophe effectively diminishes the alterity of the nephew, inscribing him in the familiar language of Enlightenment morality, and thus succeeds in reestablishing a hermeneutic *relation* with the nephew, whose rhapsodic performance brought him to the brink of madness.

In his article on admiration in the *Encyclopedia*, Diderot defended the cultivation of admiration, cautioning the reader, though, about its unruly potential: "we must guard to an extent against our soul's first reaction to present objects, giving ourselves over to it once we are reassured by our knowledge, and above all by models to which we can relate the object before us."[41] Like Descartes — who had stressed the importance of separating "admiration" from "astonishment," the latter being an undesirable excess of the former — Diderot insists on the need to bring admired objects back into the epistemological fold. As if to contain further the dangers of admiration — to ensure that it does not devolve into a paralyzing form of astonishment,[42] something more akin to the sublime — the philosophe evokes the moral concept of pity. Philosophical discussions of pity date back to Aristotle and the Stoics, but it was the Enlightenment that brought pity to the forefront as a positive term for ethical discourse.[43] Descartes exemplifies well the pre-Enlightenment philosophical tradition and its attitude toward pity:

> Those who feel very weak and very much subject to fortune's adversities seem to be more inclined to [Pity], because they represent the misfortune of others to themselves as possibly happening to them; thus they are moved to Pity by the Love they bear to themselves rather than by that which they have for others.[44]

The philosophe thus figures as anti-Cartesian, or better yet, as an updated Cartesian self, a humanized *cogito*, a caring Mind. Yet it remains unclear whether his feelings of admiration and pity make him more or less hospitable to the nephew's *alterity*. By identifying with the nephew — the basis for pity — the philosophe tacitly acknowledges the other's performative powers, his aesthetic genius, but he also fixes *Lui* as an object of *admiration*, canceling his potential transmutation into an object of *astonishment*. The philosophe ostensibly reintroduces difference between self and other immediately after identifying with the nephew by distancing himself from what he refers to as *Lui*'s ridiculousness. The type of distance envisioned here, however, does little to counterbalance the assimilation of the nephew.

Does the philosophe, then, succeed in providing the reader a way out of the *dialogue des sourds*? Any success (as the reader discovers with him) proves fleeting, for as soon as the text shifts back to the dialogical mode, to the face-to-face exchange, the nephew's unruly presence returns, seemingly oblivious to the philosophe's internal interpretive struggles. Toward the end of the dialogue, *Moi* lashes out at *Lui*: "[Y]ou are a lazy, greedy lout, a coward and a rotting soul" (85) ["[V]ous êtes un fainéant, un gourmand, un lâche, une âme de boue" (659)]. *Lui*'s response, "I believe I told you so much" ["Je crois vous l'avoir dit" (659)], beautifully neutralizes the charge.

Mastery of the other turns out to be yet another, albeit more subtle, fantasy of possession. The reader undoubtedly develops some sympathy toward the philosophe, feeling a similar kind of inhospitality toward Diderot's own sublime work.[45] Part of the frustration — and of the exhilarating joy — that the reader feels stems from the dialogue's parallactic demands, its request that the reader shift from *Moi*'s perspective to *Lui*'s and vice versa without the comfort of a conceptual synthesis, and its inventiveness in its relentless recasting of the scene of interpretation. To do justice to *Rameau's Nephew*, to be hospitable to Diderot's text, means to be receptive and responsive to the dialogue's sublime short-circuiting ways — we might say, its inhospitality to hermeneutic mastery — to the ways it solicits and blocks allegory, and to the ways it encourages and disparages the reader's desire for identification, guidance, and resolution. Mining *Rameau's Nephew* for its philosophical import, or allegorical potential, privileges containment and sameness (reducing Diderot's work or characters to a version of the reader's self — *the friend as another self*) at the expense of the dialogue's irreducible particularity, its unruly difference. If *Rameau's Nephew* starts as an allegory of the Cartesian mind-and-body problem — with the reader invited to hear both sides of the epistemological dispute — its putative philosophical concern irresistibly gives way to unforeseen questions, while its allegorical mechanisms spiral into madness, unsettling the very foundations the work had laid for itself.

Translating *Modernité*

NARRATIVE, VIOLENCE, AND AESTHETICS
IN BAUDELAIRE'S *SPLEEN OF PARIS*

> Paradoxically, it is not possible for us as ethical agents
> to imagine otherness or alterity maximally. We have to turn
> the other into something like the self in order to be ethical.
> To surrender in translation is more erotic than ethical.
> GAYATRI CHAKRAVORTY SPIVAK

Involving questions of fidelity and distance, and the inevitable reduction of the foreign to the familiar, translation enacts an ethical relation, a relation to an otherness — be it an idea, a text, or a person. Perhaps because of its potential to provoke ethical questioning, translation — as both a practice of interpretation and a self-reflexive discovery of alterity — preoccupied Charles Baudelaire throughout his career, from his early rendering of Edgar Allen Poe into French to his "retranslation," in a larger sense, of modern life in his move from poetry to prose, from *The Flowers of Evil* to *The Spleen of Paris*. This chapter explores Baudelaire's ethical engagement with translation as a means to unsettle received understandings of reality and poetry and to rethink the relationship between modern life and its aestheticized image. Beginning with an analysis of Baudelaire's profound attraction to the visual arts, I will consider the powerful insights into human suffering and modern life that painting and caricature inspired in him, insights that he sought, in turn, to translate into poetic language. Turning to the ethical dilemmas of translation that increasingly concerned Baudelaire, this chapter then considers his later unruly prose poems, which betray a growing attention to his poetry's ideological complicity with the forms of violence it often narrates, and even explicitly condemns, thus staging for the reader what can be described as the limits of translatability.

Visualizing Suffering: From the Human Condition to Bourgeois Life

In painting, no artist, for Baudelaire, surpassed Delacroix's imaginative and moving depictions of the human condition. Delacroix stands as an unmatched witness to man's eternal violence and suffering.[1] As early as the *Salon of 1846*, Baudelaire asserts that "Delacroix is universal" (SW 68) ["Delacroix est universel" (OC 2:435)], placing him alongside two masters of literature, Dante and Shakespeare:

> Delacroix is an admirer of Dante and Shakespeare, two other great painters of human suffering; he knows them thoroughly and *can interpret them freely*. To look with penetrative attention at the whole series of his pictures is to feel as though we were present at the celebration of a tragic rite. (SW 74, emphasis added)

> Delacroix affectionne Dante et Shakespeare, deux autres grands peintres de la douleur humaine; il les connaît à fond, et il sait *les traduire librement*. En contemplant la série de ses tableaux, on dirait qu'on assiste à la célébration de quelque mystère douloureux. (OC 2:440)

The translation metaphor (translation as imaginative interpretation) is telling since it underscores the literariness of Delacroix's art (establishing a "correspondence" between his images and their texts), as well as his creative (free) approach to the originals, which stand out themselves as excellent translations in their own right. Delacroix's *re*translation of Dante and Shakespeare — his artistic interpretation of their own poeticized perception of the human condition — is not an act of duplication or slavish fidelity but an imaginative practice in itself. Translation creates as it transfigures the original, and it is this act of *poiesis* that Baudelaire admires and will seek to imitate. But what is perhaps most significant here is what brings these three figures together: "human suffering," or more specifically, the *painting* of "human suffering." By describing Dante and Shakespeare as "great painters of human suffering,"

Baudelaire complicates not only the notion of fidelity but also the priority of any one medium over another, troubling any straightforward understanding of "originals" and "translations."

As a painter with a literary sensibility, Delacroix, in Baudelaire's eyes, is aptly poised to capture the moral suffering, or existential anguish, of the human condition. In the *Salon of 1846*, Baudelaire describes this capacity more precisely in his reading of *Femmes d'Alger*:

> Most are sickly, and glow with an inner beauty. He expresses strength not by depicting powerful muscles but nervous tension. He excels in expressing not only suffering but especially — and therein lies the prodigious mystery of his painting — moral suffering. (SW 74)

> Presque toutes sont malades, et resplendissent d'une certaine beauté intérieure. Il n'exprime point la force par la grosseur des muscles, mais par la tensions des nerfs. C'est non seulement la douleur qu'il sait mieux exprimer, mais surtout, — prodigieux mystère de sa peinture, — la douleur morale!" (OC 2:440)

In *The Universal Exposition of 1855*, he reiterates his admiration for Delacroix, as well as his fascination with the *suffering* of the painter's female subjects:

> All of them seem to have in their eyes some secret suffering that cannot be locked away in the secret depth of the soul. Their pallor seems to betray their inner struggle.... [T]hese women, sick at heart or in mind, have in their eyes a leaden look of fever, or the abnormal glint of their sickness, in their glance a supernatural intensity. (SW 136)

> On dirait qu'elles portent dans les yeux un secret douloureux, impossible à enfouir dans les profondeurs de la dissimulation. Leur pâleur est comme une révélation des batailles intérieures.... [C]es femmes malades du cœur ou de l'esprit ont dans les yeux le plombé de la fièvre ou la nitescence anormale et bizarre de leur mal, dans le regard, l'intensité du surnaturalisme. (OC 2:594)

The beautiful strangeness that marks Delacroix's work violates the expectations of his bourgeois beholder, this "poor man" ["pauvre homme"], who, Baudelaire tells us, "has quite lost sight of the differences that mark the phenomena of the physical and the moral worlds, the natural and the supernatural" (SW 121) ["a perdu la notion des différences qui caractérisent les phénomènes du monde physique et du monde moral, du naturel et du surnaturel" (OC 2:580)]. The French bourgeois has forgotten that *"Beauty always has an element of strangeness"* (SW 119, italics in the original) [*"le beau est toujours bizarre"* (OC 2:578)]. In a utilitarian society driven by the spirit of positivism, Delacroix exemplifies those exceptional painters who manage to translate the bizarre successfully, who are able to make the souls of their contemporary audience "vibrate with conjecture and anxiety" (SW 120) ["faire vibrer, conjecturer et... inquiéter" (OC 2:579)].

Like Delacroix, Baudelaire understands "suffering" — in all its "strangeness" — as being inextricably tied to modernity and, strictly speaking, impossible to ignore or escape fully. He translates this insight first in his art criticism, where he invites his readers to imagine the experience and perception of *douleur* differently. Extending poetic sensibility to the realm of the everydayness of modern life, Baudelaire imagines the possibility that simply perceiving an unnatural color could become an aesthetic experience producing "exquisite pain" (SW 58) ["une douleur délicieuse" (OC 2:425)]. This oxymoron jars with bourgeois utilitarianism, unsettling readerly expectations about what constitutes pleasure and pain. Yet the mediation of the Delacroixian intertext is perhaps most visible in Baudelaire's poem "A Former Life ("La Vie antérieure"), when the narrator, in the last line, attests to his "secret douloureux," the same secret that haunts Delacroix's women. The lyrical sonnet describes a harmonious paradise in which happiness unexpectedly consists in nourishing this "secret grief":

> I once lived under vast and columned vaults
> Tinged with a thousand fires by ocean suns,
> So that their grand, straight pillars would become,
> In evening light, like grottoes of basalt....
>
> So there I lived, in a voluptuous calm
> Surrounded by the sea, by splendid blue,
> And by my slaves, sweet-scented, handsome, nude,
>
> Who cooled my brow with waving of the palms,
> And had one care — to probe and make more deep
> What made me languish so, my secret grief.[2]
>
> J'ai longtemps habité sous de vastes portiques
> Que les soleils marins teignaient de mille feux,

> Et que leurs grands piliers, droits et majestueux,
> Rendaient pareils, le soir, aux grottes basaltiques. . . .
>
> C'est là que j'ai vécu dans les voluptés calmes,
> Au milieu de l'azur, des vagues, des splendeurs
> Et des esclaves nus, tout imprégnés d'odeurs,
>
> Qui me rafraîchissaient le front avec des palmes,
> Et dont l'unique soin était d'approfondir
> Le secret douloureux qui me faisait languir. (OC 1:17–18)

No content is given to the secret, which is only revealed in the final line. The bourgeois reader is left surprised and languishing after a more precise knowledge of the poet's metaphysical malaise; the reader, in his or her desire to "deepen" the secret, becomes a kind of slave to the poet. If the reader really wants to delve deeper into this mysterious pain, however, he or she must paradoxically relinquish a sense of individuality and control, and abandon an economy of consumption and mastery in favor of an aesthetic one. In such an economy, works of art are judged by "the sum of ideas or the day-dreams" (SW 120) ["la somme d'idées ou de rêveries" (OC 2:579)] that they provoke, by their ability to defamiliarize their readers and compel them to attend to their own disquieting experience of *human suffering*.

To be sure, Baudelaire anticipates that his invitation for *rêveries* may fall on deaf ears, remaining skeptical that the typical bourgeois reader (such as the "pauvre homme" evoked above) would respond to the poet's demands.[3] Yet he does hint at the existence of a different kind of reader, one who is not a fellow poet or artist, nor an unimaginative member of the bourgeoisie; rather, this reader is one who allows himself or herself to be affected and changed by art in unforeseen ways. This is the reader whom Delacroix's paintings cannot fail to affect: "It is impossible for an art-lover with a dash of the poet in him not to feel his imagination struck, not by a historical, but a poetic, religious and universal impression" (SW 312) ["Il est impossible qu'un amateur un peu poète ne sente pas son imagination frappée, non pas d'une impression historique, mais d'une impression poétique, religieuse, universelle" (OC 2:634)]. In *The Painter of Modern Life*, Baudelaire links these altering effects of paintings to the work of translation: "The moral reflections and musings that arise from the drawings of an artist are in many cases the best translation that the critic can make of them" (SW 422, translation modified) ["Les considérations et les rêveries morales qui surgissent des dessins d'un artiste sont, dans beaucoup de cas, la meilleure traduction que le critique en puisse faire" (OC 2:712)]. In this light, we could say that Baudelaire's preferred reader would not only be an amateur poet but also an amateur translator. Or perhaps being a poet and a translator here amounts to the same thing, requiring the same type of ethical openness to the *bizarrerie* of modern aesthetics.

What precisely makes modern aesthetics bizarre is not immediately clear, however. For Baudelaire, the ambiguity of modern art ultimately resides in its dualistic nature: "*Modernité* is the transient, the fleeting, the contingent; it is one half of art, the other being the eternal and the immutable" (SW 403, translation modified) ["La modernité, c'est le transitoire, le fugitif, le contingent, la moitié de l'art, dont l'autre moitié est l'éternel et l'immuable" (OC 2:695)].[4] Baudelaire's neologism *modernité* can be translated as either "modernity" or "modernism." The justification for using modernity is fairly straightforward. The term *modernité* appears in an essay discussing the painters of *modern life*, suggesting that its subject matter is a historical reality in flux (the scene of modernity) and its aesthetic representations (by nineteenth-century painters). Walter Benjamin captures well the traumatic force of the historical, the rapid changes in technology and urbanization, famously describing Baudelaire as the poet who "placed [the] shock experience" of modern urban life "at the very center of his art."[5] At the same time, as Benjamin's description also makes clear, Baudelaire inscribes *modernité* in an observation about aesthetics and the task of the modern artist, making Baudelaire a kind of proto-figure of modernism. Marshall Berman observes: "If we had to nominate a first modernist, Baudelaire would surely be the man."[6] Similarly, Gerald Bruns notes: "It was Baudelaire who gave the term 'modernism' (or *modernité*) its first formal articulation."[7] By taking the imperfect (what is ephemeral, fugitive, contingent) as an *essential* aspect of art Baudelaire undermines the classical and neoclassical understandings of Beauty (all versions of the Platonic *eidos*) as that which is by definition perfect, complete, located outside the destructive forces of space and time. Aesthetics is no longer conceived in traditional terms of transcendence and universality; rather, its subject matter is the unruliness of the here and now, that is, the unruliness of modern life.

The second half of Baudelaire's definition, "the eternal and immutable," arguably recuperates the first half and domesticates its disruptive edge. It might, however, be more productive, and more faithful to the subversive kernel of Baudelaire's formulation, to read *modernité* as a parallax, as the radical noncoincidence of both its halves. The contingent element is what makes Baudelairian aesthetics always incomplete, ontologically lacking. If *modernité* were to become identical to itself, it would no longer be *modernité*. Modern art, for Baudelaire, is not identical to itself.

In the modern city, beauty can no longer pretend to be eternal but must also incorporate the transitory. If beauty is *always* bizarre (and in this aspect, timeless), what makes *any given particular* work of art bizarre (what would make the soul of its beholder "vibrate with conjecture and anxiety"), the source of astonishment — "Beauty is *always* astonishing" (SW 294, translation modified) ["Le Beau est *toujours* étonnant" (OC 2:616)] — is relative to a historically contingent horizon of expectations. Likewise, *human suffering* is an ontological condition of man (beginning with the Fall in Judeo-Christian narrative), while the way in which this suffering is actually manifested, framed, and addressed remains historically and ideologically mediated.

For this reason Baudelaire can praise the great painters of *human suffering* while at the same time pointing to their limitations and to the need to translate the present *otherwise than eternal*. Ironically, Baudelaire's praise of Delacroix as universal comes to signify his limitation as a translator of modernity. While credited for the primacy they give to "intimacy, spirituality, colour, yearning for the infinite" (SW 53) ["intimité, spiritualité, couleur, aspiration vers l'infini" (OC 2:421)], Delacroix's paintings — "modern in sensibility" though "not in subject matter," as J. A. Hiddleston puts it[8] — ultimately did not adequately capture the changing reality of the period. For more faithful portraits of modern life, Baudelaire turned to other artists, among them the caricaturist Honoré Daumier.

Fully engaged with the subject matter of his times, Daumier takes the bourgeois as his foremost subject. "No one better than he has known and loved (in the manner of the artists) the bourgeois" (SW 221) ["Nul comme celui-là n'a connu et aimé (à la manière des artistes) le bourgeois" (OC 2:555)], writes Baudelaire in *Some French Caricaturists*. The function of caricature is of course to satirize, that is, to distort, exaggerate, and sharpen the object of representation so as to reveal to its spectator a more profound, "hidden" moral ugliness in the subject (both the spectator and the object represented). Daumier's lithograph *Rue Transnonain*, which depicts a semi-nude man whose murdered body is crushing that of his infant, exemplifies the subversive force of caricatures. Produced in the period of social unrest following the first years of Louis-Philippe's reign, Daumier's lithograph refers to an event that took place on April 14, 1834, when government troops, thinking a shot was fired on them from a neighboring house at 12 rue Transnonain, barged in and ruthlessly massacred its innocent inhabitants, including two children.[9]

What Baudelaire, however, borrows from Daumier is not so much the didactic message about the oppression of the poor (of the Proudhonian type that Baudelaire will later ridicule in "Let's Beat Up the Poor!" ["Assommons les pauvres!"]),[10] nor the unjust accumulation of power by the bourgeoisie (which would make aesthetics subservient to a political cause), but the artist's critique of bourgeois complacency as well as the lithograph's potential to solicit both an aesthetic and a political judgment, a judgment that necessarily implicates the observer in the satire.[11] Moreover, it is Daumier's brand of *serio ludere* that Baudelaire celebrates. The grotesqueness of the represented object together with the banality of the scene — "It is not what you would call caricature exactly, it is history, it is reality, trivial and terrible" (sw 218) ["Ce n'est pas précisément de la caricature, c'est de l'histoire, de la triviale et terrible réalité" (oc 2:552)] — creates a unique *mélange*, a beautiful mixing of art and politics, that produces an uncanny moment of self-reflexivity in the beholder.

Unsettling his audience's yearning for an undisturbed aesthetic experience is a technique that Baudelaire translates and deploys quite effectively in his later prose poems, which were published posthumously in 1869 as *Petits Poèmes en Prose (Little Prose Poems)*, more widely known today as *Le Spleen de Paris (The Spleen of Paris)*. Critics have argued that Baudelaire's inventive turn to this new genre stems from a general dissatisfaction with lyricism and the conventions of poetry.[12] Whereas *The Flowers of Evil* still dreamed of an aesthetics of plenitude, Baudelaire's prose poems are unfinished artwork, "belong[ing] hopelessly to the contingent real world of time and becoming."[13] In a letter-dedication to his editor Arsène Houssaye, Baudelaire describes his collections of poems as having no pretension of *telos* or finality: "I do not bind the [reader's] recalcitrant will to the endless thread of a superfluous plot"[14] ["je ne suspends pas la volonté rétive de celui-ci [du lecteur] au fil interminable d'une intrigue superflue" (oc 1:275)]. *The Spleen of Paris* resembles less a finished product marked by authorial design than a monstrous serpent, a "tortuous fantasy" (129) ("tortueuse fantaisie" [275]) where "everything in it is both tail and head" (129) ["tout ... y est à la fois tête et queue" (275)], "something (if that can be called *some thing*) peculiarly different" (130) ["je faisais quelque chose (si cela peut s'appeler *quelque chose*) de singulièrement différent" (276)]. Their envisioned effects on the reader are only suggested. Baudelaire claims to offer Houssaye the "entire serpent," a whole collection rather than isolated individual poems. As a metaphor for the collection, it is quite an ambivalent one, however. While it acknowledges, on one hand, the cutting hermeneutic will of his addressee — "chop it up into many fragments, and you will find that each one can exist separately" (129) ["*hachez-la en nombreux fragments, et vous verrez que chacun peut exister à part*" [275]] — the metaphor conjures up, on the other hand, the image of a biting and venomous serpent, one capable of literalizing the "jolts of consciousness" (129) ["*soubresauts de la conscience*" (276)] experienced by the poet of modern life. Translating modern life — or as he qualifies it, "*a modern and more abstract life*" (129) ["*une vie moderne et plus abstraite*" (275)] — as a series of "jolts of consciousness" ties Baudelaire's prose poems back to Daumier's art of caricature: the poems "play with the possibilities of the fragmented and the journalistic; they isolate an image and from it generate new meaning; they are dynamic rather than stable; and they distort and exaggerate."[15]

The Spleen of Paris: Looking Awry at Violence

Violence permeates the prose poems. Yet Baudelaire rarely confronts violence in a straightforward way. As Žižek insightfully puts it, "there is something inherently mystifying in a direct confrontation with [violence]: the overpowering horror of violent acts and empathy with the victims inexorably function as a lure which prevents us from thinking."[16] To think critically about violence is to think about it *obliquely*, to look at it *awry*, to look at it, that is, from a multiplicity of incommensurable perspectives.

Baudelaire's "The Bad Glazier" narrates violence in unsettling ways. The prose poem opens with a puzzling observation about human behavior:

> There exist characters, purely contemplative and completely unsuited for action, who, however, influenced by a mysterious and unknown impulse, sometimes act with a speed of which they would not have believed themselves capable. (13)

> Il y a des natures purement contemplatives et tout à fait impropres à l'action, qui cependant, sous une impulsion mystérieuse et inconnue, agissent quelquefois avec une rapidité dont elles se seraient crues elles-mêmes incapables. (OC 1:285)

The narrator inquires further into this "irresistible force" (13/285), insisting on its untranslatability into the authoritative language of science and morality:

> The moralist and the physician, who claim to know everything, cannot explain the cause of this crazy energy which hits these lazy and voluptuous souls. (13)

> Le moraliste et le médecin, qui prétendent tout savoir, ne peuvent pas expliquer d'où vient si subitement une si folle énergie à ces âmes paresseuses et voluptueuses. (285)

Indeed, not all are subject or vulnerable to these interruptions in "character" — only these *lazy and voluptuous souls*. After a few anecdotes that illustrate this general pattern, the narrator adds his name to the list:

> More than once I have been victim of such attacks and outbursts, which justify our belief that some malicious Demons slip into us and, without us knowing it, make us carry out their most absurd wishes. (14)

> J'ai été plus d'une fois victime de ces crises et de ces élans, qui nous autorisent à croire que des Démons malicieux se glissent en nous et nous font accomplir, à notre insu, leurs plus absurdes volontés. (286)

Yet here the narrator does not simply record another example of the inexplicable force, but explains it by pointing to its demonic origins. Reasserting his opposition to medical discourse, the narrator underscores that his "spirit of mystification" (14/286) is a natural or spontaneous compulsion to act, something akin to a mood that is better understood metaphysically as satanic than pathologically as hysterical.

Awaking in a state of boredom — "One morning I had awakened sullen, sad, and worn out with idleness" (14) ["Un matin je m'étais levé maussade, triste, fatigué d'oisiveté" (286)] — the narrator feels an urge to perform "a brilliant action" (14) ["une action d'éclat" (286)]. He tells us of his encounter with a glazier. Baudelaire clearly has in mind Houssaye's own prose poem *The Song of the Glazier*, which Baudelaire ironically evokes as a model for his textual practice in the letter-dedication: "You yourself, my dear friend, did you not try to translate the *Glazier*'s strident cry into a song, and to express in lyrical prose all the woeful associations that cry sends all the way up to attics, through the street's thickest fogs?" (129–30). In Houssaye's telling, the narrator encounters a *poor* glazier (in the double sense of economically destitute and pathetic), and reacts in good humanitarian fashion with an act of charity:

> His soul inhabited nothing more than a phantom, who, as if at his last breath, exclaimed once more in his fading voice:
> Oh! Glazier!
> I approached him. "My dear chap, you must not die of hunger." He had leaned into the wall like a drunken man. "Come, come!" I continued, taking his arm. And I guided him toward the cabaret, as if I knew the way. A little child at the counter cried out gaily in his youthful voice:
> Oh! Glazier! [my translation]

> Son âme n'habitait plus qu'un spectre, qui comme un dernier soupir, cria encore d'une voix éteinte:
> Oh! vitrier!
> J'allai à lui. "Mon brave homme, il ne faut pas mourir de faim." Il s'était appuyé sur le mur comme un homme ivre. "Allons! allons!" continuai-je en lui prenant le bras. Et je l'entraînai au cabaret, comme si j'en savais le chemin. Un petit enfant était au comptoir, qui cria de sa voix fraîche et gaie:
> Oh! vitrier! (OC 1:1309–10)

This charitable act of drinking with the other proves sadly ineffective:

> I drank to his health. But his teeth knocked against his cup, and he fainted; ... which caused him three francs ten sous's damage, half of his capital, for I could not prevent his glass panes from breaking. The poor man came to, still repeating:
> Oh! Glazier! [my translation]

> Je trinquai avec lui. Mais ses dents claquèrent sur le verre, et il s'évanouit; ... ce qui lui causa un dégât de trois francs dix sous, la moitié de son capital car je ne pus empêcher ses carreaux de casser. Le pauvre homme revint à lui en disant encore:
> Oh! vitrier! (OC 1:1310)

Despite the failure of charity, the poem is through and through recuperative, ending with both glazier and narrator gaining something from the encounter: the former, an exposure to fraternity; the latter, a painful but morally valuable experience.

In his parodic retranslation of the glazier's "strident cry," Baudelaire explodes the ethical scene of "bourgeois philanthropy" envisioned by Houssaye.[17] As the title of the poem announces, we are about to meet a *bad* glazier. But what makes him "bad" is not some moral viciousness. The glazier's sin lies in his failure to carry with him any "colored panes," any windowpanes capable of transforming (that is, distorting) his impoverished reality, of transfiguring it into a phantasmatic object, into something beautiful:

> What? You have no colored panes? no pink panes, no red, no blue, no magic panes, no panes of paradise? You are shameless! You dare walk through poor neighborhoods, and you don't even have panes which make life beautiful! (15)

> Comment? vous n'avez pas de verres de couleur? des verres roses, rouges, bleus, des vitres magiques, des vitres de paradis? Impudent que vous êtes! vous osez vous promener dans des quartiers pauvres, et vous n'avez pas même de vitres qui fassent voir la vie en beau! (287)

Despite the reference to "poor neighborhoods," the narrator, as Maria C. Scott observes, "unlike the poor glazier, evidently has the luxury of leisure."[18] The narrator's suffering or malaise appears more abstract and elusive. He is "worn out with idleness" — not physical labor. The glazier's inability to offer a remedy, to satisfy the narrator's *aesthetic* appetite (his voracious and hysterical desire for a *mystified* reality) results in a harsh retribution. The narrator first pushes the glazier toward the stairway and then, seeing him emerge into the street, drops with Cartesian precision ("perpendicularly" [15/287]) a small pot of flowers — which he calls his "engine of war" (15/287) — that shatters all of the man's merchandise. These events leave the poet utterly "drunk with [his] madness" ["ivre de [s]a folie"], and repeating deliriously, "Make life beautiful! Make life beautiful!" (15) ["La vie en beau! la vie en beau!" (287).

The movement from the narrator's yearning for "colored panes" to his violence toward the glazier parallels the movement from the poet's religious desire for transcendence — he refers to the "colored panes" as "panes of paradise" — to his demonic behavior in the world. The textual tension between elevation (heaven) and descent (hell) reappears at the end of the poem when the narrator demonstrates lucid but ironic awareness of the moral consequences of his sadistic behavior: "But what does an eternity of damnation matter to someone who has experienced for one second the infinity of delight?" (15) ["Mais qu'importe l'éternité de la damnation à qui a trouvé dans une seconde l'infini de la jouissance?" (287)].[19] This irony however is not limited to the narrator but spills over into a reading of the poem as well, contaminating the reader's proximity to the narrative. Like Daumier's "Rue Transnonain," Baudelaire's "The Bad Glazier" implicates the reader in its subject matter. He or she is presented with a dizzying and unruly hermeneutic universe in which one is called upon to entertain a *double vision*[20] — to identify with both the lazy artist and the productive merchant, both the escapist idealist and the hapless victim.[21] Through its multiplication of discourses and mixing of registers, "The Bad Glazier" performs its modern universe; it ironically juxtaposes the serious metaphysical question of salvation and damnation with the ludic confrontation between a bored artist and a pathetic, unwitting glazier, and situates its famous *universal* depiction of man's two allegiances — "In every man, at every turn, there are two simultaneous tendencies, one toward God, and the other toward Satan" (*My Heart Laid Bare* [*Mon cœur mis à nu*], my translation) ["Il y a dans tout homme, à toute heure, deux postulations simultanées, l'une vers Dieu, l'autre vers Satan" (OC 1:682)] — in its historically *contingent* nineteenth-century context, positing the Satanic pull as an alternative not so much to Christian spirituality as to the authoritative discourses of science and morality (reinvesting, as in "A Former Life," an uneasy sense of mystery into bourgeois reality). In short, we can say that "The Bad Glazier" solicits translations into political, ethical, theological, and aesthetic messages, yet renders each of these explanatory frameworks insufficient through its proximity and tension with the others.[22]

It is not difficult to see that Baudelaire's narrative also raises significant meta-reflections about its own activity, implicating its own author and the poeticization process. The physical violence performed by the narrator of "The Bad Glazier" finds its figurative counterpart in another prose poem, "The Rope." As we shall see, what is at stake in this prose poem is the act of figuration, or more precisely, the translatability of the other.

Baudelaire's poem opens with a distancing gesture: "'Illusions,' my friend was telling me, 'are perhaps as countless as relationships between people, or between people and things'" (77) ["'Les illusions', — me disait mon ami, — sont aussi innombrables peut-être que les rapports des hommes entre eux, ou des hommes avec les choses" (OC 1:328)]. In two of the three published versions of the poem, the words "my friend was telling me," which frame the story we're going to be told, are the only actual words of the poem that can be attributed to the poet-narrator of *The Spleen of Paris*.²³ It is important, then, to keep in mind that "The Rope" is reported speech.

The poem recounts his friend's demystifying tale about maternal love. We discover in the second paragraph that this "second" narrator, the friend, is a painter, and as a painter, he claims to have cultivated a keener sense of perception, which elevates him above the typical individual in his capacity to read people:

> My profession as a painter prompts me attentively to examine faces, physiognomies, turning up on my path, and you know what *delight* we gain from that faculty which makes life appear more lively and more meaningful to us than to other people. (77, emphasis added)

> Ma profession de peintre me pousse à regarder attentivement les visages, les physionomies, qui s'offrent dans ma route, et vous savez quelle *jouissance* nous tirons de cette faculté qui rend à nos yeux la vie plus vivante et plus significative que pour les autres hommes. (329)

In his ability to derive aesthetic *jouissance*, or bliss, from the self's exposure to others, the painter resembles Baudelaire's modernist figure of the *flâneur* as described in *The Painter of Modern Life*. For him,

> The crowd is his domain, just as the air is the bird's, and water that of the fish. His passion and his profession is *to merge with the crowd*. For the perfect idler, for the passionate observer it becomes an immense source of enjoyment *to establish his dwelling in the throng, in the ebb and flow, the bustle, the fleeting and the infinite*. (399, emphasis added).

> La foule est son domaine, comme l'air est celui de l'oiseau, comme l'eau celui du poisson. Sa passion et sa profession, c'est d'*épouser la foule*. Pour le parfait flâneur, pour l'observateur passionné, *c'est une immense jouissance que d'élire domicile dans le nombre, dans l'ondoyant, dans le mouvement, dans le fugitif et l'infini*. (OC 2:691)

In the prose poem titled "Crowds" ("Les Foules"), first published in 1861, three years before "The Rope," Baudelaire's speaker makes the link between the poet and the *flâneur* more explicit:

> The poet enjoys the incomparable privilege of being able, at will, to be himself and an other. Like those wandering souls seeking a body, he enters,

when he wants, into everyone's character. For him alone, everything is empty.... The solitary and thoughtful stroller draws a unique intoxication from this universal communion. (21)

Le poète jouit de cet incomparable privilège, qu'il peut à sa guise être lui-même et autre. Comme ces âmes errantes qui cherchent un corps, il entre, quant il veut, dans le personnage de chacun. Pour lui seul, tout est vacant.... Le promeneur solitaire et pensif tire une singulière ivresse de cette universelle communion. (OC 1: 291)

The world of the masses — the domain of the multitude — emerges for him as a tantalizing source of endless *jouissance*. To be sure, the painter and Baudelaire's ideal *flâneur* diverge on the full implications of such encounters. Whereas the painter limits his exposures to those who happen to cross his path, the *flâneur* immerses himself intentionally in the crowd, yearning to lose himself in the alterity of the other: "It is an ego athirst for the non-ego" ["C'est un *moi* insatiable du *non-moi*" (OC 2:692)], writes Baudelaire of the *flâneur*. Yet neither the painter nor the *flâneur* ever seems to doubt the other's malleability and availability to pleasurable translation. No barrier of otherness is so great as to prevent empathic identification or understanding for either the *flâneur* or the painter. If the *flâneur*'s translation takes the form of an *intoxicating empathy*,[24] the narrator's is a product of his *techne*, that is, an effect of his painterly habitus. It is the artistic gaze itself, and modernist art's phantamastic pretension to translate the other effectively that "The Rope" scrutinizes along with the more blatant form of indifference displayed by the callous characters surrounding the artist.[25]

The painter's story revolves around a particular encounter with a peculiar child, whom he befriended and who soon became for him the object of artistic fascination — the ideal model. After painting him several times, the narrator develops a fondness for the child and, with the consent of his poor parents, takes him under his care. Soon after, the child begins to behave strangely. The painter reports that "this little fellow sometimes surprised me with peculiar fits of precocious sadness, and ... he soon showed an immoderate craving for sugar and liquors" (78) ["ce petit bonhomme m'étonna quelquefois par des crises singulières de tristesse précoce, et ... manifesta bientôt un goût immodéré pour le sucre et les liqueurs" (329)], a craving that prompts him to steal. The child's mental state and behavior astonish the painter yet fail to provoke the same kind of fascination that he had initially felt for the child;

instead the painter threatens to send the boy home if he does not give up his unruly ways. Later that day, he discovers to his dismay the lifeless body of the child, who has hanged himself from an armoire in his studio.

The painter's first response is to lament the indifference of his neighbors during this moment of crisis. More outrageous still for him is the father's reaction when he learns of his son's death: "After all, it's probably better this way. He still would've come to a bad end!" (79) ["Après tout, cela vaut peut-être mieux ainsi; il aurait toujours mal fini!" (330)]. If the mother's cold silence also surprises him, he just assumes that it is a normal effect of trauma, acknowledging that "[t]he deepest griefs are silent" (79) ["Les douleurs les plus terribles sont les douleurs muettes" (330)]. Her one request to keep "the rope" puzzles him, but, naïvely still, he rationalizes her behavior, speculating that she wants to preserve the instrument of her child's death as "a horrible and cherished relic" (80) ["une horrible et chère relique" (331)]. He becomes aware of her true interest only after a number of his neighbors (and not all of them belonging to "the lowly and common class" (80) ["la classe infime et vulgaire" (331)]) ask him for "a piece of the deadly and beatific rope" (80) ["un morceau de la funeste et béatifique corde" (331)], reflecting the morbid belief that the rope of a hanged person is a good luck charm. The actual demystification of maternal love, then, is deferred until the end of the poem. Driven by self-interest, the child's mother embodies the despicable values of bourgeois modern life: "I understood why the mother was so eager to grab the string from me and *by what sort of trade* she meant to console herself" (80, emphasis added) ["[J]e compris pourquoi la mère tenait tant à m'arracher la ficelle et *par quel commerce* elle entendait se consoler" (331)].

The poem multiplies scenes of what Žižek calls "subjective violence," violence that is "performed by a clearly identifiable agent ... [and] ... is seen as a perturbation of the 'normal,' peaceful state of things."[26] "The Bad Glazier" stages this model of violence, framing the narrator as victimizer and the glazier as victim, and inviting critique of the latter's mistreatment. A concern for visible acts of violence, however, helps *to sustain* a more insidious form of violence, one that Žižek terms "objective violence," a form of violence that includes both "symbolic violence" (the violence of racist rhetoric, for example, or more generally, language as the hegemonic imposition of a given universe of meaning) and "systemic violence" (the violence of capitalism, for instance, as a naturalized, oppressive, impersonal, smoothly functioning sociopolitical reality). "Objective violence is invisible," Žižek maintains, "since it sustains the very zero-level standard against which we perceive something as subjectively violent."²⁷ "The Rope" makes manifest the workings of this hidden, oppressive force.

At first glance, the narrative invites the reader *to identify* with the painter's naïvety and his implicit moral superiority to his neighbors and the child's parents. Yet such a laudatory portrait crumbles upon closer examination. The reader begins to hesitate. Skepticism emerges upon rereading the narrator's first words themselves, which alert us to his unreliability as a moral example:

> When the illusion disappears, that is, when we perceive the creature or the fact such as it exists outside of us, we experience a weird feeling, complicated half with regret for the vanished phantom, half with pleasant surprise at the novelty, the real fact. (77)

> Quand l'illusion disparaît, c'est-à-dire quand nous voyons l'être ou le fait qu'il existe en dehors de nous, nous éprouvons un bizarre sentiment, compliqué moitié de regret pour le fantôme disparu, moitié de surprise agréable devant la nouveauté, devant le fait réel. (328)

If one is to take this quote literally, the demystification of "maternal love" — the "real fact [*le fait réel*]" of maternal love — must have produced within the painter an unusual feeling of both regret and pleasure. One can accept that when faced with the immorality of a mother, the painter would feel a kind of aristocratic nostalgia for a pure maternal love uncorrupted by the evils of bourgeois commerce, yet in what sense could this tragic event have brought him a "pleasant surprise"? Baudelaire's poem draws attention to such a perverse enjoyment — to its modernist fetishization of astonishment — by ironizing the narrator's moralizing gaze, disclosing the illusion of recognition and care, as well as his own complicity with the bourgeois culture he criticizes.

While the painter purports to set himself apart in his ethical treatment of the child (implicitly affirming a sense of moral superiority that parallels his professed hermeneutic supremacy), the terms of his economic arrangement with his model tell a different story. The painter claims that it is the singularity of the child that triggers his initial interest in him: "I often watched a child whose fervent and mischievous physiognomy, more than any others, immediately seduced me" (77) ["J'observai souvent un enfant dont la physionomie ardente et espiègle, plus que toutes les autres, me séduisit" (329)]. But it is ostensibly the child's easy translatability, that is, his openness to being fashioned at will, that ultimately compels the narrator to take the boy in. As he notes, "[The child] posed for me more than once, and I sometimes transformed him into a little gypsy, sometimes into an angel, sometimes into a mythological Cupid. I had him carry a vagabond's violin, the Crown of Thorns and Nails of the Passion, and the torch of Eros" (77) ["[L'enfant] a posé plus d'une fois pour moi, et je l'ai transformé tantôt en petit bohémien, tantôt en ange, tantôt en Amour mythologique. Je lui ai fait porter le violon du vagabond, la Couronne d'Epines et les Clous de la Passion, et la Torche d'Éros" (329)]. *The child*'s emotional unruliness becomes an issue when it starts to jeopardize or interfere with his ability to be a good model, that is, to be docile and malleable. Recognizing the child's aesthetic worthiness thus goes hand in hand with instrumentalizing the boy's body — with commodifying and silencing him. Moreover, the painter reveals no genuine desire to know the child: he never asks why the child is suffering. Nor does he express any curiosity about the reasons for the child's suicide. And perhaps most disturbing to the reader, the painter feels no guilt or responsibility for the child's suicide, even though it was arguably psychological violence — the threat of being returned to his "paternal hovel" — that drove the poor child to his tragic end. The painter's relation to the child pre- and post-suicide thus makes it quite clear that narcissistic self-absorption is not only compatible with bourgeois commerce but emblematic of it.

Baudelaire's dedication of "The Rope" to his fellow artist and friend, the painter Edouard Manet, provokes yet another moment of hesitation, another instance of interpretive puzzlement. The dedication might, in fact, be an ironic one, since Baudelaire may be alluding here to the real suicide of Alexandre, the model-child represented in Manet's *The Child with Cherries*. So what is the significance of this "dedication"? Is it some sort of clue for those readers who are aware of this extratextual reality? Should we read it as an indictment of Manet's art in particular, or of painting in general? Or is it more fruitful to interpret the poem as a further questioning of art — the use and abuse of translation, of an aesthetics of *modernité*?[28] As with "The Bad Glazier," the irony of "The Rope" undercuts any attempt at interpretive containment of the poem. Appeals to contextual explanations might very well shed light on certain aspects of Baudelaire's poem, but they can never fully pin down its unruly meaning any more than the painter can fully exorcise the child from his unruly mind, or expunge this "little corpse" ["petit cadavre"], as he puts it, from "the folds of [his] brain" (80) ["les replies de [son] cerveau" (331)].

Indeed, the potential referential reality to which the painter-narrator may refer does not so much negate as complicate Baudelaire's proximity to the figure of the painter. We must persist in asking: What are we to make of the resemblance between the painter-narrator and the poet-*flâneur*? Is it a *mise en abyme*, an example of a text drawing attention to its own activities, a calling into question of the artistic gaze itself? The poet-narrator who framed the story at the beginning does not return to comment at the end.[29] Is his silence a sign of his complicity with the painter's representational violence? The absence of a commentary surely disconcerts the more traditional ethical reader who yearns for a message: Who is the object of critique? Is it the indifferent neighbors of the painter, the babbling father, his loveless mother (in keeping with the explicit message of the poem)? Is the object of critique the self-absorbed painter (the implicit message of the poem), or the self-effacing poet-narrator (what we might call the meta-message of the poem)? Choosing the last culprit — the vanishing poet-narrator — would rightly emphasize Baudelaire's self-reflexive poetic bent, his constant reminder to the reader that no one is immune from critique and irony, not even the poet himself as embodied in Baudelaire's idealized figure of the poet-*flâneur*.

Yet we must resist the temptation to merely update the poem, to claim that it is not the mother who is the object of critique, that the "true" target of the poem is the painter, or that in a self-ironizing gesture the "true" subject of violence is none other than Baudelaire himself. This fake hermeneutic epiphany must be actively blocked. The poem enjoins us to recalibrate our interpretive focus and overcome the ideological traps of subjective violence to which ethical readings are so easily prone. The questions *who is to blame? who is to be praised? with whom do I need to identify?* etc. must be set aside, even if momentarily, in order to consider the poem's figuration of systemic violence. This figuration deploys irony, but an ideologically unsettling irony better understood, as Žižek puts it, "in the precise *Mozartian* sense of taking statements more seriously than the subjects who utter them themselves."[30] Such an irony bursts through the father's lines when he says: "After all, it's probably better this way. He still would've come to a bad end!" (79). The father's stupid, insensitive, and fatalistic observation is something of a moral failure or "moral error" intended to be negated in favor of the painter's allegedly more ethical reaction (he is appropriately disturbed by the child's death). However, a dialectical reading would entreat us to return to the father's first impression (namely, that *the child was condemned to a life of misery*) and look at it awry.[31] Isn't the father's observation in fact true? Doesn't it gain a new meaning once the child's situation is reconceptualized in terms of objective violence, or systemic violence, to be more precise?

Indeed, this more fundamental, systemic violence of capitalism is precisely what the painter's *personal* narrative masks and represses from the start. As we have seen, the painter does not to hesitate to expose the mother's subjection to market forces, but he merely glosses over her consent to have the child stay with him:

> At last that kid's every whimsy gave me such lively pleasure that one day I asked his parents, poor people, if they would agree to hand him over to me, promising to dress him well, give him money and not to impose any hardship other than cleaning my brushes and running my errands. (77–78)

> Je pris enfin à toute la drôlerie de ce gamin un plaisir si vif que je priai un jour ses parents, de pauvre gens, de vouloir bien me le céder, promettant de bien l'habiller, de lui donner quelque argent et de ne pas lui imposer d'autre peine que de nettoyer mes pinceaux et de faire mes commissions. (329)

This is not to say that the mother (or the father for that matter) could not have been acting out love for her child, only that the consent to the offer should have occasioned a moment of pause and reflection: under what socioeconomic conditions, under what life of misery, is such a consent a "normal" option?[32] Again, we must resist the Neo-Aristotelian humanist remedy, that the reader, in contrast to the painter, needs to do a better job empathizing with the powerless poor, to *understand* their precarious predicament: to view suicide as the child's only way out (his tragic resistance), or even to forgive the mother (to see her selling of the rope as an act of economic desperation, one that does not exclude the authenticity of her trauma). The text invites us to probe further. Baudelaire does not settle for negative exemplarity; his ideological critique is far more trenchant.

Ethics in/of the Gap

Baudelaire's "The Rope" dramatizes what Žižek describes as the hypocrisy of humanists who, "while combating *subjective violence*, commit *systemic violence* that generates the very phenomena they abhor."[33] Nevertheless, the relation of criticism to ideology cannot be reduced to one of subordination, where one can talk only of an *ideology* of reading rather than a *reading* of ideology. Baudelaire's narrative interpellates us as readers of ideology, as readers confronted with an insoluble double bind: to care for particulars, to respond to the child's unheard cry for help and protest, to object to his "subjective violence," to the painter's instrumentalization of the child (which is, of course, repeated in the telling of the story), *and* to reject the pervasive violence that invariably sustains the first critique, that is, to equally object to the "systemic violence" implicit in moralizing tales, occasions for empathic imaginings, which tend to depoliticize the scene of reading as a *personal* growth moment.

Though "The Rope" tells a demystifying tale of "the life-enhancing powers of art,"[34] exposing pure aesthetics' dubious separation of the artwork and its material source (the latent ideology underlying *modernité*), it does not simply suspend or condemn the translation of life into art. On the contrary, artistic translation not only continues to mediate Baudelaire's perception of modern life but also serves as a parallax, elucidating the gap between modern life and its aestheticized image. Rather than opting out of translation, we could say that Baudelaire chooses instead to translate ironically (modernizing Delacroix's *translate freely*), building into his work a reflection of this irreparable but immensely fertile gap.

IV

Living with Nausea

SARTRE AND ROQUENTIN

> The state of nausea that precedes vomiting, and from which vomiting will deliver us, encloses us on all sides. Yet it does not come from outside to confine us. We are revolted from the inside; our depths smother beneath ourselves; our innards "heave."
>
> EMMANUEL LEVINAS

The "undated pages" ["feuillet sans date"] that open Antoine Roquentin's diary in Sartre's *Nausea* reveal the circumstances that led their author to writing.[1] Plagued by an overwhelming sense of estrangement, Roquentin decides to keep a diary in the hope that it will help him "to see clearly" (1) ["voir clair" (5)] and ameliorate his troubled condition. Bracketing all presuppositions about the nature of the external world, Roquentin proceeds to observe and represent objects *as* he perceives them, *as* they are revealed to his consciousness in their "pure" immediacy:

> Let none of the nuances or small happenings escape even though they might seem to mean nothing. And above all, classify them. I must tell *how I see* this table, the street, the people, my packet of tobacco. (1, emphasis added)

> Ne pas laisser échapper les nuances, les petits faits même s'ils n'ont l'air de rien, et surtout les classer. Il faut dire *comment je vois* cette table, la rue, les gens, mon paquet de tabac. (5)

Roquentin's epistemological desire "to see clearly" sets the philosophical tone of the novel, inviting the reader to situate Sartre's protagonist within the long-established Cartesian tradition of self-knowledge. Yet what Sartre is actually doing with this familiar tradition is decidedly less clear.

The note from "the Editors" that precedes the diary and purportedly guarantees, in terms that hark back to eighteenth-century literary conventions, the authenticity of the work at hand, already casts doubts on the timeliness and success of the epistemological project that readers are about to witness. For some critics, Sartre's attitude toward his philosophical subject matter qualifies as parodic. Georges Poulet, for example, remarks: "The Sartrean *Cogito* appears . . . as a sort of tragic caricature of Descartes' *Cogito*. Sartre is well aware of this, moreover, and deliberately conceived his novel as a parody of the *Discourse on Method*."[2] For others, the kernel of truth lies in the novel's disclosure of the nature of consciousness. Geneviève Idt, for example, argues that once Roquentin's subjectivity is stripped of all facticity or accidental attributes, what is left is nothing but an anonymous consciousness: "Over the course of the text, Roquentin seems to lose the individual characteristics of his self. In the end, when he says "I," he uses an empty form, a purely grammatical subject. It is the abstract "I" used by philosophers from Descartes to Husserl to describe the workings of a pure consciousness."[3] As evidence she cites Roquentin's sudden and lucid awareness of the hollowness of the word "I": "Now when I say 'I,' it seems hollow to me" (170) ["A présent, quand je dis 'je,' ça me semble creux" (200)]. Whatever the philosophical message attributed to it, what remains undeniable is the novel's irresistible philosophical lure and appeal. Sartre himself has, of course, greatly contributed to the novel's *accommodation* of (existentialist) philosophy, describing *Nausea* as the "expression [*la mise en forme*] of a philosophical idea,"[4] a prelude, as it were, to his philosophical tome *Being and Nothingness*, which he published five years later, in 1943.

Reading *Nausea* with *Being and Nothingness* has obvious interpretive benefits; aside from helping to elucidating confusing passages, such a reading situates *Nausea* within a well-established philosophical tradition and its author's own intellectual trajectory. Moreover, the novel ostensibly allegorizes, through the "adventures" of his protagonist, something eternal (that is, truthful) about the existential condition, the absurdity of life and the ultimate meaninglessness of the world. Or to quote the summary blurb on the back cover of the English translation: "Roquentin's efforts to come to terms with life, his philosophical and psychological struggles, give Sartre the opportunity to dramatize the tenets of his Existentialist creed." By emphasizing the novel's humanist or timeless question of individual struggle, along with its author's existentialist philosophy (which had been well established by 1964, the year the English translation came out), the blurb functions to legitimize the novel's exemplarity and canonical value.

Reading the novel this way, however, is invariably to submit to what Foucault has described as the work's "author function" — an effect through which works are seen as fitting into the larger, coherent "thought" of a unified author. Submitting to the author function precludes seeing *Nausea* as an inventive work. Such an approach to *Nausea* yields too easily to the temptation of paraphrasing, remaining all too faithful and indebted to what Serge Doubrovsky has aptly called the "Sartrean metatext."[5] In Foucauldian parlance, Sartre *the author* often functions as a "principle of thrift" in the proliferation of *Nausea*'s meaning.[6] This chapter heeds Doubrovsky's advice not to succumb to the hegemonic "Sartrean metatext," to push back against Sartre's own appropriative identification with his protagonist — "I *was* Roquentin," he famously wrote in his autobiography *The Words*[7] — and strives not to fall prey to the hermeneutic convenience of the author function: affirming the unity of Sartre's body of works by minimizing contradictions, which translates as a disciplining of the literary work. At the same time, this chapter does not simply eclipse the question of the author's philosophy altogether. The challenge is not to refuse to read the novel's existentialist qualities, but to read them differently, to read them in a way that both accounts for and unsettles Sartre's philosophical grammar. It aims, that is, to sign and countersign Sartre.[8] This chapter, then, reads *Nausea* not merely as Sartre's primer — as his "factum on Contingency," as he described it in a letter to Simone de Beauvoir[9] — but as his unruly progeny, an inventive literary work that insists on its relative autonomy and irreducible strangeness, a novel that stages nausea rather than communicates its meaning, that narrates the drama of Roquentin's nausea in a manner that accommodates and exceeds Sartre's existentialist philosophy.

The Example of Roquentin

The phenomenological project upon which Roquentin embarks, and which will eventually lead to existentialist insights, is triggered by a disorienting encounter with seemingly ordinary things. No longer feeling at home in the provincial town of Bouville (Mudville), where he has spent the last three years researching the life of the Marquis de Rollebon, a minor eighteenth-century diplomat, Roquentin wonders why he suddenly experiences a sense of uneasiness in the presence of innocuous objects, like the pebble he picks up at the beach, causing his first attack of nausea. As he notes with consternation:

> Objects should not *touch* because they are not alive. You use them, put them back in place, you live among them: they are useful, nothing more. But they touch me, it is unbearable. I am afraid of being in contact with them as though they were living beasts. (10)

> Les objets, cela ne devrait pas *toucher*, puisque cela ne vit pas. On s'en sert, on les remet en place, on vit au milieu d'eux: ils sont utiles, rien de plus. Et moi; ils me touchent, c'est insupportable. J'ai peur d'entrer en contact avec eux tout comme s'ils étaient des bêtes vivantes. (16)

Roquentin's confrontation with an alien world, where objects are devoid of any meaning or instrumental value, contrasts sharply with the experience of Bouville's inhabitants, who, he observes, appear to have no difficulties discovering continuity and coherence in their relations with their environment and with each other. An economy of sameness underwrites the Bouvillois' mode of being. Roquentin derides their propensity to adhere to established knowledge, to exclude anything that does not conform to established *doxa*:

> They explain the new by the old — and the old they explain by the older still, like those historians who turn Lenin into a Russian Robespierre, and a Robespierre into a French Cromwell: when all is said and done, they have never understood anything at all. (69)

> Ils expliquent le neuf par l'ancien — et l'ancien, ils l'ont expliqué par des événements plus anciens encore, comme ces historiens qui font de Lénine un Robespierre russe et de Robespierre un Cromwell français: au bout du compte, ils n'ont jamais rien compris du tout. (83)

Highlighting the constructed character of these associations — pointing out that it is not necessary to see Cromwell in Robespierre, and Robespierre in Lenin — Roquentin questions the compulsion to reduce difference (otherness) to the order of the Same (the familiar and the known), then seeks to expose the mechanisms by which Bouville's homogenizing ideology exercises its influence in everyday life, scrutinizing its social institutions and public space. Social spaces are not value neutral but help produce a bourgeois vision of the world: an essentialist world where everything is already preestablished and necessary.

At the Bouville museum, for instance, home to more than 150 portraits of the city's historical elite, Roquentin observes how the museum as public space functions to perpetuate a specific type of self-understanding, how it produces ideological subjects, individuals who think of themselves as beings with rights: to life, to wealth, to immortality, and so on. Standing before the portrait of Pâcome, Roquentin becomes acutely aware of his otherness, his nonbourgeois identity. If Pâcome justified his authoritative social status as a *right* assigned to him by God — alleging that he is only fulfilling his *duty* by governing others: "For a right is nothing more than the other aspect of duty" (85) ["Car un droit n'est jamais que l'autre aspect d'un devoir" (101)] — Roquentin, for his part, finds no justification for his existence: "I hadn't the right to exist. I had appeared by chance, I existed like a stone, a plant or a microbe" (84) ["je n'avais pas le droit d'exister. J'étais apparu par hasard, j'existais comme une pierre, une plante, un microbe" (101)]. More than simply illustrating bourgeois values, however, all the portraits reinforce social order by subtly coopting the very discourses of resistance that might otherwise work to contest it.[10] Rémy Parrottin, for instance, who is honored in the second painting Roquentin encounters, may have given the illusion of preaching rebellious ideology, of being ideologically *different* ("'Socialists?' Well, I go further than they do!" (87) ["'Les socialistes?' Eh bien, moi, je vais plus loin qu'eux!" (104)]), but the outcome of his teachings was unquestionably a return to the status quo, a return to the rule of the Same (tradition). Parrottin's transgressive rhetoric was a mere sham; playing the role of a confidential counselor resulted, repulsively, in helping to normalize and neutralize Bouville's rebellious youths — the real threats to the social order. After just a few conversations with Parrottin, any young rebel became *spiritually* transformed by this mystifying rhetoric and "saw clearly within himself, he learned to know the deep bonds which attached him to his family, to his environment; at last, he understood the admirable role of the élite" (88) ["voyait clair en lui-même, il apprenait à connaître les liens profonds qui l'attachaient à sa famille, à son milieu; il comprenait enfin le rôle admirable de l'élite" (105)]. Roquentin remembers what a doctor once told him about Parrottin: "'He cured more souls . . . than I've cured bodies'" (88) ["'Il a guéri plus d'âmes . . . que je n'ai guéri de corps'" (129)]. By working on their souls, Parrottin taught his students their social duties, inculcating in them the appropriate rules of behavior; he thus helped to perpetuate — and continues symbolically to perpetuate — the normalizing practices of Bouville.

Roquentin's attitude toward the present-day Bouvillois reflects a similar contempt for their fatuous social existence. Happily dwelling in their well-regulated city, Bouvillois actively participate in their well-established routines: "On Sunday you go to the memorial cemetery or you visit your parents, or, if you're completely free, you go for a walk along the jetty" (51) ["Le dimanche on va au cimetière monumental, ou bien l'on rend visite à des parents, ou bien, si l'on est tout à fait libre, on va se promener sur la Jetée" (62)]. Yet what Roquentin finds most contemptible (recalling his critique of Bouville's museum) is their belief in a *necessary existence*, that is, the way in which each Bouvillois believes him- or herself to be "indispensable to something or someone" (111) ["indispensable à quelqu'un ou à quelque chose" (132)]. Roquentin feels no shared existence with them; he is their utmost counterexample: "It seems as though I belong to another species" (158) ["Il me semble que j'appartiens à une autre espèce" (186)].

But how, one might ask, can Roquentin consider himself immune from bourgeois ideology? Why is he not a conformist, another normalized subject? Why is he not simply formed or disciplined like the rest of the Bouvillois? Moreover, what allows him to take a certain pride in his marginal position as an outsider? Roquentin takes great pains to stress his singularity, not wanting his voice to be engulfed and effaced by a background of sameness and predictable idle talk of the kind he repeatedly observes, transcribes, and derides in his diary. From an existentialist perspective, Roquentin's privileged position ostensibly emerges from the *authentic* recognition of his transcendence or ontological freedom (his "for itself"). Unlike the Bouvillois, who flee from their *absolute* freedom by believing that their existence is somehow purposeful (that they are fulfilling their essence), Roquentin *exemplifies* an existentialist ethos in accepting the absurdity of his condition; he is acutely self-aware that he is in excess, superfluous, "*de trop*" (122/152).

This acute consciousness of his condition comes both from his concerted efforts to "see clearly," to bracket his assumptions, and from the pre-reflexive crisis that prompted him to adopt this method of inquiry in the first place. Roquentin's existential crisis begins in part as a professional one. As a would-be biographer of the Marquis de Rollebon, he comes to have serious doubts about the validity of his endeavor. After reviewing the work already accumulated on the life of this minor figure, Roquentin discovers to his dismay that his arrangements of events do not correspond to any deep hidden truth:

> What is lacking in all this testimony is firmness and consistency. They do not contradict each other, neither do they agree with each other; they do not seem to be about the same person. (13)

> Ce qui manque dans tous ces témoignages, c'est la fermeté, la consistance. Ils ne se contredisent pas, non, mais ils ne s'accordent pas non plus; ils n'ont pas l'air de concerner la même personne. (18)

The disparity in the testimonies leads him to consider the idea that continuities are not *in* history, but come from the biographer himself, from his manipulation of contingent historical events:

> And yet other historians work from the same sources of information. How do they do it? ... These are honest hypotheses which take the facts into account: but I sense so definitely that *they come from me*. (13, emphasis added)

> Et pourtant les autres historiens travaillent sur des renseignements de même espèce. Comment font-ils? ... Ce sont des hypothèses honnêtes et qui rendent compte des faits: mais je sens si bien qu'*elles viennent de moi*. (18–19)

Remarking further that the hypotheses "are simply a way of unifying my own knowledge" (13) ["sont tout simplement une manière d'unifier mes connaissances" (19)], Roquentin becomes keenly aware that history has no inherent meaning. As a result, he realizes that his project of portraying the actual events of Rollebon's past is essentially a sham. In fact, his biographical work turns out to resemble more a work of fiction than history:

> I have the feeling of doing a work of pure imagination. (13)
> I'd be better off writing a novel on the Marquis de Rollebon. (58)

> J'ai l'impression de faire un travail de pure imagination. (19)
> Il fallait plutôt que j'écrive un roman sur le marquis de Rollebon. (71)

Roquentin blurs the line between history (the realm of facts) and story (the realm of fictions) that had once seemed clear and firm. Writing about the past and creating fiction appear to be one and the same: he discovers that he cannot represent Rollebon's past without simultaneously altering, or better yet, fictionalizing it.

Having problematized the object of his quest (Rollebon) and his identity *qua* biographer (his objectivity and disinterested pursuit of truth), Roquentin refuses to perpetuate the lies of his discourse, that is, to play the role *prescribed* by his discourse, and consequently jettisons his biographical project — killing Rollebon symbolically: "M. de Rollebon had just died for the second time" (96) ["M. de Rollebon venait de mourir pour la deuxième fois" (115)].[11]

Narrating Existence and Its Vicissitudes

Hoping to avoid the pitfalls associated with his writing of Rollebon, Roquentin submits his writing of self to close scrutiny. Ideally, his diary writing must simply describe, adding nothing to the external world which is not proper to it: "I must not put in strangeness where there is none" (1) ["Il ne faut pas mettre de l'étrange où il n'y a rien" (5)]. Reflecting on his writing, Roquentin remarks to his dismay, however: "I have just filled up ten pages and I haven't told the truth — at least, not the whole truth. . . . I have re-read what I wrote . . . and I am ashamed" (9) ["Je viens de remplir dix pages et je n'ai pas dit la vérité — du moins pas toute la vérité. . . . j'ai relu ce que j'écrivais . . . et j'ai eu honte" (14–15)]. And when writing begins to truly interfere with his reflections, with a strictly descriptive approach, Roquentin associates writing with philosophy's unruly other: literature. "I do not need to make phrases. I write to bring certain circumstances to light. *Beware of literature*" (68, emphasis added) ["Je n'ai pas besoin de faire des phrases. J'écris pour tirer au clair certaines circonstances. *Se méfier de la littérature*" (68)]. Roquentin is particularly critical of Balzacian literature, which creates an illusory image of a necessary and structured universe in which one finds a preestablished beginning, development, and end.[12] Roquentin flatly rejects narrative: "There are no beginnings. . . . Neither is there any end" (39) ["Il n'y a jamais de commencements. . . . Il n'y pas de fin non plus" (49)]. The inference is clear: literature (the art of "making phrases") is an ideological lie. Literature falsifies the raw experience of reality by imposing an artificial order upon one's lived experience (*le vécu*) and hence is inadequate for his Cartesian-like meditations.

Accordingly, Roquentin is wary of all that corrupts the clarity of language. He dismisses, for example, the kind of metaphors evoked by his former lover, Anny:

> The rain has stopped, the air is mild, the sky slowly rolls up fine black images: it is more than enough to frame a perfect moment; to reflect these images, Anny would cause dark little tides to be born in our hearts. I don't know how to take advantage of the occasion: I walk at random, calm and empty, under this wasted sky. (70)

> La pluie a cessé, l'air est doux, le ciel roule lentement de belles images noires: c'est plus qu'il n'en faut pour faire le cadre d'un moment parfait; pour refléter ces images, Anny ferait naître dans nos cœurs de sombres petites marées. Moi, je ne sais pas profiter de l'occasion: je vais au hasard, vide et calme, sous ce ciel inutilisé. (85)

But as Christopher Prendergast points out, while rejecting Anny's Proustian metaphor — dismissing her inclination toward the aestheticization of the natural world — Roquentin himself evokes the metaphor of a "wasted sky": "There is ... a paradox: the paradox whereby Roquentin deploys metaphor to reject metaphor."[13]

Roquentin's resistance to literature parallels his resistance to bourgeois discourse. Like the former, the effectiveness of the latter is repeatedly compromised. If Roquentin is quite unforgiving about the way in which the Bouvillois take the most banal event and transform it into an adventure —

> I marvel at these young people: drinking their coffee, they tell clear, plausible stories. If they are asked what they did yesterday, they aren't embarrassed: they bring you up to date in a few words. If I were in their place, I'd fall over myself. (7)

> Ces jeunes gens m'émerveillent: ils racontent, en buvant leur café, des histoires nettes et vraisemblables. Si on leur demande ce qu'ils ont fait hier, ils ne se troublent pas: ils vous mettent au courant en deux mots. A leur place, je bafouillerais. (12)

— he himself falls prey to this ideological tendency, seeing himself as a *character* in a "life story": "at last an adventure happens to me ... I am as happy as the hero of a novel" (54) ["enfin une aventure m'arrive ... je suis heureux comme un héros de roman" (66)]. While on the one hand Roquentin is enraged by their mystification of the given and wants to distinguish himself from them by representing his experiences without transforming them into adventures, on the other hand, he constantly undermines his own critique — expressed in his ultimatum, "you have to choose: live or tell" (39) ["Il faut choisir: vivre ou raconter" (48)]—through his compulsion to narrate: "So I asked for some paper and *I am going to tell* what happened to him" (161, emphasis added) ["Alors j'ai demandé du papier et *je vais raconter* ce qui lui est arrivé" (190)]. This last statement is especially problematic since it occurs towards of the end of his diary, leaving the reader wondering: Has Roquentin been falsifying (that is, narrating) lived experience all along?

While it is tempting here to accuse Roquentin of hypocrisy or "bad faith" (*mauvaise foi*) for having contradicted his earlier insights into the nature of human existence (his experience of the world as absurd), these relapses into conformity (his resemblance to the Bouvillois) exceed the framework of a strict existentialist reading. They are not fully amenable to a Sartrean explication, in which the boundaries separating authenticity and bad faith, resistance and complicity, are clearly delimited and upheld. In this respect, we might consider Roquentin as existentialism's unruly example, and *Nausea* as muddying the philosophical picture of *Being and Nothingness*. More than a falsification of reality—instances of false consciousness—Roquentin's relapses testify to the *subtle* workings of ideology and its pervasiveness in everyday life (ideology's manipulation of social reality): they testify to the way ideology shapes Roquentin's beliefs, attitudes, desires, and actions. Although Roquentin knows quite well that the *idea* of narrative is problematic, that narratives distort life by imposing an artificial structure on one's lived experience, ideology is relentless in its ability to produce *within* Roquentin a desire for coherence and meaning that disposes him to structure his fluctuating identity through the proliferation of narratives. Above all, ideology produces within Roquentin a disposition to act in accordance with what might be called a "bourgeois ethos" — a constant yearning for a familiar mode of being, for "a regular world" (3) ["un monde . . . régulier" (7)] — a world that is *plausible*. Indeed, it is not a mere coincidence that when Roquentin feels at ease with his environment he refers to himself as feeling *bourgeois*: "I am quite at ease this evening, quite solidly *terre-à-terre* [*bien bourgeoisement*, or "quite bourgeois-ly"] in the world" (2) ["Ce soir, je suis bien à l'aise, bien bourgeoisement dans le monde" (6)].

This is not simply Roquentin's problem. The reader is also subjected to ideology's pull and reach. In a key scene of the novel where Roquentin's alienation pushes him to extreme measures, Sartre's protagonist cannot even rely on his own body as a source of knowledge and stability. His hand appears as *other*; as a thing in the midst of the world, from which he finds no escape:

> I see my hand spread out on the table.... no matter where I put it it will go on existing; I can't suppress it, nor can I suppress the rest of my body. (98–99)

> Je vois ma main qui s'épanouit sur la table.... où que je la mette, elle continuera d'exister et je continuerai de sentir qu'elle existe; je ne peux pas la supprimer, ni supprimer le reste de mon corps. (117–18)

Unable to bear its sight, his estrangement heightens and Roquentin mutilates himself:

> My saliva is sugary, my body warm: I feel neutral. My knife is on the table. I open it. Why not? It would be a change in any case. I put my left hand on the pad and stab the knife into the palm. (100)

> Ma salive est sucrée, mon corps est tiède; je me sens fade. Mon canif est sur la table. Je l'ouvre. Pourquoi pas? De toute façon, ça changerait un peu. Je pose ma main gauche sur le bloc-notes et je m'envoie un bon coup de couteau dans la paume. (119)

With this mutilation, Roquentin seeks at once to revolt against the absurd presence of his body and alleviate his discomfiture by reaffirming himself as an active subject in the world. This act of revolt is, however, quickly appropriated by contingency:

> I wonder. I watch the small, monotonous trickle of blood. Now it is coagulating. It's over. My skin looks rusty around the cut. Under the skin, the only thing left is a small sensation exactly like the others, perhaps even more insipid. (100)

> J'hésite. Je regarde la petite coulée monotone du sang. Le voilà justement qui coagule. C'est fini. Ma peau a l'air rouillée, autour de la coupure. Sous la peau, il ne reste qu'une petite sensation pareille aux autres, peut-être encore plus fade. (119)

On a first reading this passage thematizes Roquentin's absurd condition and reveals the force of the diary form in communicating the affective immediacy of ontological nausea — his "*insipid* taste"[14] of contingency. Yet, on a second reading, as Denis Hollier points out, the verisimilitude of the above passage breaks down:

> It should be recalled here that Roquentin, who is writing this at the same time he is doing it, knows quite well ... that in order to write one has to

make use of both hands, one to hold the pen, the other to prevent the paper from moving. All of which gives him four in this case: two real — or better, plausible — ones, those that are before his eyes and that he evokes on this page (one with the knife, the other with the wound), and then their shadowy twins, which give them utterance, the phantom hands of his double.[15]

What was presented as Roquentin's phenomenological experience — the novel's "subjective realism" — turns out to be a ruse of sorts. Such a self-reflexive moment is as much a warning against the reader's inclination to embrace one form of realism over another as a critique of the ideology of *verisimilitude*.

Roquentin's resistance to ideology likewise merits a careful (re)reading. Upon reflection, Roquentin emerges as a split subject. On the one hand, Roquentin displays a measure of self-reflexivity, some level of resistance to authoritative discourses. As we have seen, he decides to abandon his project of biography rather than to accept and perpetuate the *doxa* of traditional historiography (the belief that a coherent and objective representation of Rollebon is possible). Similarly, Roquentin exhibits resistance to Bouville's social norms: he does not consider himself an anonymous "case," a useful and docile body, someone like Bouville resident M. Achille, for whom power is naturalized and uncontested. Whereas M. Achille conforms to social forces blindly, unable to think critically about his status *qua* subject — "M. Achille is simply a case and lets himself be brought back easily to the accepted ideas" (68) ["M. Achille est un cas, tout simplement, et qui se laisse aisément ramener à quelques notions communes" (82)]) — Roquentin practices self-reflection; he deliberates and chooses, expressing a desire to fashion himself *differently*. On the other hand, Roquentin's power of disidentification — his capacity to distance himself from the socially prescribed mode of being — functions as a *pharmakon*: it is an antidote to ideology (allowing him to resist the gaze of Bouville's elites at the museum) and it is ideology's most seductive form of manipulation. Žižek calls the latter "ideological disidentification":

> One should turn around the standard notion of ideology as providing a firm identification for its subjects, constraining them to their "social roles": what if, at a different — but no less irrevocable and structurally necessary — level, ideology is effective precisely by way of constructing a space of false disidentification, of false distance towards the actual coordinates of the subject's social existence?[16]

The practice of disidentification both undermines and supports ideology, feeding Roquentin's — and, we might say, the existentialist's — fantasy of his own singularity, his cultivation of a quasi-heroic, defiant will.

A Resistance without a Subject

There is yet another side to Roquentin's form of resistance, a form that is ostensibly not predicated on Roquentin's "enlightened" will or on the negating powers of his consciousness. What interrupts Roquentin's social existence, what provokes transgression from the Bouville norms, is seldom a self-generated, purely autonomous act. The Lucienne episode proves particularly useful for a further exploration of Roquentin's will to transgress. This episode takes place shortly after the abandonment of the biography project, the "second death" of Rollebon, and Roquentin's own death as biographer — which opens up, in turn, a space to reconfigure his *social* identity: "I'm not writing my book on Rollebon any more; it's finished, I can't write any more of it. What am I going to do with my life?" (94) ["Je n'écris plus mon livre sur Rollebon; c'est fini, je ne *peux* plus l'écrire. Qu'est-ce que je vais faire de ma vie?" (113)]. After having heard of the rape and death of little Lucienne, Roquentin *displaces* his sexual identity in a fantasy rape. Shortly after his initial identification with the rapist — "I flee. The criminal has fled, the violated body" (101) ["Je fuis, l'ignoble individu a pris fuite, son corps violé" (146)] — Roquentin identifies with Lucienne, the object of rape, as his body becomes feminized:

> Existence takes my thoughts from behind and gently expands them *from behind*; someone takes me from behind, they force me to think from behind, therefore to be something... little Lucienne assaulted from behind, violated by existence from behind. (102)

> L'existence prend mes pensées par derrière et doucement les épanouit *par-derrière*; on me prend par derrière, on me force par-derrière de penser, donc d'être quelque chose... la petite Lucile assaillie par-derrière, violée par l'existence par-derrière. (148)

At first, it would seem that Roquentin evacuates his freedom by a process of desubjectivization (moving from an active "I" to a passive "they"). He surrenders his role of subject by becoming feminine (object), a passive recipient rather than a dynamic agent. This interpretation seems, however, too restrictive: it reduces the feminization of the body to a state of passivity while leaving unquestioned the social dimension of sexuality. Rather, Roquentin's identification with Lucienne's body can better be understood as a "radical subversion of the norms of the *logos*,"[17] as a defiance of Bouville's censoring discourse. By becoming homosexual, or losing the voice of the heterosexual — subjecting himself to the illogic logic of "both and yet neither" — Roquentin transgresses the social boundaries defining his masculinity. No longer disciplined, Roquentin's body escapes the established bourgeois norms of Bouville. His *assigned* heterosexual identity is (un)consciously altered and subverted by his fantasy rape, and as a result, he ceases, momentarily, to be a knowable and predictable sexual subject — even to himself. As Lawrence Kritzman notes, "The self-contradictory rhythms of this narrative reveal a subject who no longer knows precisely who he is and engages in a process of self-reinvention by playing on the in-between."[18] Moreover, the Lucienne episode is significant because it illustrates that Roquentin's transgressive act of identification and "self-reinvention" reflects only a *gradation* of freedom; the *will* behind the transgression is not that of a pure consciousness but one that is enmeshed within the play of power and conditioned by the constraints of language.

In his dialogue with the Self-Taught Man, Roquentin faces and resists another paradigmatic model of subjectivity, that of the humanist self. Appearing at first as the object of ridicule (his project is to read the entire contents of the municipal library in alphabetical order in the hope of acquiring universal knowledge), the Self-Taught Man emerges as the unequivocal voice of a long and serious ethical tradition stressing "love" for human beings. Distraught over Roquentin's resistance to humanism, the Self-Taught Man accuses him of being an "anti-humanist," which in turn infuriates Roquentin, who rages: "I don't want to be integrated, I don't want my good red blood to go and fatten this lymphatic beast: I will not be fool enough to call myself 'anti-humanist.' I *am not* a humanist, that's all there is to it" (118) ["Je ne veux pas qu'on m'intègre, ni que mon beau sang rouge aille engraisser cette bête lymphatique: je ne commettrai pas la sottise de me dire 'antihumaniste.' Je ne *suis pas* humaniste, voila tout" (140)]. The aim of the Self-Taught Man is clear: he seeks either to homogenize or to exclude the other.

Roquentin, however, does not enter the humanist's discourse, refusing to be enslaved by his taxonomies, for oppositional thinking would only invert the humanist tradition and consequently reinstate its logic: "If you oppose him head on, you play his game; he lives off his opponents" (118) ["Si l'on s'oppose à lui de front, on fait son jeu; il vit de ses contraires" (140)]. Roquentin reverses their power relation — originally constituted by the Self-Taught Man's desire to direct or govern the behavior of Roquentin — through his refusal to participate in his language game, to conform to the latter's expectations. By circumventing his interlocutor's logic, Roquentin exposes the poverty of the Self-Taught Man's rhetoric and its latent binarism.

This proto-deconstructive move did not escape the notice of Jacques Derrida, who acknowledged the importance of Roquentin's counter-hegemonic stance: "It is in the dialogue with the Self-Taught Man that Roquentin levels the worst charges against humanism, against all humanist styles."[19] Roquentin's encounter with the Self-Taught Man also recalls Foucault's exchange with the so-called defenders of the Enlightenment:

> But that does not mean that one has to be "for" or "against" the Enlightenment. It even means precisely that one has to refuse everything that might present itself in the form of a simplistic and authoritarian alternative: you either accept the Enlightenment and remain within the tradition of its rationalism . . . or else you criticize the Enlightenment and then try to escape from its principles of rationality.[20]

Like Foucault's critique of the "blackmail" of the Enlightenment, Roquentin eludes the victimizing nature of humanist thinking while at the same time remaining unflagging in its denunciation. Roquentin's subversion of the Self-Taught Man's binary logic is especially, if not paradoxically, applicable to his own earlier formulation, "you have to choose: live or tell" — and, we might add, its corollary, "you have to choose: resist or conform."

The encounter with the Self-Taught Man and the Lucienne episode invite us to consider a *resistance without a subject*. Yet the novel also makes clear Roquentin's lasting psychic investment in philosophy, in its luring model of subjectivity. Despite, or because of, his repeated setbacks, Roquentin does not waiver in his project to "see clearly," in his quest for "self-knowledge" (4) ["connaissance de moi-même" (8)] — nor in his faith in the representational capacity of language. Gerald Prince expresses Roquentin's enduring optimism and commitment to the powers of the *logos*: "It seems . . . that language is a faithful and illuminating mirror for things and that the order of discourse and that of the real are one and the same."[21]

Roquentin in Language

Halfway through the diary, an anguished Roquentin trusts that his words will elucidate the nature of things, that his phenomenological *epoché* — his bracketing of presuppositions about the objective world, or what Husserl calls the "natural attitude"[22] — will prove successful in curing him of his nausea:

> As long as I could stare at things nothing would happen: I looked at them as much as I could, pavement, houses, gaslights; my eyes went rapidly from one to another, to catch them unaware, stop them in the midst of their metamorphosis. They did not look natural, but *I told myself forcibly*: this is a gaslight, this is a drinking fountain, and I tried to reduce them to their everyday aspect by the power of *my gaze*. (78, emphasis added)

> Tant que je pourrais fixer les objets, il ne se produirait rien: j'en regardais le plus que je pouvais, des pavés, des maisons, des becs de gaz; mes yeux allaient rapidement des uns aux autres pour les surprendre et les arrêter au milieu de leur métamorphose. Ils n'avaient pas l'air trop naturels, mais *je me disais avec force*: c'est un bec de gaz, c'est une borne-fontaine et j'essayais, par la puissance de *mon regard*, de les réduire à leur aspect quotidien. (94)

This passage clearly reveals Roquentin's investment in the purity of speech. By *telling himself* that this is a gaslight, Roquentin's voice hopes to stabilize the gaslight and render its meaning fully present. Roquentin's *logos* in its spontaneous immediacy expresses what is *present* for his consciousness and more importantly guarantees that the phonemes of "g-a-s-l-i-g-h-t" correspond to the concept (meaning) "gaslight." Roquentin assumes here the position of a meaning-giving subject, situating his perception (and tacitly his *logos*) as something outside the realm of discursivity. However, to maintain such a privileged space, Roquentin must master the world of things, denote the physically real and prove to himself the originary and authoritative voice of his discourse: he must be the Adam of his world.[23]

But Roquentin's *logos* fails to rise to the task. A seemingly innocuous tramway seat subverts his semiotic universe. After losing its social (instrumental and utilitarian) function, the seat is unable to be subdued by Roquentin's gaze and speech. By resisting Roquentin's nominalization, the seat in question breaks free from linguistic domestication and instrumentality. Roquentin murmurs: "'It's a seat,' a little like an exorcism" (125) ["'c'est une banquette,' un peu comme un exorcisme" (148)]. "But the word stays on [his] lips," no longer corresponding to some putatively natural extralinguistic entity:

> It refuses to go and put itself on the thing. It stays what it is, with its red plush, thousands of red little red paws in the air, all still, little dead paws. This enormous belly turned upward, bleeding, inflated — bloated with all its dead paws, this belly floating in this car, in this grey sky, is not a seat. It could just as well be a dead donkey tossed about in the water, floating with the current, belly in the air in a great grey river, a river of floods; and I could be sitting on the donkey's belly, my feet dangling in the clear water. (125)

> Mais le mot reste sur mes lèvres: il refuse d'aller se poser sur la chose. Elle reste ce qu'elle est, avec sa peluche rouge, milliers de petites pattes rouges, en l'air, toutes raides, de petites pattes mortes. Cet énorme ventre tourné en l'air, sanglant, ballonné — boursouflé avec toutes ses pattes mortes, ventre qui flotte dans cette boîte, dans ce ciel gris, ce n'est pas une banquette. Ça pourrait tout aussi bien être un âne mort, par exemple, ballonné par l'eau et qui flotte à la dérive, le ventre en l'air dans un grand fleuve gris, un fleuve d'inondation; et moi je serais aussi sur le ventre de l'âne et mes pieds tremperaient dans l'eau claire. (148)

Stupefied to see that the meaning that he tries to impute orally has failed miserably — and this right after his unconventional metaphorization of the seat: a tramway seat *is like* the belly of a dead donkey floating in a river of blood — Roquentin, in the midst of this linguistic flux, is forced to conclude that his words (figurative and otherwise) are ultimately inadequate, that things are in fact unnameable:

> *Things are divorced from their name. They are there*, grotesque, headstrong, gigantic and it seems ridiculous to call them seats or say anything at all about them: I am in the midst of things, *nameless things*. (125, emphasis added)

> *Les choses se sont délivrées de leurs noms. Elles sont là*, grotesques, têtues, géantes et ça paraît imbécile de les appeler des banquettes ou de dire quoi que ce soit sur elles: je suis au milieu des Choses, *les innommables*. (148)

Shortly after the episode with the tramway seat, Roquentin finds himself in the public park, the site of his philosophic epiphany: his encounter with the root of a chestnut tree. In contrast to the previous encounters with the gaslight and the bench, here Roquentin fails to produce a transparent representation of the present state of affairs, and is forced to use a *non*present tense to express what he has just *perceived*: "In vain to repeat: 'This is a root' — it didn't work any more" (129) ["J'avais beau me répéter: 'C'est une racine' — ça ne prenait plus" (153)]. During this linguistic crisis, the spoken sign did not coincide with the *presence* of the chestnut tree's being. Despite his powerlessness to express immediately what he perceived, Roquentin describes his experience as a "vision" (127) ("illumination" [150]). He has finally attained his goal: "And suddenly, suddenly, the veil is torn away, I have understood, I have *seen*" (126) ["Et tout d'un coup, d'un seul coup, le voile se déchire, j'ai compris, j'ai *vu*" (150)]. Roquentin announces that his illuminating experience was pre-verbal:

> The word absurdity is coming to life under my pen; a little while ago, in the garden, I couldn't find it, but neither was I looking for it, I did not need it: I thought without words, *on* things, *with* things. (129)

> Le mot d'Absurdité naît à présent sous ma plume; tout à l'heure, au jardin, je ne l'ai pas trouvé, mais je ne le cherchais pas non plus, je n'en avais pas besoin: Je pensais sans mots, *sur* les choses, *avec* les choses. (152)

After this remark, the reader expects that Roquentin will share, clearly and distinctly, as would a philosopher, his unadulterated perception of reality: a reality, according to Mark Bertrand, in which objects are liberated from their social and linguistic domestication, and revealed to the knower in their "natural state" (*état sauvage*).[24] At the precise moment when Roquentin is about to provide his reader with a lucid account of naked existence, the "real" state of things, he frustrates the latter's expectations by reintroducing the kind of exaggerated metaphors evoked in the case of the tramway seat:

> Absurdity was not an idea in my head, or the sound of a voice, only this long serpent dead at my feet, this wooden serpent. Serpent or claw or root or vulture's talon, what difference does it make. (129)

> L'absurdité, ce n'était pas une idée dans ma tête, ni un souffle de voix, mais ce long serpent mort à mes pieds, ce serpent de bois. Serpent ou griffe ou racine ou serre de vautour, peu importe. (152)

While constantly invoking unconventional metaphors, Roquentin appears to distance himself from his initial philosophical project of purifying his language of all semantic opacity. Rereading Roquentin's encounter with the tramway seat, we can see that far from providing a clear and distinct meaning for the word "seat," in comparing it to a "dead donkey" Roquentin reveals (even if unintentionally) the word's semantic fluidity. Similarly, his experience at the public garden is as much textual as it is metaphysical.[25] The episode both accommodates and exceeds a Sartrean interpretation. Roquentin does not stop with the philosophical insight that it is "impossible to grasp facticity in its brute nudity"[26] but rather translates his "horrible ecstasy" (131) ["extase horrible" (155)] *poetically*.[27] The "experience" of absurdity (the absence of inherent meaning in the world) provokes a proliferation of conspicuous metaphors — "wooden serpent," "claw," and "vulture's talon" — that pull the reader's attention away from the referential reality of the event to its traumatizing *effects* on Roquentin. The event of the epiphany undergoes even further displacement when Roquentin confesses his inability to determine whether his "epiphanic" moment was lived or imagined: "Had I dreamed of this enormous presence?" (134) ["Est-ce que je l'ai rêvée, cette énorme présence?" (159)].

Alain Robbe-Grillet was one of the first critics to draw attention to Roquentin's use of metaphor, which he maintains is "never an innocent figure of speech."[28] Though *Nausea* admirably highlights human contingency, the novel's critique of essentialism falls short of evacuating *all* human significance from its narrative, that is, of producing a pure and neutral description of the world. For Robbe-Grillet, *Nausea*'s metaphors — Roquentin's "fatal complicity"[29] with the world of objects — have the contradictory effect of humanizing the world, of anthropomorphizing nature, to the extent that they impose relations where none are present. Sartre himself would later confirm Robbe-Grillet's critique, seeing his early work as symptomatic of a deeply ingrained idealism: "In Platonic fashion, I went from knowledge to this subject. I found more reality in the idea than in the thing.... From that came the idealism which it took me thirty years to shake off."[30]

Both Robbe-Grillet's objections and Sartre's belated self-critique, however, flatten *Nausea*'s staging of figurative language, neutralizing its metaphors' short-circuiting potential. Roquentin's metaphors do establish a relation with the world of objects, yet it is a relation that we might say is *otherwise than humanizing*, since the metaphors themselves yield no positive knowledge about the root of the chestnut tree. Roquentin's unruly metaphors produce a *surplus of meaning*; they overwhelm his phenomenological reduction, effectively disrupting his narrative of the event. Desperately wanting to name Being — to ontologically unveil and hermeneutically gain control over Being — Roquentin can only *register* Being's intransigence discursively, at the symbolic level, through his dizzying display of metaphorical excess.[31] In Lacanian parlance, the Real of Being is not a substance; it is "not an external thing that resists being caught in the symbolic network, but the fissure within the symbolic network itself."[32] Once Roquentin's language fails to function as he wishes (to signify in moderation), once his *logos* is no longer able to nail things down in their place, to capture the immediacy and presence of the world, and to integrate adequately the raw content of his perception, all description of reality (of the referent) ceases to be unproblematic. Unable to close the gap between words and things, Roquentin has lost his referential foothold. Textually dispossessed of his *logos*, verbally impotent, a failed Adam, Roquentin discovers that his living speech lacks the power to guarantee the presence of things. Baffled by the discovery that the semantic order imposed by his metaphysical language is illusory, Roquentin tries desperately to recenter himself, to regain his sovereignty.

Having "begun" his project with a view of language as an unproblematic medium for self-expression, Roquentin "ends" this project by resolving to write a work of art, "another type of book" (178) ["un autre espèce de livre" (210)], thus turning from one extreme to another, from a literal language to a figural one, from a referential language to a self-referential one. He models this book *à venir* after the jazz song *Some of These Days*, the creation (or so imagines Roquentin) of a Jewish composer and a black singer, whose refrain, "Some of these days/you'll miss me honey," and euphonious melody — it has nothing *de trop* — help him "transcend" his nausea and cope with reality by allowing him to take momentary refuge in an imaginary realm away from the contingencies of life. What attracts him to this jazz piece is the song's being (its status as being), its ideal ontological status, its teleological nature, the way in which each element has a fixed and necessary value — giving Roquentin, in turn, a sense of finality.

If the Sartre of *Being and Nothingness* declared that man is condemned to be free, the Sartre of *Nausea* could have claimed that man is condemned to remain *in* language.[33] Far from being a thing exterior to him, something that he merely *uses* (something that faithfully *serves* his perception), language, Roquentin comes to realize, is a system that also works *on* and *through* him. Having failed to master his referential reality hermeneutically and secure adequate grounds for claims about self-knowledge, he finds that the role of perception, privileged at the outset of the diary for its unmediated and immediate access to the object, ends up significantly demoted by the time we reach the dénouement of the work.[34] Indeed, Roquentin's perception, once conceived as originary, will play no part in the book *à venir*—since the book will *not* take as its object an existent:

> It would have to be a book: I don't know how to do anything else. But not a history book: history talks about what has existed—an existant can never justify the existence of another existant. ... Another type of book. I don't quite know which kind—but you would have to guess, behind the printed words, behind the pages, at something which would not exist, which would be above existence. A story, for example, something that could never happen, an adventure. It would have to be beautiful and hard as steel and make people ashamed of their existence. (178)

> Il faudrait que ce soit un livre: je ne sais rien faire d'autre. Mais pas un livre d'histoire: l'histoire, ça parle de ce qui a existé—jamais un existant ne peut justifier l'existence d'un autre existant. ... Un autre espèce de livre. Je ne sais pas très bien laquelle — mais il faudrait qu'on devine, derrière les mots imprimés, derrière les pages, quelque chose qui n'existerait pas, qui serait au-dessus de l'existence. Une histoire, par exemple, comme il ne peut en arriver, une aventure. Il faudrait qu'elle soit belle et dure comme de l'acier et qu'elle fasse honte aux gens de leur existence. (210)

Roquentin's vision recalls Flaubert's desire to write "a book about nothing, a book dependent on nothing external, which would be held together by the strength of its style, just as the earth, suspended in the void, depends on nothing external for its support; a book which would have almost no subject, or at least in which the subject would be almost invisible, if such a thing is possible."[35] Opting to write a book of pure fiction, to create a work of pure art, Roquentin adopts here what seems to be an all-or-nothing attitude toward referentiality: either language will express or represent authentically the "thing itself" (where words and things have a one-to-one correspondence), or language will aim at what is "above existence," that is, what is beyond the referential world. But the language envisioned by Roquentin here has not really changed. Even if his language is no longer referential, he continues to aspire to a monological, univocal, and transparent language, to a book whose writing would render it a closed, autonomous, and necessary system, absent of all play and contingencies.

The meaning of the ending remains nonetheless paradoxical. On a literal reading, Roquentin's aesthetic solution — his overcoming of solitude through an abandonment of the referential world in favor of an imaginary realm capable of guaranteeing meaning and necessity — echoes utopian, modernist projects: art transubstantiates the contingent/absurd self into a purposeful aesthetic object. Terence Keefe defends the seriousness of the aesthetic solution, asserting that "it is a grave error to see [Sartre] looking on Roquentin's 'solution' to his own problems ironically or with derision and still a graver one to claim that the unelaborated character of the ending indicates that Sartre did not take it seriously, or was not interested in it."[36] Keefe justifies his reading by appealing to "external" sources, namely Sartre's *Words* and his other works more or less contemporary with his publication of *Nausea*: "Even when we concentrate on the ending of *La Nausée* in our narrow sense, *we need to remember that evidence external to the novel as such can come into play*."[37] By relying heavily on authorial intentionality, such a reading — although well documented and instructive — domesticates the novel's corrosive irony, ignoring the self-contesting impulse of *Nausea*. Against the argument that *Nausea*'s ending is based on "a train of thought that is clearly intended to be fallacious as an argument" and that consequently there is no "genuine conclusion,"[38] such a reading accepts Roquentin's prose at face value, minimizing the novel's ambiguity and self-contesting character, the way in which it consistently subverts the expectations of his readers. As Dominick LaCapra observes: "By its end, the reader is almost programmed to expect an expectation of meaning to be frustrated."[39]

Ironic Hesitations

We might conclude, then, that the obvious meaning of the ending (pure art as Roquentin's Proustian redemption) must be renounced or ironically interpreted by *Nausea*'s attentive reader, for whom the problem of representation raised throughout the text cannot simply be forgotten, ignored, or resolved by Roquentin's aesthetic "solution" (the ironic ending referring the reader back to the parodic beginning of *Nausea*). Yet such a response to the ending imposes its own kind of finality, one that is not so qualitatively different from the straightforward reading. To be sure, recognizing structural irony adds another layer of meaning to the text; by the same token, it also risks neutralizing the play of the ending and its potential for hesitation, that is, its capacity to solicit and resist an array of interpretations. As with Baudelairian irony, *Nausea*'s ironic ending does not deliver meaning (irony *as* the contrary of what Roquentin says), or rather, the meaning that it delivers resists hermeneutic mastery. If the reader has his or her suspicions about the plausibility of Roquentin's new project, along with the type of aesthetics it entails, Roquentin himself complicates further this ironic reversal by disrupting the very division between art and existence on which such a reversal is predicated. Roquentin's book *à venir* is not absolutely divorced from referentiality, since he considers what *effect* his artwork would have on his future readers, hoping — we might say fantasizing — that his book will make its readers "ashamed of their existence" (178) ["qu'elle fasse honte aux gens de leur existence" (210)], creating in them a desire for its author: "'Antoine Roquentin wrote it, a red-headed man who hung around cafés,' and they would think about my life as I think about the Negress's: as something precious and almost legendary" (178) ["'C'est Antoine Roquentin qui l'a écrit, c'était un type roux qui traînait dans les cafés,' et ils penseraient à ma vie comme je pense à celle de cette Négresse: comme à quelque chose de précieux et d'à moitié légendaire" (210)]. Roquentin's consideration of his potential reception can, of course, be brushed aside as a narcissistic wish for authorial grandeur or immortality, a desire for his prose to have an impact on the literary world. Conversely, the timing of his consideration might be said to register an unsettling moment of hesitation or self-doubt in his dream of artistic transcendence. By evoking his reader *à venir* precisely after announcing his book *à venir*, Roquentin reinscribes his aesthetic work, unwittingly perhaps, in the nauseating world of existence: the world of both ontological and hermeneutic unruliness.

V

Intoxicating Meaning

ALAIN ROBBE-GRILLET'S *JEALOUSY*

> If it intoxicates me, nonmeaning indeed
> has this meaning — *it intoxicates me.*
> GEORGES BATAILLE

Published in 1957, as the *nouveau roman* was rising on the Parisian literary scene, Alain Robbe-Grillet's novel *Jealousy* produced in many of its first readers a reaction of puzzlement and consternation. One critic from the newspaper *Le Monde* believed "that he had surely received a copy whose pages had been mixed up by the printer, that it was a jumbled mess."[1] *Jealousy*, in many ways, can be said to illustrate Robbe-Grillet's modernist, if not postmodernist, bias against classical realism and narration,[2] his view that "tell[ing] a story has become strictly impossible [*raconter est devenu proprement impossible*]."[3] Making these remarks in an article aptly entitled "On Several Obsolete Notions," published the same year as *Jealousy* and republished a few years later in his influential 1963 manifesto *For a New Novel*, Robbe-Grillet made clear his intention to renovate both the novel form and the critical reading practices used in approaching the genre as a whole.

Robbe-Grillet's call for a radicalization of the novel — for a "new novel" that "refuses to conform to our habits of apprehension and to our classification"[4] — proved more difficult to translate into new protocols of reading, however, and the question of how one can or should read *Jealousy*'s unruliness, its intentional challenge to hermeneutic containment and cognitive mastery, remains open. The question of how to respond to a work that stubbornly insists on its refractory otherness — a question that *Jealousy* itself allegorizes or stages in several key scenes — is not just an intellectual or epistemological challenge but also an ethical one. Taking up this challenge, this chapter looks awry at the reception of Robbe-Grillet's work — viewing the familiar fault lines in criticism askance — identifying the forms of readerly responsibility that the novel stages and elicits, and evaluating the very possibility of meeting the work's ethical and interpretive demands.

Another Realism or Realism's Other

"No novel, no matter how avant-garde, can succeed without engaging its readers' desires and expectations, and readers cannot desire or expect anything in a world totally alien from their own," writes Peter J. Rabinowitz.[5] *Jealousy* unmistakably engages its readers' desires and expectations, yet how this acknowledgment relates back to the novel's strangeness is a decidedly more complicated question. Confronted with *Jealousy*'s alien and alienating unruliness, some critics have sought to tame the novel — that is, to fix its promiscuous slippage of meaning — through recourse to well-established modes of inquiry. In his 1963 work, *The Novels of Robbe-Grillet*, Bruce Morrissette offered the first systematic and explanatory study of the novel, basing his reading in part on the authority of its jacket blurb, which he faithfully paraphrased as follows: "The story with its three characters — the husband, the wife, the presumed lover — is 'narrated' by the husband, a tropical planter who, from the vantage points in his banana plantation house, surrounded on three sides by its wide veranda, suspiciously keeps watch over his wife."[6]

According to Morrissette, two chronologies control the novel's action: an external chronology (which is impossible to determine) and a chronology of the husband's psychological states. The novel's disconcerting chronological impasses can be explained as symptoms of the inner psychic unity governing the order of the novel's events. This psychic unity ultimately refers us to a stable, coherent subject and a readable subject/work, one situated in the tradition of the psychological novel. *Jealousy*'s initial disturbing effects are thus eliminated through a critical rereading, one that naturalizes the contradictions and restores the comforting sense of comprehension and mastery.

Prioritizing referential interpretation does not necessarily lead to a psychological reading of *Jealousy*, however. In his 1973 *Lecture politique du roman* (*Political Reading of the Novel*), Jacques Leenhardt proposed an illuminating sociological analysis of the novel, unsettling Morrissette's influential contention that *Jealousy* is about erotic jealousy, and more specifically, about the psychic reality of a jealous husband. Leenhardt's Marxist reading of *Jealousy* purports to make visible what Fredric Jameson describes as the novel's language or, to be more precise, its signifiers' "material and referential *preconditions*."[7] Privileging the social, in turn, enables the reader to escape the psychologization of the husband in order to better attest to his ideological subject position. Leenhardt reads the novel allegorically as a textual site of tension between two competing colonial models: the husband, who stands for the old racist French empire, and the new, more utilitarian, neocolonial model, allegorized in the figure of Franck.[8]

On Leenhardt's account, the motor of the story is not erotic jealousy per se, but the husband's fear of losing his material possessions and patriarchal privilege. The narrator's obsessive, depersonalized gaze, for instance, is not merely an index of the husband's isolated pathology; rather, it reflects the anxieties of late French colonialism on the eve of the 1960 accessions to independence in West Africa. Leenhardt historicizes the Cartesian subject and its desire for control, situating this subject (embodied here by the husband) in the early moments of decolonization, an era that confirmed the death of a traditional French imperialism based on territorial conquest and control, while also witnessing a rise in neocolonial capitalist systems of domination.[9] On this reading, the narrator-husband's obsessive gaze, exemplified in his geometrical descriptions of his banana plantation — for example,

> The bulge of the bank also begins to take effect starting from the fifth row: this row, as a matter of fact, also possesses only twenty-one trees, whereas it should have twenty-two for a true trapezoid and twenty-three for a rectangle (uneven row).

> La courbure de la rive entre à son tour en jeu à partir de la cinquième rangée: celle-ci en effet ne possède également que vingt-et-un individus, alors qu'elle en aurait vingt-deux pour un vrai trapèze, et vingt-trois pour un rectangle (ligne d'ordre impair).[10]

— is symptomatic of his uneasiness and loss of footing in the changing field of power. "Looking and being looked at ... places jealousy at the center of the plantation problem, which is a microcosm of the colonial problem," Leenhardt concludes.[11] For Leenhardt, neither *Jealousy*'s textual self-reflexivity nor its psychological realism should blind the reader to the novel's historical frame of reference or its ideological content. Accordingly, *Jealousy*'s realism, its epistemological claims about the referential world, lie not so much in the evocation of the narrator's psychic reality but in the novel's representation of a colonial mentality, or more precisely, in its staging of the ideological tension inherent in the devolution and devaluation of Western colonialism.

Already in 1959, however, literary critic and novelist Maurice Blanchot was warning against any referential reading of the novel, that is, a reading in which the primary goal is to explicate and domesticate Robbe-Grillet's unruly narration by imposing a hermeneutic order, a reading whose attempt at comprehensive mastery raises both aesthetic and ethical questions. In *The Book to Come*, Blanchot not only questions the primacy of the husband's jealousy but also problematizes the very existence of such a central character. Taking objection, in particular, to the jacket blurb's characterization of the narrator as a jealous husband,[12] Blanchot underscores the novel's radical alterity, its irreducibility to a thematic analysis, and its departure from preexisting literary models. More importantly, noting the "powerful absence [at] the center of the plot and of the narration," he reminds the reader that no character is ever in fact named as the narrator and that what we have instead is an *absent I*:

> According to the critics, we are to understand that what is speaking in this absence is the very character of the jealous one, the husband who watches over his wife. I think this misunderstands the authentic reality of this narrative as the reader is invited to approach it. The reader indeed feels that something is missing; he has the premonition that it is this lack that allows everything to be said and everything to be seen — but how could this lack be identified with someone? How could there still be a name and an identity there? It is nameless, faceless; it is pure anonymous presence.[13]

For Blanchot, the anonymity of the narrative voice reflects the demands of writing and crystallizes the singular experience of literature, that is, literature's resistance to readerly cognitive demands: "The essence of literature is precisely to escape any essential determination, any assertion that stabilizes it or even realizes it: it is never already there, it always has to be rediscovered or reinvented."[14] The event of literature not only frustrates comprehension but also alters and dispossesses its readers: "It is what divests me of myself and of any being, just as it makes language no longer what speaks but what is; language becomes the idle profundity of being, the domain where the word becomes being but does not signify and does not reveal."[15] In "Maurice Blanchot: The Thought from Outside," Michel Foucault similarly underscores the noninstrumentality of literary language, the way that (modernist) literature

> is no longer discourse and the communication of meaning, but a spreading forth of language in its raw state, an unfolding of pure exteriority. And the subject that speaks is less the responsible agent of a discourse (what holds it, what uses it to assert and judge, what sometimes represents itself by means of a grammatical form designed to have that effect) than a non-existence in whose emptiness the unending outpouring of language uninterruptedly continues.[16]

The event of literature is an exposure to the outside, to the raw being of language, the experience of language as a dissolution: "the being of language only appears for itself with the disappearance of the subject."[17]

During a conference on the status of the *nouveau roman* in the fall of 1982 at New York University, Robbe-Grillet responded directly to Blanchot's concerns about the jacket blurb, as well as the type of readings that it authorizes:

> Blanchot was right. I wrote to him that he was right, but that it was I who had written this blurb and that, in fact, it was not intended for him, but for those hurried critics who do not have time to read the books they have to write about in papers. The blurb was, of course, not addressed to Maurice Blanchot who, in the cell of his tower, *actually reads books*.[18]

Those who actually read the book, moving beyond the jacket to the text itself, immediately encounter its narrative unruliness, an unruliness that raises a number of perplexing questions: How does one perform a reading of or a commentary on *Jealousy* without at the same time displacing its eventness by assimilating it to an economy of the Same? If the ethical relation with the other is fundamentally irreducible to a relation of knowledge (in which the other becomes merely an object of contemplation or comprehension), how does one think *Jealousy*'s realism *otherwise than being*?

At the heart of the controversy surrounding the reception of *Jealousy* lies the perception of its mimetic intent, since its "retrievability" or recuperability depends on the extent to which one views it as inviting or refusing referential interpretation.[19] And it is precisely against the tendency to read literature as a representation of a referential or extratextual (psychic and/or sociological) world that the polemical theorist Jean Ricardou conceptualized the *nouveau roman* less in terms of "the writing of an adventure [*l'écriture d'une aventure*]" than in terms of "the adventure of writing [*l'aventure d'une écriture*]."[20] Yet the *nouveau roman*, at least in its beginnings, did not a priori rule out mimetic or realist concerns. Quite the contrary, far from being hostile to realism, the New Novelists tended to privilege a phenomenological relation to the external world. In *For a New Novel*, Robbe-Grillet vacillates between (and conflates) two versions of realism: an objective realism (which accords primacy to objects) and a subjective one (stressing the primacy of perception). At times, he considers the anthropomorphization of the world anathema to the aesthetics of the *nouveau roman*. Yearning to escape from nineteenth-century Balzacian realism and its "tyranny" of signification, he underscores in categorical terms the neutrality of the external world: "The world is neither significant nor absurd. It *is*, quite simply. . . . Man looks at the world, and the world does not look back at him."[21] Barthes, commenting on Robbe-Grillet's cinematic realism, notes: "The author's entire art is to give the object a *Dasein*, a 'being-there,' and to strip it of a 'being-something.'"[22] Yet at other times, Robbe-Grillet underscores the subjective character of realism, privileging the individual's fragmented, precarious, and contingent perception of reality:

> Man is present on every page, in every line, in every word. Even if many objects are presented and are described with great care, there is always, and especially, the eye which sees them, the thought which examines them, the passion which distorts them. The objects in our novels never have a presence outside human perception, real or imaginary. . . . In our books . . . it is a *man* who sees, who feels, who imagines, a man located in space and time, conditioned by his passions, a man like you and me. And the book reports nothing but his experience, limited and uncertain as it is. It is a man here, now, who is his own narrator, finally.[23]

Both versions of realism are noticeably manifest in *Jealousy*, from the husband's camera-like recording of events to his unreliable, hallucinatory recollections. These multiple ways of enacting realism are so pervasive that they have led one critic to ask: "Are the construction of the novel and the description of objects and events to be read as signs of a deforming vision, or as objective representations of a material and non-signifying world?"[24]

Later novels by Robbe-Grillet and other New Novelists conform more or less to Ricardou's formalist, aesthetic sensibility, ostensibly doing away with mimetic concerns in favor of postmodern antirealism. Robbe-Grillet's preoccupation with a purely self-reflexive textuality is already apparent in *Jealousy*, however. The most obvious example is the word *jalousie*, which in French signifies both "jealousy" and "Venetian blind." The two disparate meanings of the word can be linked insofar as the reader postulates a jealous husband spying on his wife through the slats of a window blind. Yet by choosing this ambiguous, multivalent title, Robbe-Grillet twists meanings and destabilizes representations, implicitly cautioning his readers against subscribing to any one totalizing approach — be it mimetic or self-reflexive.[25] Likewise, Robbe-Grillet both grants and denies us access to the narrator-husband. Through the process of what Kaja Silverman calls "heteropathic identification," which enacts "an ethical or nonviolent relation to the other" by simultaneously soliciting and blocking empathic identification, Robbe-Grillet's novel creates the possibility of a referential reading that is *otherwise than being*.[26] Such a reading — which stages the relation between reader and narrator as a "relation without relation" — does not deny, absorb, or flatten the subversive elements and discursive possibilities of his *writing* by positing and affirming a reality prior to or unaltered by the novel's textual performance.

Doing justice to *Jealousy*'s inventiveness (to its realism as an event), sustaining its generic unruliness, requires, then, an interpretive oscillation between mimetic and self-reflexive modes of interpretation. Both modes are undeniably necessary, yet each on its own is incomplete. Read parallectically, neither the mimetic code nor the self-reflexive code adequately translates Robbe-Grillet's novel. Without a metalanguage to mediate or surmount their incommensurable differences and the irreconcilable perspectives afforded by each mode, the reader confronts the novel's dizzying shifts and oscillating movement from the mimetic to the self-reflexive. Barthes's observation that there are "*two* Robbe-Grillets: on one hand, the Robbe-Grillet of immediate things, destroyer of meaning..., and on the other hand, the Robbe-Grillet of mediate things, creator of meaning"[27] brings to attention the way in which a shift in the epistemological perspective (*how* one interprets) reflects an ontological change in the "author" of *Jealousy* (*who* and *what* one interprets). Morrissette single-handedly inaugurated the latter Robbe-Grillet, though at the unfortunate expense of the former. The problem with such an analysis is *not* that it distorts an essential, true, unchanging Robbe-Grillet, but that it overcomes the aporetic hesitation solicited by the text, foreclosing, as it were, our ethical exposure to the novel. Fearing the narrative's contaminating potential,

Morrissette cautions against the reader's passive fusion with the narrator, his or her desire to coincide with the husband's consciousness:

> We must constantly separate ourselves from this jealous husband that we *become* as we read, whose tormenting emotion we share, whose perceptions and ideas haunt us, who drags us with him into his eternal cycle of obsessive visions that annihilates all chronology. It becomes necessary, in a word, for the reader, having become a man sick with jealousy, to be cured of his disease, to be brought back to normal.[28]

Morrissette's ideal reader is one who renounces or overcomes the identification with the narrator-husband. Yet this abjection still does not reflect an ethical sensibility, only a defensive strategy — one originating from the desire to safeguard the autonomy and sovereignty of the reader's ego from the text/husband's pathological discourse, its threat of displacement. For the reader to be cured of such contamination, then, he or she would have to separate facts from fiction, perception from imagination. And even if Morrissette acknowledges the difficulty or impossibility of this interpretive task, the imperative to normalize, which is synonymous with the pursuit of intelligibility, itself distorts the text with its demands for clarity: "To salvage and place, with any degree of exactitude, the 'facts' of the plot of *Jealousy* in chronological order, it becomes necessary to clarify the images seen in the distorting mirror of the husband's vision, in which events and objects are caught and reflected."[29] This jealousy thus becomes a purely psychological matter — that is, a purely mimetic concern — something to elucidate, contain, and correct in order for genuine acts of comprehension to take place.

The Subject of Fascination

Jealousy in Robbe-Grillet's novel, however, is more of an ontological experience than simply a psychological one. Akin to Blanchot's notion of fascination, jealousy is an uncanny event that radically disturbs the narrator's memory and narrative, altering his perception and relation to the external world. In *The Space of Literature*, Blanchot argues, "What fascinates us robs us of our power to give sense. It abandons its 'sensory' nature, abandons the world, draws back from the world, and draws us along. It no longer reveals itself to us, yet it affirms itself in a presence foreign to the temporal present and to presence in space."[30] Regaining in *Jealousy* the strong etymological sense of "charm" or "enchantment," fascination renders problematic the classic Cartesian opposition of subject and object, as well as models of perception based on a clear separation between the two. "It can be said," writes Blanchot, "that a person who is fascinated does not perceive any real object, any real form, because what he sees does not belong to the world of reality, but to the indeterminate realm of fascination."[31] The fascinated subject par excellence is, of course, the writer. He or she is obsessed with and overwhelmed by language, for "to write is to let fascination rule language."[32] Far from upholding the romantic view of the author as demiurge, the absolute source of meaning, Blanchot repeatedly points to the *disempowerment* of the literary process:

> The writer's mastery is not in the hand that writes, the "sick" hand that never lets the pencil go — that can't let go because what it holds it doesn't really hold.... Mastery always characterizes the other hand, the one that doesn't write and is capable of intervening at the right moment to seize the pencil and put it aside. Thus power consists in the power to stop writing, to interrupt what is being written, thereby restoring to the present instant its rights, its decisive trenchancy.[33]

Analogous to fascination, jealousy — as it is staged in Robbe-Grillet's novel — is a figure of dispossession, a challenge to the autonomy of consciousness. It is what robs the narrator's gaze of its habitual sense of power, what makes the narrator's objectivizing consciousness fail to contain the objects that fall within its horizon of intelligibility. This alienation is illustrated in what is perhaps the most famous scene of the novel: the crushing of the centipede by Franck, a neighbor and fellow plantation owner, who is suspected of having an adulterous affair with the wife, A.... This "primal" scene, the one that the reader is invited to reconstruct from the numerous fragmented descriptions, takes place in the dining room. When Franck "bravely" kills the centipede that is upsetting A..., he boldly usurps the husband's power, undermining his position as dutiful protector of his wife/possession. The overtly sexual description of A...'s hand clenching the knife handle, a phallic symbol, further highlights the husband's emasculation. The image of the centipede (and the stain that it leaves on the wall) haunts the narrator, who continually reimagines the scene. His most dramatic fantasy emerges after A... accompanies Franck on a shopping trip while he looks for a new truck. Left alone on his plantation, the narrator becomes obsessed by the image of the centipede in the Blanchotian sense; his fascination is "a passion for the image,"[34] a fervent desire or zeal (jealousy is itself etymologically derived from the ancient Greek *zelos*) for an object that lies beyond his mastery.[35] The image's unruly plasticity reaches its apogee when the centipede — said earlier to be "of average size" (64) ["une scutigère de taille moyenne" (61–62)] — becomes transmuted into a monstrous insect: "It is enormous: one of the largest to be found in this climate. With its long antennae and its huge legs spread on each side of its body, it covers the area of an ordinary plate" (112) ["Il est gigantesque: un des plus gros qui puissent se rencontrer sous ces climats. Ses antennes allongées, ses pattes immenses étalées autour de corps, il couvre presque la surface d'une assiette ordinaire" (163)]. It is as if the image becomes imbued with agency just as the narrator becomes devoid of his. In this Kafkaesque rendering of the scene, not only the centipede but also the location of the event, have undergone a radical transformation: as if caught *in flagrante delicto*, A . . . and Franck have been transported to a hotel room, in a scene that the narrator-husband appears to be *imagining*, and not, strictly speaking, perceiving. Nevertheless, deviating from Robbe-Grillet's ideal vision of "reality" as something that can be experienced in a pure, immediate state (as he describes it in *For a New Novel*), the episode is related in the present tense, in a disturbing conflation of perception and imagination that reflects the inaccessibility of the external world.

According to Robbe-Grillet's manifesto, perception, this "cleansing power of the sense of sight," should enable the subject to describe things as they are ("neither significant nor absurd") and leave "things in their respective place."[36] If perception truly had a cleansing function, however, the narrator's representation of the centipede should remain constant in each retelling of the episode instead of falling prey to the husband's distorting, anthropomorphic hallucinations. The centipede should have simply been, in the words of Barthes, "an optical resistance."[37] Instead, it fails to conform to the phenomenological tenets that Robbe-Grillet himself favors in his essays. *Jealousy* ironically confirms the disturbing insights of Sartre's *Nausea*: perception is compromised through and through by language.

Not unlike the bouts of nausea that alter Roquentin's relation to the world, the bouts of jealousy in Robbe-Grillet's work render the narrator's relation to the real highly problematic, especially the unmediated apprehension of it. What *Nausea* and *Jealousy* have in common, then, is a certain dramatization of the relation between the subject and object of consciousness. Both novels stage the disruption of the Cartesian subject as well as the phenomenological subject, enacting what Foucault was to term "the death of man."[38] If Roquentin, once removed from the event, from the traumatic site of the public park, reemerges as a narrating subject, albeit one whose agency is precarious at best, Robbe-Grillet further pushes the breakdown of the subject/object boundaries through fascination, taking as a point of departure a husband who is denied a first-person pronoun, thus troubling the very possibility of a contrast between a fascinated state and a nonfascinated one (a contrast *Nausea* upholds, as Roquentin moves from moments of enchanted self-dissolution to moments of controlled self-consciousness and back). The *being* of the narrator-husband is not only linguistically absent (marked by the absence of an "I") but also fascinated, robbed of its sovereignty, stripped of the possessive quality of intentionality. Robbe-Grillet's *Jealousy*, even more than its predecessor, illustrates and performs the unruliness of consciousness (an unruliness heightened by jealousy), and underscores the difficulty that it poses both for reflection and for narration.

This resistance to narrative control reaches its peak at the very moment when the husband attempts to restore a presiding subjectivity over his property and wife by fantasizing about her death during her ride with Franck:

> In his haste to reach his goal, Franck increases his speed. The jolts become more violent. In the darkness, he has not seen the hole running halfway across the road. The car makes a leap, skids. . . . On this bad road the driver cannot straighten out in time. The blue sedan goes crashing into a roadside tree whose rigid foliage scarcely shivers under the impact, despite its violence. The car immediately bursts into flames. The whole brush is illuminated by the crackling, spreading fire. (113–14)

> Dans sa hâte d'arriver au but, Franck accélère encore l'allure. Les cahots deviennent plus violents. Il continue néanmoins d'accélérer. Il n'a pas vu, dans la nuit, le trou qui coupe la moitié de la piste. La voiture fait un saut, une embardée. . . . Sur cette chaussée défectueuse le conducteur ne peut redresser à temps. La conduite-intérieure bleue va s'écraser, sur le bas côté, contre un arbre au feuillage rigide qui tremble à peine sous le choc, malgré sa violence. Aussitôt des flammes jaillissent. Toute la brousse en est illuminée, dans le crépitement de l'incendie qui se propage. (166–67)

Expressing his desire to punish A . . . and her lover for their betrayal, the narrator imagines a sort of divine retribution for his suffering. While it is tempting to see this wish as an (unconscious) desire on the part of the narrator to restore control over his chaotic world, the stability or order that he establishes is short-lived because, through a kind of free association, he moves from the "crackling fire," to the "sound the centipede makes" as it is crushed against the wall, to the sound of A . . . 's hairbrush "moving down [her] loosened hair" (114) ["le long de la chevelure défaite" (167)]. Ironically, imagination thwarts rather than abets the husband's sadistic desires, quickly eluding his authorial control.

The scenes following this episode hint at the possibility of closure yet impede facile resolution. The narrator's obsession with the couple's day trip appears to wane upon their return, for example, when his fantasy confronts the reality of their presence. The reader, like the husband, does not know for certain what has actually transpired between A . . . and Franck, although questions surrounding Franck's "mechanical troubles" (127) ["des ennuis mécaniques" (195)] suggest that his failure is not only mechanical but amorous, a link that A . . . makes more explicit in her comparison of engines to women. An ambiguous reference to a "dark liquid" (111) ["liquide foncé" (161)], which is later depicted in even more suggestive language as a "reddish streak" (134) ["trainée rougeâtre" (210)], also suggests that foul play ensues. Yet the plausibility of such a tragic ending is itself quickly invalidated on the next page when A . . . observes that "the spot has always been there, on the wall. For the moment there is no question of repainting anything but the blinds and the balustrade — the latter a bright yellow. That is what A . . . has decided" [135] ["la tache a toujours été là, sur le mur. Il n'est question de repeindre, pour l'instant, que les jalousies et la balustrade — cette dernière en jaune vif. Ainsi en a décidé A . . ." (211)].[39] The circular structure of the novel ultimately short-circuits any definitive sense of closure, halting any progression from textual obscurity to interpretive clarity. Moreover, in the absence of a linear unfolding of the narrator's jealousy, we could say that the reader enters the state of jealousy, itself a state of anxiety and irresolution, *in medias res*.

Resisting Reverence

Jealousy demands that the reader be alert to its fundamental resistance to comprehension, its defiance of hermeneutic commentary or symbolic mastery; yet at the same time, the reader must also counterbalance and supplement that Blanchotian reverence for the text — its irreducible otherness — with an actual interpretation of the events, thus crafting his or her own reading of *Jealousy*, if only provisionally. While any such interpretation of *Jealousy* can be said to betray the novel (just as would any recuperative deciphering of the work's meaning and "secrets"),[40] a reading of the novel that is *otherwise than being*, however tenuous or impossible, seems imperative. If one interpretive current reads the novel mimetically or referentially (as a story about a jealous husband or as an allegory of political struggle, for example), Blanchot, as we have seen, denies the novel's mimetic intent altogether, interpreting the narrative voice as a figure for the anonymity of language itself. It is arguably only Blanchot's account, in its refusal to name the unnameable, as it were, "to think of reading as either appropriation or domination,"[41] that takes *Jealousy*'s alterity seriously. Blanchot's reading preserves the irreducible distance between the reader and Robbe-Grillet's novel; it "does not comprehend (strictly speaking)" but "attends,"[42] as he writes in *The Infinite Conversation*. Reading *as such* is prior to or beyond comprehension and meaning. In *The Writing of the Disaster*, Blanchot formulates his ethical mode of reading as an act of testimony: "There is the reading that is no longer passive, but is passivity's reading. It is without pleasure, without joy; it escapes both comprehension and desire. It is like the nocturnal vigil, that 'inspiring' insomnia when, all having been said, 'Saying' [*le Dire*] is heard, and the testimony of the last witness is pronounced."[43]

To be sure, the act of comprehension involves a degree of power and violence in the hermeneutic gesture of grasping (com-*prendre*) the narrative. Yet in presenting the reader with what amounts to two basic, opposing modalities of reading (one that comprehends versus one that attends), Blanchot rules out the possibility of a different kind of comprehension and, by extension, a different kind of ethics. Most importantly, while Blanchot's call to respect the Saying of the work is ostensibly Levinasian, it ignores how Levinas himself productively complicates this ethical notion. For Levinas, the choice that one must make is never simply a choice between Saying and the Said, between ethics and epistemology. Levinas constantly returns to the ways that philosophy interrogates itself in *unsaying* and *resaying* the ontological Said: "The greatest virtue of philosophy is that it can put itself into question, try to deconstruct what it has constructed, and unsay what it has said."[44] The same holds true for literary criticism: its greatest virtue, or, we might say, its ethical force, lies in its self-critique and refusal to confer closure, and in its perpetual return to the demands of the artwork, to its Saying. An ethical reading of *Jealousy*, then, does not opt for nonmeaning over meaning, a "letting-go" over "active engagement."[45] Rather, it remains alert to the work's recalcitrant ways — Robbe-Grillet once referred to his novel as an "engine of war against order"[46] — and to its irresolution, an irresolution that requires a continual, if not obsessive, return to the work — to its Saying and (the critic's) Said.

The novel itself stages this return to the text, foregrounding the problematic of irresolution, in two of its numerous *mises en abyme*: the native song and the African novel that both A... and Franck have been reading. Juxtaposing competing models of interpretation in these episodes, *Jealousy* throws into question the viability and completeness of either. In the first example, the native song challenges comprehension completely, possessing no identifiable meaning; it is described as a "native tune, with incomprehensible words, or even without words" (83) ["un air indigène, aux paroles incompréhensibles, ou même sans paroles" (99)].[47] The song sparks the narrator's curiosity; he wonders about its internal logic while recognizing the melody's intrinsic opacity ("it is difficult to determine if the song is interrupted for some fortuitous reason ... or whether the tune has come to its natural conclusion" [83] ["il est difficile de déterminer si le chant s'est interrompu pour une raison fortuite ... ou bien si l'air trouvait là sa fin naturelle" (100)]). The narrator also suggests that his experience of its opacity is due, at least in part, to his own cultural horizon of expectation:

> The poem is at moments so little like what is ordinarily called a song, a complaint, a refrain, that the western listener is justified in wondering if something quite different is involved. The sounds, despite apparent repetitions, do not seem related by any musical law. There is no tune, really, no melody, no rhythm. It is as if the man were content to utter unconnected fragments as an accompaniment to his work. (127, translation modified)

> Le poème ressemble si peu, par moment, à ce qu'il est convenu d'appeler une chanson, une complainte, un refrain, que l'auditeur occidental est en droit de se demander s'il ne s'agit pas de tout autre chose. Les sons, en dépit d'évidentes reprises, ne semblent liés par aucune loi musicale. Il n'y a pas d'air, en somme, pas de mélodie, pas de rythme. On dirait que l'homme se contente d'émettre des lambeaux sans suite pour accompagner son travail. (194–95)

From the perspective of the Westerner, the song appears unintelligible, beyond interpretation, as if the song's Saying and literariness are intimately tied to its agrammaticality — its lack of conformity to "musical law." In fact, the song-poem appears profoundly antirepresentational, devoid of any constative utterances (utterances of which the truth or falsity can be determined), since it neither describes nor communicates anything about the world. If the reader's subject position parallels that of the narrator, then any reading of the novel (realist or antirealist) would effectively be ruled out: the reader confronts an artwork that is wholly other, utterly inaccessible.

In the second example, the African novel also draws attention to the interpretive act — the event of reading. Thematically analogous to *Jealousy*, the novel tells the story of an adulterous wife and her negligent husband. Like *Jealousy*, it also displays a lack of verisimilitude and a potential to generate multiple readings. Interpretive differences between Franck and A... emerge, for example, with respect to female sexuality. Franck finds one female character's sexual escapades shocking, while A... does not:

> "After all," he says, "sleeping with Negroes..." A... turns toward him, raises her chin, and asks smilingly: "Well, why not?" (126)

> "Quand même, dit-il, coucher avec des nègres..." A... se tourne vers lui, lève le menton, demande avec un sourire: "Eh bien, pourquoi pas?" (194)

In contending that women can sleep with whomever they choose (in this case, the colonized other), A..., in her playful rebuke, sets herself apart from Franck, implicitly refusing to conform to his masculinist desire to control or possess her fully — leaving him quite speechless ("Franck smiles in his turn, but answers nothing" [126] ["Franck sourit à son tour, mais il ne répond rien" (194)] and wearing an awkward facial expression: "The movement of his mouth ends in a sort of grimace" (126) ["Le mouvement de sa bouche s'achève en une sorte de grimace" (194)]. At other points, however, she and Franck delight in the novel's ability to outrage and spark imagination:

> They... sometimes deplore the coincidences of the plot, saying that "things don't happen that way," and then they construct a different probable outcome starting from a new supposition, "if it weren't for that." Other possibilities are offered, during the course of the book, which lead to different endings.... They seem to enjoy multiplying these choices, exchanging smiles, carried away by their enthusiasm, probably a little intoxicated by this proliferation. (75)

> Ils déplorent... quelquefois les hasards de l'intrigue, disant que "ce n'est

pas de chance," et ils construisent alors un autre déroulement probable à partir d'une nouvelle hypothèse, "si ça n'était pas arrivé." D'autres bifurcations possibles se présentent, en cours de route, qui conduisent toutes à des fins différentes.... Ils semblent même les multiplier à plaisir, échangeant des sourires, s'excitant au jeu, sans doute un peu grisés par cette prolifération. (83)

This interpretive play is short-lived. Franck reestablishes hermeneutic order, reaffirms signifying conventions, putting an end to textual *jouissance* and interpretive "intoxication": "Franck sweeps away in a single gesture all the suppositions they had just constructed together. It's no use making up contrary possibilities, since things are the way they are: reality stays the same" (75) ["Franck balaye ainsi d'un seul coup les fictions qu'ils viennent d'échafauder ensemble. Rien ne sert de faire des suppositions contraires, puisque les choses sont ce qu'elles sont: on ne change rien à la réalité" (83)]. Unlike the native song, then, the African novel both produces and resolves interpretive anxieties — at least for Franck.

What is the reader to make of these two models of reading? Each one serves to illustrate the two extreme poles of interpretation: the native song is unreadable, whereas the African novel is all too hermeneutically containable. At which end of the interpretive pole do we situate *Jealousy*? Or is the question itself misplaced? Some critics, wanting to underscore the poetics of *Jealousy* against its thematics or psychological preoccupations (which others use to recuperate the novel under the label of realism), have understandably stressed its proximity to the native song-poem. As Ann Jefferson writes, for example, "In reading the narrative as the expression of the husband's jealousy, we are making it impossible to read it as a 'poem,' as literature."[48] Yet this type of reading also restricts *Jealousy*'s "literariness," defining it too narrowly as poetry — a reified, self-enclosed, timeless, and autonomous aesthetic object — resistant to knowledge, impenetrable to the reader's interpretive and appropriating gaze. As Fredric Jameson notes, "the very concept of the work of art *qua* aesthetic object is itself a fetishization and an abstraction."[49] To situate *Jealousy* beyond *any* cognitive horizon — a consequence of identifying the novel purely with the poem-song — is to mystify and reify the (non)meaning of Robbe-Grillet's text — and thus to arrest the ethics of hesitation elicited by the novel under the ethico-aesthetic pretense of attending and safeguarding its literariness, its alterity.

Reading the native song along *with*, rather than simply *against*, the African novel gives a fuller account of the ways that the novel allegorizes, or rather stages, its own allegorization of irresolution, and might offer in turn a more ethical approach to *Jealousy*. If we shift focus from the intrinsic properties of the song-poem to its horizon of intelligibility, then a *rapprochement* can be made with the African novel. The two models are not mutually exclusive, for both highlight the relational quality of otherness. That is to say, the alterity of the song-poem and the African novel is not affirmed in abstraction but is experienced as an interruption of otherness, a rupture, a textual disturbance, *relative to* listener-readers' understanding and expectations. The native song is perceived as agrammatical, as other, mainly because it disrupts the narrator-husband's grammar,[50] his familiarity with music; similarly, the excitement that the African novel initially provokes stems from its ability to unsettle A . . . and Franck's expectations ("things don't happen that way"). When Franck strips the African novel of its potential for inventiveness, denying its reception "as an other that opens up new possibilities,"[51] he effectively displaces and destroys the experience of the novel's alterity, along with its transformative and *dis*organizing potential, returning it to the logic of the Same and reinscribing the work of art within the established norms of readability.

If Franck serves as an example to avoid, the ethical reader of *Jealousy* cannot simply negate this mode of reading or posit the work outside the realm of interpretation. As Robbe-Grillet himself put it, a literary work that could theoretically "escape from this system of recuperation . . . would not be an interesting text, because it would be an angelical text, that is, a text which is in and for itself. One cannot be outside of ideology."[52] The danger of simply upholding the otherness of *Jealousy* is that conceiving of it as pure alterity — as an "angelic text" — falsifies it, denying it any impact on the reader, leaving his or her ideological and hermeneutic habits intact. As a fruitful alternative, Robbe-Grillet proposes an open-ended dialectic, a dialectic without synthesis, whereby the readerly impulses of order and disorder interact playfully to create a productive tension, "a sort of mutual recuperation."[53] Such a reading practice is *not* inimical to realist, or antirealist, interpretations of *Jealousy*; indeed, it fosters a parallactic sensibility, attracting and defying the reader's will to interpret by urging him or her to join and disjoin incongruous positions and incommensurable meanings. And it is in this spirit that we can read *Jealousy*, alternating between mastery over and reverence for the work. Preserving the irresolution at the heart of the novel does not require the reader to retreat into a paralyzing, skeptical void, remaining silent or simply affirming the unsayability of the work — the Blanchotian temptation. On the contrary, readers must engage with the unruly work; they must give it particular shape and meaning, and yes, inevitably betray the novel's inexhaustibility. The ethical reader can, however, *reduce* this betrayal and persevere in his or her response to the provocation and demands of the work by diligently attending to the moments of self-reflexivity, fascination, and dispossession that give pause in *Jealousy* — moments, if you will, that resist thematization, demand reconsideration, and prolong readerly intoxication.

VI

Fidelity to Sexual Difference

MARGUERITE DURAS'S
THE RAVISHING OF LOL STEIN

> Let us note in passing that *Totality and Infinity* pushes
> the respect for dissymmetry so far that it seems to us
> impossible, essentially impossible, that it could have been
> written by a woman. Its philosophical subject is man (*vir*).
> JACQUES DERRIDA

Emmanuel Levinas's reception among feminists has been tumultuous from the outset. Jacques Derrida's musings on the hypervirility of the author of *Totality and Infinity* point to one major objection leveled against Levinasian thought within feminist circles. Only a man, Derrida notes, could advocate an ethics that foregrounds asymmetry (nonreciprocity) as the condition for the ethical proper, and subordination to the other as its enactment. Compounding this displacement of a universalist framework affirming *equality* among the sexes — a position that might well be deemed detrimental to feminist ethics and politics — are Levinas's actual writings on women, such as his problematic association of *female* alterity with "mystery": "The transcendence of the feminine . . . is a movement opposed to the movement of consciousness, . . . and I see no other possibility than to call it mystery."[1] Simone de Beauvoir was perhaps the first to identify and critique Levinas's masculinist blindness. In *The Second Sex*, she comments: "When [Levinas] writes that woman is mystery, he assumes that she is mystery for man. So this apparently objective description is in fact an affirmation of masculine privilege."[2] For Beauvoir, Levinas's representation of woman effectively reduces her once again to an *object* of male philosophical investigation: "He is the Subject; he is the Absolute. She is the Other."[3]

In the decades following Beauvoir's groundbreaking work, feminist interpretations of Levinas have shifted and diverged. Though Levinas's relevance for feminism remains a disputed matter, engaging with his thought has almost become unavoidable.[4] Some continue to view Levinas's ethical model as anathema to feminism,[5] while Luce Irigaray and others have pursued a more dialogic engagement with his work, drawing heavily from Levinasian rhetoric, for example, in critiquing Western phallocentric thought:

> This domination of the philosophic logos stems in large part from its power to *reduce all others to the economy of the Same.* The teleologically constructive project it takes on is always also a project of diversion, deflection, reduction of the other in the Same. And, in its greatest generality perhaps, from its power to *eradicate the difference between the sexes* in systems that are self-representative of a "masculine subject."[6]

For Irigaray, Levinas's philosophy of alterity opens up the possibility of a radical ethics of sexual difference, an ethics that insists on the incommensurability between the particular and the universal.[7]

Irigaray grounds her ethics of sexual difference on the feminine's "*disruptive excess.*"[8] The title of her book already performs, as it were, the unruliness of the feminine. A *sex which is not one* does not itself mean only one thing; it refers to woman's lack (her absence of ontology; according to the dictates of patriarchal ideology, she is not a full-fledged subject, fully whole) and to her doubleness (as opposed to the oneness of the phallus); she is multiple — the object of male discourse, *and more* ("She is neither one nor two"[9]). Likewise, to understand woman's unruliness only ontologically (claiming that her anarchic *being* exceeds its containment within the symbolic order) deemphasizes the discursive supplement at work in Irigaray's feminist calculus, which she articulates through her injunction to other women "to speak woman," "*parler-femme*," or translated less literally, "to speak feminine," "to speak [as] woman," and, punning on *par les femmes*, "by women."[10]

Marguerite Duras's 1964 novel, *The Ravishing of Lol Stein*, arguably engages in what Irigaray would later term *parler-femme*, subtly interweaving the psychoanalytic and feminist registers that were to form the explicit basis of Irigaray's hermeneutics. Radically rewriting the male fantasy narrative about female madness — the definitive example being André Breton's 1929 surrealist autobiographic novel, *Nadja* — Duras's new novel provided an unruly example that has repeatedly commanded the attention of critics drawn in by the ambiguities of its title and its disputed subject matter. Is this a novel "of" Lol Stein, a novel about a woman who desires to perpetually relive the night of her abandonment or/as ravishment at the ball of T. Beach? Or is it of Jacques Hold, the ravished or ravishing male narrator/lover of Lol, who obsessively desires to know his beloved *object*? For many feminist readers, Duras's paradigmatic illustration of the dynamics of sexual difference foregrounds the irreducibility of Lol's difference to Jacques Hold's scopic drive (the narrator's own surname suggests the phallocentric wish *to hold* — that is, to contain, to pin down — the unruly feminine[11]). From this point of view, Levinas's philosophy of the other provides the feminist reader primarily with a grammar with which to read the ethical resistance of Duras's female protagonist.[12] Simply stated, Duras's novel exposes Jacques Hold as a colonizer of sexual difference, a "usurper"[13] of Lol's place and voice. What Jacques says of Lol's experiences and world "concerns his own universe."[14] Extrapolating from Levinas's *Totality and Infinity*, we could say that the ethical moment of reading unfolds in the recognition that Lol (as the feminine other) exceeds *the idea of* Lol that Jacques reproduces but ultimately fails to master in his narrative of her ravishing.

Reading Lol/*The Ravishing of Lol Stein* from the perspective of Levinas's other major philosophical text, *Otherwise than Being*, affords, however, an alternative ethics of Duras's work. To recall, Levinas, in *Otherwise than Being*, places the ethical moment within language. The Saying (the desire to communicate) still precedes the Said (meaning), but the ethical injunction now lies in the short-circuiting of the Said, in "an incessant unsaying of the said" (181). From this Levinasian optic, then, the ethical question no longer lies in (the determination of) the author's gender politics but in the intersubjective demands of the novel, in the reader's attentiveness and responsiveness to Lol's Saying, a Saying that, as we shall see, invariably passes through the scene of language/Jacques's narrative.

In reading Duras's novel *with* Levinas's *Otherwise than Being*, this chapter aims to highlight the work's inventiveness for feminism, the ways it elicits and frustrates familiar hermeneutic schemes: utilitarian or overdetermined responses to sexual difference. More specifically, the chapter reframes the terms of the debate surrounding *The Ravishing of Lol Stein*, asking to what extent a faithful feminist reading depends on the reader's ability to share Lol's "experience," and to what extent the complexity of the male narrator's writing of Lol — that is, his writing of her ravishing and the ravishing of his writing — resists or exceeds any straightforward identification with the female character, or with the "feminine," more generally.

The Saying of Duras/Lol or the Said of Jacques

Duras's choice of a male narrator raises an immediate concern for the reader; no conflation between author and narrator will take place in this novel. The original French reveals the gender of the narrator in the second paragraph; in the English, the gender indeterminacy is prolonged for a few pages. Does this information authorize, or at the very least orient the reader toward, a feminist reading? Even if we assume that it does (appeals to extratextual or biographical information about Duras's strong feminist leanings are typically deployed as justification for such an approach), just what a feminist reading of *The Ravishing of Lol Stein* would actually entail remains nonetheless unclear.

In *Gynesis: Configurations of Woman and Modernity*, Alice Jardine firmly asserts that the true subject of Duras's novel is Lol V. Stein. To give Jacques Hold Lol's place as the real matter of her story, that is, to claim that the novel is really about the teller of the tale — as does Lacan, for example, when he states in his "Homage to Marguerite Duras" that Jacques Hold is not only "display[ing] the machinery" of the novel but is "one of its mainsprings"[15] — amounts to violently silencing the feminine voice, turning a deaf ear to the Saying of Duras and Lol. Jardine takes issue in particular with Lacanian hermeneutics, which she considers non-/antifeminist, finding Lacan's comments and his identification with Jacques Hold highly problematic.[16] Critical of Jacques Hold/Lacan's reduction of Duras's otherness to Lacan's master discourse of the Same, of his arrogance and usurpation of Lol/Duras's story (Jacques Hold writes, "I shall relate *my* own story of Lol Stein" [4, emphasis added] ["je raconterai *mon* histoire de Lol V. Stein" (14)], while Lacan marvels, "Marguerite Duras knows, without me, what I teach"[17]), Jardine affirms that a feminist reader needs to identify with Lol (the woman) and not Jacques (the man): "For the feminist reader, this book written by a feminist has only one subject: Lol V. Stein."[18] Rather than reducing Lol, as Lacan does, to an object of psychoanalytical discourse, perceiving Lol *only* as a "perfect case of clinical delirium,"[19] Jardine sees in Duras's representation of Lol another kind of example, a call for a new kind of subjectivity: "For the feminist reader . . . the representation of Lol as a new kind of subject-in-the-world is *categorical*."[20]

It is at times unclear, however, whether Jardine's putative feminist reader is gender-specific, and whether her feminist reading presupposes its own version of the order of the Same.

> For to the extent that one always reads ... through identification, the woman reader has most likely been identifying, not with either of the Jacques, but rather with two highly visible if improbable others: Lol and Marguerite Duras.... For the feminist reader, it is Lol V. Stein — the entire name — which forms the potential space of the text.[21]

Jardine's conflation here of the feminist reader and the woman reader (it seems that the feminist reader of *The Ravishing of Lol Stein* is the woman reader who "correctly" actualizes the text's potential by identifying with Lol) unfortunately ignores or sidesteps questions pertaining to the male reader of Duras's novel: Can a male reader genuinely identify with Lol's subjectivity? Or to put it in Levinasian parlance, can a male reader read *The Ravishing of Lol Stein otherwise than being* (where "being" here represents a male [phallo]-centric interpretive mode)? Can the male reader actually read not *as* a woman (which would arguably efface sexual difference) but *like* a feminist?[22] Although it is unquestionable that Duras writes "about" women,[23] it is doubtful that she writes *only* for women, or more importantly, that her textual practice or *écriture* does not also have a transformative effect on her male audience. The fact that she chooses a male narrator to tell the story of a woman might alert us to the hermeneutic complexities that await us as readers.

In sharp contrast to Jardine, Martha Noel Evans does not dismiss Jacques Hold as the narrator of the story. Quite the contrary; Evans posits Jacques's narration as Duras's true target: "Duras uses this male narrator as a kind of front: first to present and explore the characteristics of traditional male narrative and then to dramatize the undoing of that very narrative."[24] Reading Jacques's love story as an "allegory" of male domination, Evans argues that Jacques's "search for truth and love" presupposes rather than rules out "the violent instincts of domination and destruction."[25] Likewise, Laurie Edson does not formulate her feminist reading around the imperative of sexual identification, but advocates a feminist reading that paradoxically removes Lol as the *subject* of Duras's novel. The matter of the novel is not "the story of the human subject that is Lol, but the story of the way any story of a human subject is mediated by cultural codes — language, desire, discourses of power, and epistemology itself."[26] What the reader confronts in the *Ravishing of Lol*

Stein, then, is not a set of characters with whom one may or may not identify, but a hegemonic system of representation. Consequently Lol as an unmediated representation is unavailable to the reader; what emerges in Duras's novel is not a subject in its own right (Lol as speaking subject) but a feminine figure produced by Jacques's male desire. Rather than creating a space for the Saying of Lol to be heard (letting the female other speak in her own voice), Jacques gives the reader the Said of Lol (*his meaning* of Lol).

Edson sees as futile any attempt to restore or recuperate Lol's voice from a psychoanalytical male discourse, which, according to Jardine, has problematically divorced the sign from the referent, reducing Lol to a trope ("the figure of Lol... is the figure of femininity — not the representation of a woman"[27]). She is more interested in examining the ways in which Duras's novel *mimes* the traditional male narrative in order to disclose and deconstruct its patterns of "patriarchal thinking — in particular, assumptions of objectifiability and knowability."[28] For Edson, Duras exploits male logic only to undermine it from within. Thus, despite the fact that both Jardine and Edson approach *The Ravishing of Lol Stein* from a feminist perspective (both recognize that men speaking about and for women has become a suspicious activity), they differ radically in their assessment of Jacques Hold. Jardine wants to rescue Duras's novel from the appropriating impulses of Lacanian psychoanalysis and to refocus attention on what she sees as the repressed but true subject of the story, Lol Stein. Edson, on the other hand, denies the possibility of any direct access to Lol, turning her focus instead to Duras's critical mimesis, to the textual mediation at work in the novel. Yet it is unclear to what extent their critique of male narrators is generalizable and applicable to male readers. Jardine's feminism — which gives primacy to sexual identification[29] — seems to put into question all male readings of Lol's story: female experience and desire are inaccessible to "bodies-coded-as-male," to the male epistemological gaze; indeed, two male perspectives are explicitly discredited by Jardine: Jacques Hold and Jacques Lacan.[30] Although Edson intentionally avoids formulating an essentialist definition of feminism (an essentialism based on sexual difference, for instance), she does seem paradoxically to essentialize and totalize the male perspective. Situating Jacques Hold firmly within an allegedly monolithic male literary tradition, she proceeds to challenge his "male logic" systematically.[31] Edson warns us that this all-powerful male logic governs even some ("contaminated") feminist readings of *The Ravishing of Lol Stein*. She argues, for example, that Evans's reading, though similar in devoting much attention to Jacques's role in the novel, accepts too readily his authority: "How can Evans know anything at all about what Lol wants or does, except through Jacques's mediation, which she herself has already called into question?"[32] In other words, Evans severely undermines her feminist argument once she diverts it from her oppositional reading and speaks as if Jacques Hold's words were truths, that is, unmediated representations of Lol's psychic state.

Like Jardine, Edson associates the problematic of male desire with psychoanalytical discourse, reinforcing in turn the difference between feminism and psychoanalysis. But according to Edson, the fundamental problem with a psychoanalytical reading of Duras's novel does not lie in a (mis)identification between the reader and the main subject of the novel (indeed, she even credits Lacan for having correctly recognized the primacy of Jacques Hold in the story of Lol: "It is not surprising that psychoanalyst Jacques Lacan ... understood the central character to be Jacques Hold, not Lol").[33] It lies instead in an uncritical analysis of Lol, one that does not take into consideration Hold's vested interest in his representation of Lol: "Any such psychoanalytical reading of Lol can only duplicate Jacques's (mis)reading of her."[34]

If Lacanian analysts indulged in abstraction with their accounts of Lol as a figure of the Real, Edson, for her part, transfigures Jacques Hold into a figure of phallocentric mediation, though she could have taken her type of feminist criticism to its logical conclusion: If the reader becomes suspicious of Jacques Hold's narrative, why should this suspicion be selective? Jacques is either fully credible or he is not credible at all (especially when it comes to deciphering the desire of the feminine other).

The feminist hermeneutics at work here models Ricoeur's "hermeneutics of suspicion." For Ricoeur, a "hermeneutics of suspicion" stands in opposition to a "hermeneutics of faith"; it contests the legitimacy of consciousness and its production of meaning: "After the doubt about things, we have started to doubt consciousness," he writes.[35] Ricoeur warns, however, that a hermeneutics of suspicion should not be conflated with the less desirable form of nihilistic skepticism:

> These three masters of suspicion [Marx, Nietzsche, Freud] are not to be misunderstood, however, as three masters of skepticism. They are, assuredly, three great "destroyers." But that of itself should not mislead us; ... All three clear the horizon for a more authentic word, for a new reign of Truth,

not only by means of a "destructive" critique, but by the invention of an art of *interpreting*.[36]

Based on the above sample of readings, a feminist hermeneutics of suspicion takes the following form: the "Truth" of Duras's novel lies in the "'destructive critique" of Jacques's Said, his narrative appropriation of Lol's voice (his phallocentric determination of her meaning).[37]

Levinas's Said and Saying perhaps map too neatly onto this feminist landscape. Is the question of Saying only to be located on the side of Duras and Lol? Is the Said of Jacques condemned to stasis? Isn't Levinas's formulation of the relation between Saying and the Said also supplemented by the double imperative of "unsaying" and "resaying" the ontological Said? Doesn't Levinas further link this double imperative to the unruly practice of skepticism?[38] To take up these questions, we must first revisit Jacques Hold's representational economy, probing further his status as a dubious, phallocentric subject of representation. Then we will be in a better position to evaluate Duras's staging of the ethical encounter in *The Ravishing of Lol Stein* as well as her staging of *The Ravishing of Lol Stein* as an ethical encounter with the reader.

As we have seen, what feminist readings of *The Ravishing of Lol Stein* seem to have in common is an essentializing propensity: Jardine essentializes identification (biological and social women need to identify with Lol) and Evans and Edson gender ontology (Jacques's narrative is an unproblematic exemplar of male logic). This essentialist dimension of the critique ironically reinscribes feminism within the tradition of ontology and its economy of the Same, decried by many of the same authors for its phallogocentric underpinnings. More specifically, it is to the notion of "experience" that much of the debate about feminism gravitates. If female experience and male experience are fundamentally incommensurable, then what chance does Jacques have of producing a faithful account of Lol? Is fidelity to Lol's sexual difference always inevitably a betrayal of that difference? Is it possible to conceive of feminism as *otherwise than being*, a feminism that does not posit the meaning of (female or male) experience as unproblematic or prediscursively given?

Such a feminist reading of Duras's novel would subsequently depend less on the reader's ability to share Lol's "experience" than on the reader's alertness to the quality of Jacques Hold's writing of Lol. Rather than exclusively focusing on Jacques Hold's writing of Lol's *ravishing* (which for some feminists is synonymous with his ravishing of Lol, that is, his violent subordination of Lol to his narrative will to know), I suggest that we ask as well: Is Jacques — or, more importantly, is his narrative — at all transformed by his encounter with Lol? Is the novel not only about Jacques's writing of Lol's *ravishing* but also the *ravishing* of his writing? While Jacques's appropriation of Lol's story is to a certain degree undeniable ("I shall relate *my own* story of Lol Stein"), one must nevertheless resist the impulse to deny or negate the singularity and heterogeneity of Jacques's character and condemn his narrative *tout court*.[39] One-sided readings of Jacques's male narrative (either by radically displacing the importance of his role [Jardine] or by treating him as a one-dimensional character/narrator [Evans-Edson]) run the risk of simply reversing the male totalizing reading of Lol (uncritical acceptance of the narrator's voice) in instituting a feminist totalizing reading of Jacques (an irresponsible dismissal of Jacques's narratorial authority). Indeed, a critical reading of Duras's *The Ravishing of Lol Stein* must avoid the false choice of being either *for* or *against* Jacques Hold.

Rather than separating the feminine and the masculine in any clear and distinct fashion, Duras's text mines the distinction intrinsic to sexual difference without, however, simply collapsing the categories. In the first pages of *The Ravishing of Lol Stein*, the text draws attention to Lol's indocility, to the way in which "part of her seemed always to be evading you" (3) ["une part d'elle-même eût été toujours en allée loin de vous" (13)], and later in the novel Jacques stresses the unidirectional relation between them. Lol is described as a fascinating and evasive individual: "There is no way of approaching Lol. One can neither get close to her or move away from her. You have to wait until she comes in search of you, until she wants to" (95) ["L'approche de Lol n'existe pas. On ne peut pas se rapprocher ou s'éloigner d'elle. Il faut attendre qu'elle vienne vous chercher, qu'elle veuille" (105)]. Analogously related to Jacques's exposure to Lol — where Lol figures as the object of radical alterity — the reader's relation to *The Ravishing of Lol Stein* takes the form of an interpellation. As we have seen, one way of understanding this interpellation is as an ethical response to Duras's invitation to dialogue. I would add that this interpellation — this call of/from the other — emanates also from Duras's *male* narrator, that is, from Jacques's Saying. What makes part of *The Ravishing of Lol Stein* seem always to be evading the reader (to echo Duras's phrasing) is arguably the perplexing qualities of Jacques Hold as lover/knower/narrator of Lol.

The Saying of Jacques

Ironically, the cover blurb for the English translation significantly diminishes, if not altogether effaces, Jacques's presence in the novel:

> *The Ravishing of Lol Stein* is a haunting early novel by the author of *The Lover*. Lol Stein is a beautiful young woman, securely married, settled in a comfortable life — and a voyeur. Returning with her husband and children to the town where, years before, her fiancé had abandoned her for another woman, she is drawn inexorably to recreate that long-past tragedy. She arranges a rendezvous for her friend Tatiana and Tatiana's lover. She arranges to spy on them. And then, she goes one step further...

What the blurb does, however, is to turn the reader's focus to the "primal scene" of the novel, the event of Lol's abandonment (that is, her ravishing), and to her subsequent attempts to cope with her "long-past tragedy." For Jacques, this event marks simultaneously the beginning of Lol's madness and *his* story of Lol:

> As for the nineteen years preceding that night, I do not want to know any more about them than what I tell, or very little more, setting forth only the straight, unadulterated chronological facts, even if these years conceal some magic moment to which I am indebted for having enabled me to meet Lol Stein. I don't want to because the presence of her adolescence in this story might somehow tend to detract, in the eyes of the reader, from the overwhelming actuality of this woman in my life. (4)

> Les dix-neuf ans qui ont précédé cette nuit, je ne veux pas les connaître plus que je ne le dis, ou à peine, ni autrement que dans leur chronologie même s'ils se recèlent une minute magique à laquelle je dois d'avoir connu Lol V. Stein. Je ne le veux pas parce que la présence de son adolescence dans cette histoire risquerait d'atténuer un peu aux yeux du lecteur l'écrasante actualité de cette femme dans ma vie. (14)

The exclusion of Lol's adolescence from the realm of investigation might seem puzzling for someone who seeks to truly understand the other. This repression of a significant part of Lol's facticity is all the more disturbing given the initial opposition of Lol's friend and Jacques's lover, Tatiana, to his reading of Lol: "Tatiana does not believe that this fabled Town Beach ball was so overwhelmingly responsible for Lol Stein's illness. No, Tatiana Karl *traces the origins of that illness back further, further even than the beginning of their friendship*" (2, emphasis added) ["Tatiana, elle, ne croit pas au rôle prépondérant de ce fameux bal de T. Beach dans la maladie de Lol V. Stein. Tatiana Karl, elle, *fait remonter plus avant, plus avant même que leur amitié, les origines de cette maladie*" (120)]. Tatiana had always perceived Lol as an unconventional subject, as always being not *there*. Unlike Jacques, and despite the importance of the ball scene at T. Beach, she does not believe that Lol had ever had a substantial and integral self that was subsequently traumatized by her *ravishment*. Lol's identity was always characterized by its fluidity and mobility. From Tatiana's perspective, then, Lol's absence *preceded* her trauma:

> Lol was funny, an inveterate wit, and very bright, even though part of her seemed always to be evading you, and the present moment. Going where? Into some adolescent dream world? No, Tatiana answers, no, it seemed as though she were going nowhere, yes, that's it, nowhere. Was it her heart that wasn't there? Tatiana apparently inclines toward the opinion that it was perhaps, indeed, Lol Stein's heart which wasn't — as she says — there; it would doubtless come, but she, Tatiana, had never seen any sign of it. (3)

> Lol était drôle, moqueuse impénitente et très fine bien qu'une part d'elle-même eût été toujours en allée loin de vous et de l'instant. Où? Dans le rêve adolescent? Non, répond Tatiana, non, on aurait dit dans rien encore, justement rien. Était-ce le cœur qui n'était pas là? Tatiana aurait tendance à croire que c'était peut-être en effet le cœur de Lol V. Stein qui n'était pas — elle dit: là — il allait venir sans doute, mais elle, elle ne l'avait pas connu. (13)

Although Tatiana suggests what seems to be a causal explanation of Lol's present condition, she is unable to locate the moment of Lol's breakdown. In contrast to Jacques's clear and distinct location of Lol's illness in her *ravishing* at the ball, the imprecision of Tatiana's analysis may well strike the reader as being less a causal explanation than an affirmation of the unknowability of Lol's identity.

Jacques, however, does not allow Tatiana to expand on her alternative reading and is quick to discredit any authority she may have had in virtue of both her friendship for/with Lol and her proximity to the so-called originary event:

> I no longer believe a word Tatiana says. I'm convinced of absolutely nothing. Here then, in full, and all mixed together, both this false impression

which Tatiana Karl tells about and what I have been able to imagine about that night at the Town Beach casino. Following which I shall relate my own story of Lol Stein. (4)

Je ne crois plus à rien de ce que dit Tatiana, je ne suis convaincu de rien. Voici, tout au long, mêlés, à la fois, ce faux semblant que raconte Tatiana Karl et ce que j'invente sur la nuit du Casino de T. Beach. A partir de quoi je raconterai mon histoire de Lol V. Stein. (14)

Tatiana will thus *only* supply Jacques Hold with the raw matter that the latter's imagination will fashion into his story of Lol Stein.

Jacques's abrupt decision to silence Tatiana is so drastic and forceful that it should raise concerns about a propensity to subdue or instrumentalize the feminine other for his own narcissistic ends. Yet, at the same time, Jacques makes clear that he is not telling *the* story of Lol (as if such a story could be told, even by Tatiana) but *his* story of Lol; remaining faithful to "the overwhelming actuality of this woman in [his] life" seems to necessitate this interpretive decision to confine the parameters of his inquiry. The reader quickly discovers that Jacques means what he says; two pages later, when inquiring about the unfolding of the traumatic event, more specifically, about Anne-Marie Stretter, the *femme fatale*, he asks: "Had she looked at Michael Richardson as she passed by? And this non-look of hers swept over him as it took in the ballroom?" (6) ["Avait-elle regardé Michael Richardson en passant? L'avait-elle balayé de ce non-regard qu'elle promenait sur le bal?" (16)]. Uncertainty about what took place in this primal scene of seduction translates into doubts about the origins of his story: "It was impossible to tell, it is therefore impossible to know when my story of Lol Stein begins" (6) ["C'était impossible de le savoir, c'est impossible de savoir quand, par conséquent, commence mon histoire de Lol V. Stein" (16)].

Jacques's assertion that he wants to tell the story of Lol's transformative impact on his life includes a seemingly unexpected but innocuous reference to the reader — "the presence of her adolescence in this story might somehow tend to detract, *in the eyes of the reader*, from the overwhelming actuality of this woman in my life" — the only reference of its kind in the novel. More than a literary convention through which the narrator establishes some intimacy with his reader, the reference might more fruitfully be seen as an intersubjective gesture, foregrounding Jacques's exposure to the reader, reflecting a deeply self-conscious narrator, that is, a narrator conscious that he is writing *about*

Lol *for* a third party (Jacques does not reveal his identity until one-third of the way into the story). This formulation, of course, reinscribes Jacques in the traditional position of the active subject (the knower) and Lol in that of the passive object (the as of yet not known).

Again, things are a bit more complicated than they initially appear. Jacques already possesses some knowledge of Lol, a knowledge that clearly precedes the narrating of his story. Jacques feels nevertheless compelled to write her story down, to inquire further into the being of Lol. Assuming something akin to a pre-ontological understanding of Lol, then, Jacques takes up the role of an archaeologist, and engages in a poetics of unearthing. He proceeds to reconstruct the object of Lol's desire in order to better understand her state of mind and silence; in short, to bridge the temporal gap between the ball and the present:

> To level the terrain, to dig down into it, to open the tombs wherein Lol is feigning death, seems to me fairer — given the necessity to fill in the missing links of Lol Stein's story — than to fabricate mountains, create obstacles, rely on chance. And, knowing this woman, I believe she would prefer that I compensate in this way for the lack of cold, hard facts about her life. Moreover, in doing so I am always relying on hypotheses which are in no way gratuitous but which, in my opinion, have at least some slight foundation in fact. (27–28)

> Aplanir le terrain, le défoncer, ouvrir des tombeaux où Lol fait la morte, me paraît plus juste, du moment qu'il faut inventer les chaînons qui me manquent dans l'histoire de Lol V. Stein, que de fabriquer des montagnes, d'édifier des obstacles, des accidents. Et je crois, connaissant cette femme, qu'elle aurait préféré que je remédie dans ce sens à la pénurie des faits de sa vie. D'ailleurs c'est toujours à partir d'hypothèses non gratuites et qui ont déjà, à mon avis, reçu un début de confirmation, que je le fais. (37)

Jacques speculates about why Lol "plays dead" and invents the links of the chain in her story. More specifically, he traces her silence after the ball scene to the inability of language to represent or translate linguistically her desire for the endless night, for what could have permitted Lol to lose her self absolutely by eternally fusing with the couple (fusion as a sort of self-dissolution). He *imagines* Lol dreaming of an absolute word that could capture or symbolize the essence of her traumatic abandonment:

> But what she does believe is that she must enter it, that that was what she had to do, that it would always have meant, for her mind as well as her body, both their greatest pain and their greatest joy, so commingled as to be undefinable, a single entity but unnamable for lack of a word. I like to believe — since I love her — that if Lol is silent in her daily life it is because, for a split second, she believed that this word might exist. Since it does not, she remains silent. It would have been an absence-word, a hole-word, whose center would have been hollowed out into a hole, the kind of hole in which all other words would have been buried. (38)

> Mais ce qu'elle croit, c'est qu'elle devait y pénétrer, que c'était ce qu'il lui fallait faire, que ç'aurait été pour toujours, pour sa tête et pour son corps, leur plus grande douleur et leur plus grande joie confondue jusque dans leur définition devenue unique mais innommable faute de mot. J'aime à croire, comme je l'aime, que si Lol est silencieuse dans la vie c'est qu'elle a cru, l'espace d'un éclair, que ce mot pouvait exister. Faute de son existence, elle se tait. Ç'aurait été un mot-absence, un mot-trou, creusé en son centre d'un trou, de ce trou où tous les autres mots auraient été enterrés. (48)

Lacking the absolute word to verbalize the "experience" of her *ravishment*, to express what she wanted to see, "all that she succeeds in 'seeing'... is the vision of a short scene in which Michael Richardson would have been undressing the other woman."[40] Lol is condemned to "act out" or repeat this untotalized scene in her mind; indeed, the scene of her *ravishment* will unfold eternally in "the cinema of Lol Stein" (39) ["le cinéma de Lol V. Stein" (49)].

Deborah N. Glassman suggestively connects Jacques's intimate poetics of unearthing to Freudian psychoanalysis:

> Freud, in "Construction in Analysis," asks: "What sort of material does [the patient] put at our disposal which we can make use of to put him on the way to recovering the lost memories? All kinds of things... fragments of these memories in his dreams... ideas... repetitions of the affects belonging to the repressed. It is out of such raw material... that we have to put together what we are in search of... [the analyst's] task is to make out what has been forgotten from the traces which it has left behind, or more correctly, to construct it."[41]

Glassman's reading of Jacques as a crypto-psychoanalyst is all the more justified given the ambiguity concerning Jacques's medical profession. Having said this, however, we must pause and not assume *a priori* that a psychoanalytic framework produces a masterful body of knowledge, to see in Lol, *à la* Lacan, a "perfect case of clinical delirium." Lol's exemplarity (not unlike Jacques's) is precisely what is at issue here. What Jacques fashions or invents about Lol at times produces insights that are peculiarly paradoxical in nature. "[T]o know nothing about Lol Stein was already to know her. One could, it seemed to me, know even less about her, less and less about Lol Stein," Jacques observes (72) ["[N]e rien savoir de Lol était la connaître déjà. On pouvait, me parut-il, en savoir moins encore, de moins en moins sur Lol V. Stein" (81)]. Knowledge of Lol is something that Jacques undergoes rather than cunningly obtains. Here *knowing Lol* does not correspond to the traditional subject/object epistemological relation: a self-detached, autonomous, and reason-driven knower in relation to his known object.[42] Unlike the "perverters of the truth" (72 ["les faussaires" (81)] who spread gossip about the details of Lol's life, Jacques cannot *will* to know Lol. Passivity — rather than willful agency — characterizes his epistemic situation; his "initial discovery" (72) ["première découverte" (81)] is that he knows that he knows nothing, and that even this insight (knowledge of the absence of knowledge) is insufficient because, as he avows, "One could, it seemed to me, know even less about her, less and less about Lol Stein" (72) ["On pouvait, me parut-il, en savoir moins encore, de moins en moins sur Lol V. Stein" (81)].

In this light, Jacques Hold's "psychoanalytic" approach to Lol would resemble more closely that of Jean Laplanche, for whom psychoanalysis is better understood as anti-hermeneutics, as a skeptical practice that foregrounds the opacity of the signifier, the untranslatability of the analysand's message into the analyst's preexisting interpretive horizon (that is, the classic Freudian language of typicality or symbols).[43] In Levinasian parlance, the Laplanchian analyst maintains a "relation without relation" with the analysand; in this nonappropriative relation, the analyst does not exert his will to decipher but ethically responds to the aporetic demands made upon him by the analysand: to be heard without being converted into an object of comprehension (made into a case and thus reduced to the economy of the Same).

Jacques's observation that "to know nothing about Lol Stein was already to know her" intimates such a "relation without relation," recording Lol's incomprehensibility from within an egological universe. Jacques's Lol emerges as an Other irreducible to the narrator's narcissistic self-projection.[44] Indeed, Lol's enigmaticity is not only uncontainable but often contagious, affecting not only Jacques's representation of Lol but also the core foundations of his own identity. After his erotic encounter with Lol, Jacques no longer feels that his ego coincides with itself; her uncanny alterity obscures his self-transparency: "But what is there about me I am so completely unaware of and which she summons me to know? Who will be there, at that moment, beside her?" (96) ["Mais qu'est-ce que j'ignore de moi-même à ce point et qu'elle me met en demeure de connaître? qui sera là dans cet instant auprès d'elle?" (105)]. A similar kind of defamiliarization reoccurs later in the novel when Lol disturbs Jacques's very process of self-nomination. After she pronounces his name, he finds himself utterly bewildered, *ravi* (captivated and enchanted): "A dazzling discovery.... For the first time my name, pronounced, names nothing" (103) ["Fulgurante trouvaille.... Pour la première fois mon nom prononcé ne nomme pas" (112–13)].[45] But Lol's linguistic contagion ostensibly reaches its apogee in her description of Tatiana as "naked beneath her black hair" (105) ["nue sous ses cheveux noirs" (115)]. Lol's sentence ravishes Jacques. He repeats it in vain: "It's true that Tatiana was as Lol has just described her, naked beneath her dark hair.... The intensity of the sentence suddenly increases, the air around it has been rent, the sentence explodes, it blows the meaning apart" (106) ["Il est vrai que Tatiana était ainsi que Lol vient de la décrire, nue sous ses cheveux noirs.... L'intensité de la phrase augmente tout à coup. L'air a claqué autour d'elle, la phrase éclate, elle crève le sens" (116)]). Overwhelming Jacques's will to narrate, the sheer excess of meaning generated by Lol's sentence obliterates the very distinction between meaning and nonmeaning: "I fail to understand it, I no longer even understand that it means nothing" (106) ["Je ne la comprends pas, je ne comprends même plus qu'elle ne veut rien dire" [116]). Indeed, the "deafening roar" (106) ["force assourdissante" (116)] of Lol's sentence profoundly alters Jacques's relationship to his material reality, both in his perception and in his writing of Tatiana's body. Her nudity now escapes the containment of Jacques's I/eye: "Tatiana emerges from herself, spills through the open windows out over the town, the roads, mire, liquid, tide of nudity" (106) ["Tatiana sort d'elle-même, se répand par les fenêtres ouvertes, sur la ville, les routes, boue, liquide, marée de nudité" (116)].

Here we might say that *ravishment* functions as an ethical category akin to Levinas's notion of persecution from his 1968 essay "Substitution": "Persecution reduces the ego to the self, to the absolute accusative whereby the Ego is accused of a fault which it neither willed nor committed, and which disturbs its freedom. Persecution is a traumatism, violence par excellence, without warning, without *a priori*, without the possibility of apology, without logos."⁴⁶ Thrown into a profoundly heteronomous state, Jacques experiences Lol's ravishment as a traumatism, as an uprooting and disappropriation of the self; Lol's sexual difference fractures Jacques's masculinist self and disrupts his patriarchal reason (compelling him to see himself as an enigmatic signifier of his own). As Susan Rubin Suleiman puts it, Lol "feminizes" Jacques's masculine narrative,⁴⁷ introducing a ravishing unruliness within his phallocentric discourse. Enmeshed in transference, deeply affected by Lol's story (evidenced by his obsessive identification with Michael Richardson, for instance), Jacques resembles a compromised analyst, a less than masterful *subject supposed to know*.⁴⁸

Seeing Jacques as wholly vulnerable, as completely transformed by his encounter(s) with Lol, though, would be to grossly overstate the situation. If Suleiman, for example, likens Jacques's "hesitant" mode of narration to Duras's own elliptical style or practice of *écriture féminine* ("feminine writing"), pointing to the development of an ethically more sensible knower,⁴⁹ other critics have sought to expose Jacques's sinister motives, calling into question the *effect* of his self-contesting assertions about his writing of Lol: "what I have been able to imagine" (4) ["ce que j'invente" (14)]; "Here is my opinion" (35) ["Ce que je crois" (45)]; "I see this" (45) ["Je vois ceci" (55)]. Rather than limiting or undermining his narratorial authority, Jacques's rhetorical maneuverings "increase our confidence in the narrator's reliability."⁵⁰ "[W]hen Jacques Hold the analyst . . . systematically engages in a reification of his own ignorance, he is striving to secure his own . . . authority."⁵¹ Jacques's uncertainty, then, only masquerades as an absence of mastery, as an openness to female alterity: *it is the latest ruse of the male hermeneut*. Yet a critical evaluation of Jacques's textual strategies must resist this false choice — between generosity and suspicion, as it were — and entertain a more parallactic mode of reading, keeping in mind that Jacques's character is not one-dimensional, that the complexity of his narrative eludes both types of totalization: *écriture féminine* and male domination. While Duras's text invariably, and infuriatingly, solicits both of these mutually exclusive readings of Jacques, it also blocks the clear dominance of either one.

Jacques's desire to know Lol — "I had to know her, because such was her desire" (75) ["Je devais la connaître parce qu'elle désirait que cela se produise" (83–84)] — is never far from his desire to control her. Well after his "epiphanic" epistemological moment, where he states that "to know nothing about Lol Stein was already to know her," Jacques reiterates his irresistible thirst for

Lol's speech/story ("Like one parched, I desperately want to drink of the hazy, insipid milk of the word which emerges from the lips of Lol Stein" [97, translation modified] ["Je désire comme un assoiffé boire le lait brumeux et insipide de la parole qui sort de Lol V. Stein" (106)]) and quickly follows this statement with a paradoxical yearning to be both possessed by Lol ("let her consume and crush me with the rest, I shall bend to her will" [97]) ["qu'elle me broie avec le reste, je serai servile" (106)] and to possess her: "My hands are becoming the trap wherewith to ensnare her, immobilize her, keep her from constantly moving to and fro from one end of time to the other" (97) ["Mes mains deviennent le piège dans lequel l'immobiliser, la retenir de toujours aller et venir d'un bout à l'autre du temps" (107)]. Jacques's bizarre mixture of phantasmatic passivity with physical/hermeneutic violence (containing Lol physically and interpretively) makes evident that the ethical encounter does not unfold in any linear fashion: first, there is Jacques's desire for comprehension (the reduction of Lol to the realm of egology), then resistance resulting from his "ethical" recognition of Lol's otherness (Lol as an enigmatic signifier). Narrating the ethical encounter complicates a teleological understanding of the Levinasian encounter. It might also reveal why Levinas was deeply suspicious of the literary as such, as he says in "Reality and Its Shadow": "The characters of a novel are beings that are shut up, prisoners. Their history is never finished, it still goes on, but makes no headway."[52] It is precisely this lack of progression that Duras's novel displays time and time again. Yet narration and the ethical encounter as such are not necessarily locked in a negative dialectic. Rather, Duras's novel persistently resists the "pathos of understanding," as Lacan puts it,[53] fostering interpretive irresolution through its constant framing and reframing of the ethical encounter. Even the most idyllic image of ethical coexistence, such as Jacques's affectionate claim of being utterly *riveted* to Lol ("Here we are, bound together inextricably" [103]) ["Nous voici chevillés ensemble" (113)], is not immune to ironic recontextualization, to its reinscription within the many twists and turns of the narrative.[54] In an exchange with Lol toward the end of the novel, for instance, Jacques (as well as the reader) is reminded of Lol's recalcitrant otherness:

"I don't love you and yet I do. You know what I mean."
   I ask:
"Why don't you kill yourself? Why haven't you already killed yourself?"
"No, you're wrong, that's not it at all." (159)

> —Je ne vous aime pas cependant je vous aime, vous me comprenez?
> Je demande:
> —Pourquoi ne pas vous tuer? Pourquoi ne vous êtes-vous pas encore tuée?
> —Non, vous vous trompez, ce n'est pas ça. (169)[55]

Lol's statement that she does not love Jacques and does love him at the same time violates, or ravishes, the principle of noncontradiction, a principle of great utility for the analytic mind. Unraveling Jacques's logic, Lol deflates his hermeneutic astuteness: "No, you're wrong, that's not it at all." Here a feminist reader is tempted to privilege Lol's sexual difference — opposing her subversive agrammaticality to Jacques's familiar grammar — and interpret Lol's unruliness as Duras's call for a heroic new female subjectivity. And this type of interpretation would do no more than confirm and strengthen what that reader already knows or feels. Yet the novel asks us to do more; or paradoxically, it incites us to do *less*. We could say that *The Ravishing of Lol Stein* creatively dramatizes Levinas's statement that "to require that a communication be sure of being heard is to confuse communication and knowledge."[56] What the novel narrates or communicates is *not* knowledge of sexual difference, of a new female subjectivity, or the like. Rather, the Saying of the novel lies in its invitation to the reader to take up the ethical imperative of "unsaying" and "resaying" — not only the Said of Jacques's discourse but also, or better yet, especially the Said produced by any reading of *The Ravishing of Lol Stein*, including one's own. Doing justice to Duras's novel, then, involves a constant alertness to one's interpretive maneuverings, precariously hesitating between competing injunctions: to interpret but not to translate Lol/Jacques/*The Ravishing of Lol Stein* into a pre-established hermeneutic code — feminist or otherwise.

Conclusion

UNRULY THEORY

> Theory does not contain answers to everything; it reacts to the world, which is faulty to the core. What would be free from the spell of the world is not under theory's jurisdiction.
>
> THEODOR ADORNO

Unruly works are things of this world; yet, at the same time, they resist the meaning the world ascribes to them. They impose their own demands on the world of readers, interrupting the flow of knowledge and commentary. Attempts at comprehending the unruly — the elusive otherness of an artwork — often meet with a barrier. The negotiation with the unruly and response to its barrier constitute the ethical scene of reading.

In "Compassion and Terror," Martha Nussbaum frames the encounter with otherness in terms of a cosmopolitan ethics, an ethics that underscores "compassionate imagining" as an antidote to the confines and comfort brought about by the nation-state. As an alternative to narcissistic investment in one's own country and culture, Nussbaum advocates for "an education in common human weakness and vulnerability," through which "students should learn to decode the suffering of others, and this decoding should deliberately lead them into lives both near and far, including the lives of distant humans and the lives of animals."[1] Nussbaum is certainly not naïve about the difficulties in realizing this ideal; she is quite aware of the dangers in grounding an ethics in the self's capacity to imagine and capture the suffering of others. She repeatedly acknowledges the dilemmas of interpretation and the double aim of her readings: recognizing otherness and understanding the other. As she argues in *Love's Knowledge*, "[Literary] stories cultivate our ability *to see and care for particulars,* not as representatives of a law, but as what they themselves are: to respond vigorously with senses and emotions before the new; to care deeply about chance happenings in the world, rather than fortify ourselves against them."[2] Accordingly, ethical criticism cannot proceed by merely applying a preexisting rule or law; it requires a care for particulars, a care for that which cannot be reduced to an example of a rule. Yet criticism must at the same time strive to recognize the exemplarity of the particular, to be attentive to its potential to yield "moral truth."[3] Indeed, criticism must endeavor to understand/decipher the particular rather than stress its unknowability or otherness:

> We always risk error in bringing a distant person close to us; we ignore differences of language and of cultural context, and the manifold ways in which these differences shape one's inner world. But there are dangers in any act of imagining, and we should not let these particular dangers cause us to admit defeat prematurely, surrendering before an allegedly insuperable barrier of otherness.[4]

What is at stake here is not simply the *feasibility* of overcoming the other's otherness, but also the *desirability* of transcending the other's difference as an ethical goal. The passage opens with a call for hesitation and recognition: the self is not the other and the other is not the self. Readers risk moral failure unless they both admit the limits of the self and recognize the linguistic and cultural differences of the other. The first ethico-interpretive injunction is *not* to cannibalize the other, or in its positive formulation, to respect the other's recalcitrant difference. Yet the passage ends with another warning, a second injunction: do not be seduced by the otherness of the other, or positively stated (the result of a double negation as it were), cannibalize that otherness — for the sake of understanding, that is, in order to make emphatic imaginings happen. To sum up Nussbaum's argument: too much attention to difference risks fetishizing the border that separates the self and the other. What sets up this quasi-reversal of focus (from not enough difference to too much otherness) is the idea of "one's shared inner world." The use of the pronoun "one" here serves a double function. First, it *ontologically* harmonizes the self's separation from the other; that is, although we may be separated by language and culture, we still share the same humanity, the same experiential makeup. Second, it provides the necessary rationale for the call to overcome "the barrier of otherness."

For Nussbaum, ethics and otherness are thus locked together in an unhappy dialectic. Knowledge of the other will *necessarily* be imperfect — hence the importance of hesitation as one proceeds in the act of reading. But such an imperfection should not result in interpretive paralysis and irresolution, nor discourage the faithful humanist or Neo-Aristotelian reader from the task at hand: the promotion of an empathic identification with the other, or "compassion within the limits of reason," as she puts it in *Upheavals of Thought*.[5]

While approaching the problem differently from within a Heideggerian framework, Hans-Georg Gadamer responds to the issues of otherness, barriers, and the potential interpretive pitfalls facing readers of literature in a surprisingly similar fashion. In "Text and Interpretation," Gadamer frames the hermeneutic question as one of understanding otherness, of determining the other's meaning through the mediation of language:

> First, How do the communality of meaning..., which is built up in conversation, and the impenetrability of the otherness of the other mediate each other? Second, What, in the final analysis, is linguisticality? Is it a bridge or a barrier? Is it a bridge built of things that are the same for each self over which one communicates with the other over the flowing stream of otherness? Or is it a barrier that limits our self-abandonment and that cuts us off from the possibility of ever completely expressing ourselves and communicating with others?[6]

For Gadamer, it is the image of linguisticality as a bridge that ultimately prevails. The emphasis for Gadamer, like for Nussbaum, resides in the *common*, in the "fusion of horizons," as he is fond of saying, in the ways "something like texts can be given to us in common."[7] At the heart of Gadamer's hermeneutic act lies a dialogic impulse, a shared notion of a good will: "Both partners must have the good will to try to understand one another."[8] The same can be said of the literary work: it wants to be read and understood. Alterity *as such*, then, is not the end of hermeneutics, only its beginning.[9]

Nussbaum and Gadamer each arrive, through different paths, at a principled and carefully conceived call for understanding that strikes many as thoroughly unobjectionable. "How could anyone not be tempted to acknowledge how extremely evident this axiom is?" comments Derrida, recognizing the persuasiveness of arguments that posit commonality as a basis for ethics. Yet he questions this basis, asking "whether the precondition of *Verstehen* ["understanding the other" and "understanding one another"], far from being the continuity of *rapport*..., is not rather the interruption of *rapport*, a certain *rapport* of interruption, the suspending of all mediation?"[10] With these questions, Derrida invites us to rethink the preconditions for understanding otherness in terms of interruption rather than continuity, to conceive of the barrier of otherness not as an obstacle to overcome or transcend through interpretive consensus, but as that which sets in motion the ethical injunction to respect and preserve difference. Indeed, to insist on "the barrier *of* otherness" is to insist on the unruly or aporetic character of my relation to the other, that is, of my relation as "an interminable experience"[11] — as a *relation without relation*.

Theorizing the event of the other — the other as an event — is paradoxically predicated on both the necessity and the failure of hermeneutics:

> Although the experience of an event... calls for a movement of appropriation (comprehension, recognition, identification, description, determination, interpretation, and so on), although this movement of appropriation is irreducible and ineluctable, there is no event worthy of the name except insofar as this appropriation *falters* at some border or frontier.[12]

Readability and unreadability are thus, strictly speaking, no longer to be conceived as distinct or opposing modalities of interpretation. An eye for the event requires a split perspective, a parallax view. The structure of appropriation is *not all* — there is always "an irreducible remainder or excess."[13] Theory — and this might constitute its greatest difference from philosophy, which "is always haunted by the dream of some foolproof self-sufficient system, a set of interlocking concepts which are their own cause"[14] — does not disavow this excess, that which short-circuits the machinery of comprehension. On the contrary, theory attends and attests to such moments of hermeneutic indigestibility; it does not interpret otherness merely or primarily as a *hindrance* to comprehension. In this respect, theory is most hospitable to skepticism's unruly ways, which, under its watch, undergo nothing short of a Nietzschean transvaluation. Skepticism *as such* is no longer something that the reader simply settles for; skepticism is not simply all that we can hope for since a complete or exhaustive reading is unrealizable in the here and now of earthly criticism,[15] nor are the hesitation and indecision that it provokes only bumpy moments in the ethical journey of understanding.

Such a hermeneutics of skepticism has informed *Reading Unruly*. Skepticism's hysterical questioning pluralizes meaning; it *perverts* (from the Latin *pervertere*, meaning to overturn, to turn upside down) philosophy's — or ethical criticism's — quest for truth, exposing the inadequacies of its "exemplary" solutions to epistemological and ethical problems.[16] Pushing back against the impulse to abstract, against the urge to construe from a range of unruly works a theory of the unruly (an essence of the unruly, of its pure agrammaticality), this book strives to be mindful of the irreducible and incommensurable demands of each singular work. It strives to be mindful of the necessity to remain alert to the ways each literary text imposes its own double bind — how it imagines and performs its barrier of otherness, its remainder or excess — compelling its reader, in turn, to *invent* his or her provisional rule of reading. Sustaining this act of invention, what we might describe as the work of ethical skepticism, is an endless task, since, as Barthes once aptly put it, "it is not *answering* which is difficult, it is questioning."[17] The responsive and responsible reader must persevere in questioning, for an ethics of reading is skeptical or it is not.

Notes

INTRODUCTION

1. Among the dominant voices in this debate, see, for example, J. Hillis Miller, *The Ethics of Reading*; Harpham, *Shadows of Ethics*; and the following volumes: Davis and Womack, *Mapping the Ethical Turn*; Garber, Hanssen, and Walkowitz, *The Turn to Ethics*; and Buell, "Ethics and Literary Study," the special issue of PMLA (January 1999).

2. The appeal to the language of turns is almost irresistible. Yet the point here is not to abandon a discussion of shifts or trends but rather to scrutinize the (conscious or unconscious) desire for the next big thing. In this respect, I find Michael Eskin's suggestion of a "double 'turn,'" one to ethics and the other to literature, equally fruitful in frustrating the readerly impulse to simplify trends. See Eskin, "Introduction: The Double 'Turn' to Ethics and Literature?"

3. Kermode, "Literary Criticism: Old and New Styles," 194.

4. "Under the old dispensation, one might choose between several methodologies which had in common only the assumptions that it was permissible to speak of literary quality and that one could read with a degree of attention that warranted the issuing of judgments, even of declarations, that some works demanded to be read by all who claimed the right to expound and instruct. Under the newer metacritical dispensation, there were now many interesting ways of banning such activities and substituting for them methods of description and analysis which might derive their force from linguistics, politics, anthropology, psychoanalysis, or what were claimed to be brand-new, unillusioned, and exciting ways of writing history" (Kermode, *Pleasure and Change*, 16).

5. Lamenting literature's contamination by Theory, Robert Alter writes: "I mean simply that the sundry versions of what Paul Ricoeur has called in connection with Freud 'the hermeneutics of suspicion' have led beyond skepticism to an attitude sometimes approaching disdain for literature. In both criticism and in debates over curriculum, one encounters an insistence that daily newspapers, pulp fiction, private

diaries, clinical case studies, and imaginative literature belong on one level, that any distinctions among them are dictated chiefly by ideology" (Alter, *The Pleasures of Reading in an Ideological Age*, 11). Martha C. Nussbaum also expresses her dissatisfaction with Theory's hegemony: "After reading Derrida, and not Derrida alone, I feel a certain hunger for blood; for, that is, writing about literature that talks of human lives and choices *as if they matter to us all*" (Nussbaum, *Love's Knowledge*, 171, emphasis added). Nussbaum's "hunger for blood" signals an aversion to a peculiar type of interpretive style, the all-too-playful kind that operates at the surface level and is fascinated by the text's words or "signifiers," failing, as it were, to attend to the rich lives of people.

6. Booth, *The Company We Keep*, 5. See also Janet Wolff, who approvingly quotes and reiterates Booth's harmonizing gesture in the last pages of her book *The Aesthetics of Uncertainty*.

7. Author, here, signifies either the flesh-and-blood writer or the "implied" author. According to H. Porter Abbott, the implied author, a concept first introduced by Wayne Booth in *The Rhetoric of Fiction* (1961), is the author that the reader posits or constructs in order to give structural order and unity to the work: "The implied author is . . . like the narrative, itself a kind of construct that among other things serves to anchor the narrative" (Abbott, *Cambridge Introduction to Narrative*, 77). James Phelan, for his part, locates the implied author outside the text: "The implied author is not a product of the text, but rather the agent responsible for bringing the text into existence" (Phelan, *Living to Tell about It*, 45).

8. See, for example, Newton, *Narrative Ethics*; Eaglestone, *Ethical Criticism*; Gibson, *Postmodernity, Ethics, and the Novel*; Shankman, *Other Others*.

9. See Levinas, *Totality and Infinity*, 69. Adam Zachary Newton writes, "one faces a text as one might face a person, having to confront the claims raised by that very immediacy, an immediacy of contact, not of meaning" (Newton, *Narrative Ethics*, 11).

10. Attridge, *The Singularity of Literature*, 130.

11. Barthes, *S/Z*, 4.

12. Barthes, *S/Z*, 4, 15.

13. Žižek, *The Parallax View*, ix.

14. "This is what Marx, among others, did with philosophy and religion . . . ; this is what Freud and Nietzsche did with morality. . . . What such a reading achieves is not a simple 'desublimation,' a reduction of the higher intellectual content to its lower economic or libidinal cause; the aim of such an approach is, rather, the inherent decentering of the interpreted text, which brings to light its 'unthought,' its disavowed presuppositions and consequences" (Žižek, *The Parallax View*, ix).

15. Tim Dean has also drawn attention to Žižek's strong model of interpretive agency: "One cannot help noticing that in his dozen or so books no cultural artifact poses any resistance to Žižek's hermeneutic energy; there is no social system or movie or opera or novel that he cannot interpret," or, for that matter, short-circuit (Dean, "Art as Symptom," 23).

16. Barthes, *The Pleasure of the Text*, 14.

17. Barthes, *The Pleasure of the Text*, 14.
18. Barthes, *The Pleasure of the Text*, 64–65.
19. Barthes, *The Pleasure of the Text*, 14.
20. As a corrective to a simple affirmation of *jouissance* as a subversive, antibourgeois category, Žižek underscores enjoyment's ideological trappings in today's permissive societies; the injunction *Enjoy!* all too often results in the self's submission to societal regulations and prohibitions. Rather than associating the superego with "symbolic castration" (the superego as a straightforward internalization of the Law), Žižek argues that the superego embodies the obscene or repressed underside of the Law, "marking a point at which *permitted* enjoyment, freedom-to-enjoy, is reversed into *obligation* to enjoy — which, one must add, is the most effective way to block access to enjoyment" (Žižek, *For They Know Not What They Do*, 237).
21. Foucault, *The Use of Pleasure*, 8.
22. Fantasy trumps cognition. Barthes boldly affirms the death of the Author, denouncing its mystifying or ideological function, but still registers his fetishistic yearning for the author: "The author is dead . . . but . . . *I desire* the author: I need his figure . . . as he needs mine" (Barthes, *The Pleasure of the Text*, 27).
23. A similar objection can be made to Wolfgang Iser's more measured brand of reader-response theory. While literary works invite their readers to interpret and dialogue with them (to act as co-creators), actualizing the text's potential and construing its intelligibility by filling in its "gaps" or "unformulated part," as Iser terms it, does not fully meet the ethical demands of reading (*The Implied Reader*, 34, 287). To prevent the "inexhaustibility" of the literary work that Iser discusses from becoming an abstraction or a truism, the reader's relation to these works must remain dynamic, and not conform to a strict logic of fidelity (nonviolence) and betrayal (violence) (*The Implied Reader*, 280). Following such a strict logic ironically elides the responsibility of reading — and the mixed feeling of anguish and delight produced by the uncertainty of judgment, the prospect of having to invent rather than mechanically apply the rules of interpretation. As Derrida insists, "there are ethics because I have to *invent* the rule" (Derrida, "Following Theory, 31").
24. Blanchot, *The Writing of the Disaster*, 101, emphasis added. Cf. Eaglestone, *Ethical Criticism*, 175–76.
25. Ann Smock points out that "le Dire" is an "expression [that] evokes Emmanuel Levinas and his conviction that speech alone sustains the relation of a subject to the Other. Speech: not any particular communication, but speech itself as an offering, the offering of language in response to the infinite obligation which the presence to me of an other person is" ("Translator's Remarks," in Blanchot, *The Writing of the Disaster*, xi–xii). This reading of the Levinasian intertext stresses Levinas's *Totality and Infinity* — for the "'saying of the Other'" takes place in the face-to-face encounter (Levinas, *Totality and Infinity*, 48); we shall see that this reading is complicated by Levinas's later work *Otherwise than Being*, which ostensibly shifts the ethical (the Saying) away from the existential encounter to the workings of language.

26. Levinas, *Totality and Infinity*, 50.

27. Levinas himself resisted this extension of otherness to the literary. As Colin Davis puts it, "Levinas attacks art because it is irresponsible and inhuman, it is a form of idolatry which puts the mind to sleep and shrouds it in darkness.... Narrative fiction falsifies the nature of the self and the experience of time and freedom" (Davis, *Critical Excess*, 97). For Levinas's most explicit treatment of the artwork, see his "Reality and Its Shadow," in Hand, *The Levinas Reader*, 129–43.

28. Take, for example, Gerald L. Bruns's stimulating book, *On the Anarchy of Poetry and Philosophy*, in which Bruns verges on collapsing the unruly with "the anarchy of the sublime" (25).

29. Badiou does make a distinction between Levinas and the more pervasive liberal, sentimentalist appropriation of Levinas: "For the honour of philosophy, it is first of all necessary to admit that this ideology of a 'right to difference', the contemporary catechism of goodwill with regard to 'other cultures', are strikingly distant from Lévinas's actual conception of things" (Badiou, *Ethics: An Essay on the Understanding of Evil*, trans. Peter Hallward, 20). The force or relevance of this distinction is, however, subsequently minimized if not displaced by Badiou's polemical reading of Levinas.

30. Badiou, *Ethics*, 22. Hereafter cited parenthetically in the text.

31. In light of the recent history of continental philosophy, Badiou's evocation of truth surely disconcerts; does he really expect his readers to have forgotten Foucault's Nietzschean claim that "truth is a thing of this world" (Foucault, *Power/Knowledge*, 131)? Yet Badiou's use of truth here is quite peculiar, and should not be confused with the language of moral realism. As Simon Critchley suggests, it might be clearer, and more useful, to replace Badiou's rhetoric of truth with that of justification: "an event is justified if and only if it is universalizable, that is, if it is in principle addressed to all" (Critchley, *Infinitely Demanding*, 48). Though subjective and relative, the truth of the event, then, is not completely devoid of a sense of normativity.

32. Peter Hallward has objected to the Levinasian language of demand when discussing Badiou's understanding of the event. Insisting that "an event does not make a demand on you" but exposes contingency, the inconsistency of existence, offering us less a demand than an opportunity to *affirm* the implication of this troubling inconsistency (Baldwin and Haeffner, "'Fault Lines': Simon Critchley in Discussion on Alain Badiou," 298–99), Hallward brings to the forefront the question of hermeneutic agency in relation to the subject and the event. Evoking the rhetoric of demand *necessarily* reintroduces, for Hallward's Badiou, a theistic framework, one that foregrounds pathos and "an inaugural passivity" on the part of the subject, a position allegedly detrimental to decision making and philosophy itself. While Hallward faithfully follows Badiou in registering the objection to the Levinasian language of passivity—reiterating Badiou's critique of French philosophy's "fetishism of literature" under the sway of the thinkers of difference (Badiou, *Manifesto for Philosophy*, 66)—I think Hallward and Badiou paint too simplistic a portrait of Levinas and his

subject of responsibility. On this matter, I agree with Simon Critchley in exploring lines of convergence between the two philosophers. (Hallward's comments come from his exchange with Critchley during a general discussion of Alain Badiou and Critchley's interpretation of his work. Jon Baldwin and Nick Haeffner recorded their exchange in "'Fault Lines'" 295–307).

33. Žižek, *The Plague of Fantasies*, 214.

34. Žižek, *Organs without Bodies*, 106. Terry Eagleton makes a similar observation: "Badiou's thought runs in the same theoretical grooves as some of the very acolytes of otherness he most scathingly opposes" (Eagleton, *Figures of Dissent*, 249).

35. Derrida, "Violence and Metaphysics," 151.

36. Derrida, "Violence and Metaphysics," 84. Similarly, after discussing the two competing "interpretations of interpretation" — a Rousseauistic one that "seeks to decipher, dreams of deciphering a truth or an origin which escapes play and the order of the sign, and which lives the necessity of interpretation as an exile" and a Nietzschean one that is "the joyous affirmation of the play of the world and of the innocence of becoming, the affirmation of a world of signs without fault, without truth, and without origin which is offered to an active interpretation" — Derrida opts for undecidability: "I do not believe that today there is any question of *choosing*" ("Structure, Sign, and Play in the Discourse of the Human Sciences," 292). Dislodging interpretation from a disjunctive logic, Derrida invites us to think of interpretation in terms of multiplicity, friction, and incommensurability. Alan D. Schrift insightfully discerns from Derrida's musings "the advantages of a pluralistic approach to interpretation" (Schrift, *Nietzsche and the Question of Interpretation*, 171).

37. Derrida, *Aporias*, 22.

38. Derrida, *Rogues*, 60.

39. Levinas and Blanchot also use the formulation of "relation without relation." See, for instance, Blanchot, *The Infinite Conversation*, 73; and Levinas, *Totality and Infinity*, 80.

40. Derrida, *The Gift of Death*, 78.

41. Spivak, *An Aesthetic Education in the Era of Globalization*, 233.

42. Levinas, *Otherwise than Being*, 42. Hereafter cited parenthetically in the text.

43. See Jakobson, "Closing Statement," 350–77. Thomas Trezise rightly acknowledges the limitation of this analogy, since, for Jakobson, "the phatic is only one of six linguistic functions . . . whereas, for Levinas, Saying is one of several terms designating a relation to alterity that is not even reducible to language as a whole" (Trezise, "Unspeakable," 66n43).

44. I am indebted here to Barthes's penetrating remarks on rereading in his *S/Z*: "Rereading, an operation contrary to the commercial and ideological habits of our society, which would have us 'throw away' the story once it has been consumed ('devoured'), so that we can then move on to another story, buy another book, and which is tolerated only in certain marginal categories of readers (children, old people, and professors), rereading is here suggested at the outset, for it alone saves

the text from repetition (those who fail to re-read are obliged to read the same story everywhere)" (15–16).

45. Derrida, "'Eating Well,' or the Calculation of the Subject," 115. Derrida's formulation of an ethics of "eating well" echoes his own "fail well" and Beckett's "fail better": "In order to succeed, it [the law of mourning] would well have to *fail*, to fail well" (Derrida, *The Work of Mourning*, 144). "All of old. Nothing else ever. Ever tried. Ever failed. No matter. Try again. Fail better" (Samuel Beckett, *Worstward Ho*, 7).

46. Attridge sees this concession to relationality as eliminating the literary work's status as "other": "coming into existence [in the act of reading] necessarily involves ceasing to be other" (Attridge, *The Singularity of Literature*, 125–26). His choice for a relation to the work rather than a nonrelation, however, risks reintroducing the logic of either/other (as opposed to the logic of both/and, a logic that entails a creative hesitation between pure alterity and sameness, and compels, as I have argued, its readers to unsay and resay the Said of the artwork).

47. Derrida's injunction "to eat well," and the type of hermeneutic interaction that it elicits from the reader, recall Mikhail Bakhtin's notion of "responsive understanding" (see, for example, Bakhtin, *Art and Answerability* and *Speech Genres and Other Late Essays*. Like Levinas and Derrida, Bakhtin underscores the incompleteness of the self's discursive position, foregrounding intersubjectivity and relationality, or what he calls dialogism. Responsive understanding can be described as an empathic mode that is *otherwise than assimilative* insofar as it seeks both to respond to the other's call for hermeneutic identification, and to respect the "outsideness" of the other — to attend to what remains uncontainable from within the reader's "single consciousness" (Bakhtin, *Speech Genres*, 141). See Newton, *Narrative Ethics*, 85–86.

48. I am reminded here of Barthes's comment on literature's specificity: "What do things signify, what does the world signify? All literature is this question, but we must immediately add, for this is what constitutes its speciality, *literature is the question minus its answer*" (Barthes, *Critical Essays*, 202).

49. As Derrida observes, "When one says, 'one must do justice,' 'one has to be fair' ['*il faut être juste*'], it is often with the intention of correcting an impulse or reversing the direction of a tendency; one is also recommending resisting a temptation" ("'To Do Justice to Freud,'" 236).

50. Blanchot, *The Infinite Conversation*, 153. Cf. Bruns, *On the Anarchy of Poetry and Philosophy*, 74.

51. Gerald Graff has championed the view that gives primacy to *the way we read* — reflecting, first and foremost, a pedagogical concern — over the canon-driven *what we read*. See Graff, *Beyond the Culture Wars* and "Why How We Read Trumps What We Read."

52. As Mladen Dolar cautions, "for the very act of interpreting operates by arbitrary cuts and the alleged wealth of the object interpreted is a retroactive effect of the very interpretation that seemed to reduce it. Here, rather than claiming any fidelity to an original textual wealth, I proceed by taking up only one essential point that

interests me" (Dolar, "'I Shall Be with You on Your Wedding-Night,'" 8n7). Dolar's model of reading, however, unduly flattens the complexity of the interpretive scene, instrumentalizing the literary work by putting it purely at the service of the reader's masterful will.

53. Badiou, of course, does say that the truth event always happens *within* a situation (à la Sartre), so no event exists in the abstract. Badiou is, however, more vulnerable to objection in his insistence that knowledge (= opinion) and truth are clearly and distinctly different from one another — with the result that truth remains untranslatable back into the given discourse and its hegemony of consensus. That is to say, there is no possibility of unsaying and resaying the Said of the event (after the subject's interpellation by the Saying of the event); this is an all-or-nothing logic, with only starvation in/as fidelity.

54. Žižek, *The Parallax View*, 17. Hereafter cited parenthetically in the text.

55. Derrida, *Of Grammatology*, 158.

56. In a 2004 exchange with Žižek, Badiou made use of the notion of "relation without relation" to describe his account of the event and the ethico-political demands that it makes upon the subject. The first full articulation is given in the context of a discussion of the event of love: "What I here name the 'smile' of the lovers, for lack of a better word, is a philosophical situation. Why? Because in it we once again encounter something incommensurable, a relation without relation. Between the event love . . . and the ordinary rules of life . . . there is no common measure. What will philosophy tell us then? It will tell us that 'we must think the event'. We must think the exception. We must know what we have to say about what is not ordinary. We must think the transformation of life" (Badiou, "Thinking the Event," 11–12). For Badiou, what philosophy stages time and time again is the rupture of relation, "the break of the established natural and social bond": "So we can say that philosophy, which is the thought, not of what there is, but of what is not what there is (not of contracts, but of contracts broken), is exclusively interested in relations that are not relations" (15). Readers familiar with Derrida and Levinas will see an uncanny resemblance here.

57. Žižek alludes to a conceptual overlap between Derrida's earlier notion of *différance* and his parallax gap. See Žižek's "A Plea for a Return to *Différance*."

58. Fish, *Doing What Comes Naturally*, 146.

59. Foucault, *The Use of Pleasure*, 8.

60. Badiou, *Ethics*, 32.

61. Foucault, "What is Enlightenment?," 46.

62. Foucault, "The Masked Philosopher," 328.

63. Derrida, "Force of Law: The 'Mystical Foundation of Authority,'" in *Acts of Religion*, ed. Gil Anidjar (New York: Routledge, 2002), 252.

64. The decision also involves a certain risk, a vulnerability that comes from proceeding with no interpretive guarantees: "An ethics with guarantees is not an ethics. If you have an ethics with some insurance, and you know that if you are wrong the

insurance will pay, it isn't ethics. Ethics is dangerous" (Derrida, "Following Theory," 32). See also Derrida, *Psyche: Inventions of the Other*, 1:45.

65. Derrida, "Force of Law," 251.

66. I am adapting here Levinas's remark that "ethical exigency is not an ontological necessity"; the injunction "Thou shalt not kill" (the ultimate ethical commandment) does not make murder ontologically impossible (Levinas, *Ethics and Infinity*, 87).

67. See Badiou, *Saint Paul*.

68. "Cultural consecration does indeed confer on the objects, persons and situations it touches a sort of ontological promotion akin to transubstantiation" (*Distinction*, 6).

69. Bourdieu, *Distinction*, 7.

70. Bourdieu, *Distinction*, 66.

71. As an important corrective to Bourdieu, Jacques Rancière exposes an irony in such sociological accounts: "The very ones who say that the people are incapable of ever making a reasonable use of freedom claim that the Beautiful is a matter either of learned criteria or the pleasure of refined senses (which are, in both cases, outside the sphere of common people)" (*The Philosopher and His Poor*, 198). In other words, Bourdieu's framing of the problem risks perpetuating rather than overcoming the gap between the refined elite and the ignorant working class.

72. In *Archive Fever*, Derrida describes one's responsibility to the past in similar terms. The archive is always more than a repository of information (something to be merely instrumentalized). Moreover, one can never recover the past in some pure state — in a way that fully accounts for the past event's uniqueness. Archival documents are not simply given, whence the endless ethical task and political stakes of interpretation: "There is no political power without control of the archive, if not memory. Effective democratization can always be measured by this essential criterion: the participation in and access to the archive, its constitution, and its interpretation" (Derrida, *Archive Fever*, 4n1).

73. J. Hillis Miller, *Versions of Pygmalion*, 21.

74. As Derek Attridge nicely observes, "All canons rest on exclusion; the voice they give to some can be heard only by virtue of the silence they impose on others. But it is not just a silencing by exclusion, it is a silencing by *inclusion* as well: any voice we can hear is by that very fact purged of its uniqueness and alterity" (Attridge, *J. M. Coetzee and the Ethics of Reading*, 82).

75. Baudelaire, "The Painter of Modern Life," 403.

76. On Derrida's concept of countersignature, see "This Strange Institution Called Literature," 60–75.

77. Robbe-Grillet, *For a New Novel: Essays on Fiction*, 33.

78. Montaigne, *Complete Works*, 819.

79. "*Tout autre est tout autre*" occurs several times Derrida's *The Gift of Death* (cf. *Aporias*, 22). David Wills translates the phrase as "*every other (one) is every (bit) other*" (68), effectively conveying the difficulties that Derrida's sentence poses for translation and comprehension.

1. MONTAIGNE

1. Montaigne, *Complete Works*, II, 12, 421a, translation modified, emphasis added; Villey and Saulnier, *Les Essais de Michel de Montaigne*, 560. Henceforth all references to these editions are stated parenthetically in the text. Citations refer to book, essay, and page. The letters *a*, *b*, and *c* indicate the three major textual strata corresponding to the 1580 edition, the 1588 edition, and the manuscript additions made by Montaigne to his personal copy of the 1588 edition of the *Essays*, known as the *Exemplaire de Bordeaux* [Bordeaux Copy]. References to the book and chapter are omitted whenever they can be clearly inferred from the context.

2. Richard Regosin has also highlighted the multifaceted nature of the relation between Montaigne and his textual progeny: "Here Montaigne is writer as maker, maker of that which is and is not himself, that which has life, and its own life, and gives him life as well" ("'Mettre la theorique avant la practique': Montaigne and the Practice of Theory," 275). See also Regosin, *Montaigne's Unruly Brood*.

3. Lacan, "The Agency of the Letter in the Unconscious," 166.

4. Adorno, "The Essay as Form," 161.

5. Foucault, *The Use of Pleasure*, 9. Similarly, Tom Conley affirms that the essay, exemplified by Montaigne's "Apology for Raymond Sebond," "stands as one of the most accomplished destructions of all inherited systems of truth" (Conley, "Mapping Montaigne," 72).

6. This expression belongs to Gilles Deleuze (see, in particular, chapter 3 of *Difference and Repetition*).

7. Hoffmann, "From Amateur to Gentleman to Gentleman Amateur," 24.

8. Cave, *How to Read Montaigne*, 3–4.

9. Cave, *How to Read Montaigne*, 4, emphasis added.

10. Rigolot, "Interpréter Rabelais aujourd'hui," 270, my translation.

11. Cf. Compagnon, *Chat en poche*, 50.

12. Montaigne, as an "able reader" of Titus Livy, writes: "I have read in Livy a hundred things that another man has not read in him. Plutarch has read in him a hundred besides the ones I could read, and perhaps besides what the author had put in" (I, 26, 115c) ["J'ay leu en Tite-Live cent choses que tel n'y a pas leu. Plutarque en y a leu cent, outre ce que j'y ay sceu lire, et, à l'adventure, outre ce que l'autheur y avoit mis" (156)].

13. To be sure, Montaigne did not endorse just any type of reading, warning his reader that he would return from the dead in order to contest any deliberate or careless misreading of his work, regardless of the reader's good intentions: "I would willingly come back from the other world to give the lie to any man who portrayed me other than I was, even if it were to honor me" (III, 9, 751b) ["Je reviendrois volontiers de l'autre monde pour démentir celuy qui me formeroit autre que je n'estois, fut-ce pour m'honorer" (983)].

14. A reading of Montaigne that privileges multiperspectivism could help to attenuate the essayist's scathing indictment of the practice of interpretation: "It is more of

a job to interpret the interpretations than to interpret the things, and there are more books about books than about any other subject: we do nothing but write glosses about each other" (III, 13, 818b) ["Il y a plus affaire à interpreter les interpretations qu'à interpreter les choses, et plus de livres sur les livres que sur autre subject: nous ne faisons que nous entregloser" (1069)].

15. For an account of the pedagogical implications of Montaigne's critique of humanism, see Zahi Zalloua, "(Im)Perfecting the Self."

16. Pico della Mirandola, *Oration on the Dignity of Man*, 225.

17. Nietzsche, *On the Genealogy of Morals*, 3.18.

18. Neto, "*Epoche* as Perfection," 19.

19. Faye, *Philosophie et perfection de l'homme*, 210, my translation.

20. Faye, *Philosophie et perfection de l'homme*, my translation.

21. Faye, *Philosophie et perfection de l'homme*, 195–96.

22. Todorov, *Imperfect Garden*, 6.

23. *Essayes of Michael lord of Montaigne*, trans. and ed. John Florio (1908), 85.

24. *Essays of Michel de Montaigne*, trans. M. A. Screech (1991), 99.

25. *Complete Works of Montaigne*, trans. Donald Frame, 62.

26. "Je veux qu'on agisse et qu'on allonge les tâches de la vie autant qu'on peut, et que la mort me trouve en train de planter mes choux, mais insoucieux d'elle et encore plus de mon jardin inachevé" (Montaigne, *Essais*, trans. and ed. André Lanly, 112).

27. Nietzsche, *Twilight of the Idols/The Anti-Christ*, 51. On the influence of Montaigne on Nietzsche's own thought, see Robert B. Pippin, *Nietzsche, Psychology, and First Philosophy*; and Nicola Panichi, "Nietzsche et le 'gai scepticisme' de Montaigne."

28. Kritzman, *The Fabulous Imagination*, 36.

29. "It is a sign of contraction of the mind when it is content, or of weariness. *A generous mind never stops within itself*; it is always aspiring and going beyond its strength; it has impulses beyond its powers of achievement. If it does not advance and press forward and stand at bay and clash, it is only half alive" (III, 12, 817–18c, translation modified) ["C'est signe de racourciment d'esprit quand il se contente, ou de lasseté. *Nul esprit genereux ne s'arreste en soy*: il pretend tousjours et va outre ses forces; il a des eslans au delà de ses effects; s'il ne s'avance et ne se presse et ne s'accule et ne se choque, il n'est vif qu'à demy" (1068)]. The word "genereux" derives from the Latin *genus*, meaning of high birth, noble, and by extension, endowed with virtue — in Montaigne's formulation, the "generous mind" refers to an individual's intellectual courage to go beyond the limits and boundaries of the self.

30. Barthes, *The Neutral*, 180.

31. Pierre Charron, one of Montaigne's early disciples, rewrote and ultimately negated the motto's disrupting force, preferring the more tame and readable "I do not know" ["Je ne sçay,"] which he engraved on the title page of his revised *De la sagesse* (1604). For a comparative reading of Montaigne and Charron, see Thierry Gontier, "Charron face à Montaigne: Stratégies du scepticisme."

32. Eaglestone, *Ethical Criticism*, 139.

33. Taking Montaigne's moment of self-discovery (as an "accidental philosopher") as her point of departure, Ann Hartle systematically proceeds to elucidate the full meaning of Montaigne's observation. What emerges from her reading is a radical thinker who breaks with ancient philosophy and medieval theology. As would be expected in a book about Montaigne's philosophy, skepticism plays a major role in Hartle's positive assessment of the essayist. She asks: "Does skepticism provide us with a complete and adequate understanding of Montaigne's philosophical activity?" (Hartle, *Michel de Montaigne: Accidental Philosopher*, 15). She thinks that it does not. "Montaigne is not a skeptic," as she clearly puts it (15). Yet Hartle never really considers skepticism as something proper to the Montaignian essay, where skepticism *as such* is reducible neither to a doctrine or instrumentality. Seeing Montaigne as an *accidental theorist* is, in this respect, an attempt to imagine a kind of skepticism that would be coextensive with the unruly movement of the essay.

34. "Nothing can overcome the resistance to theory, since theory *is* itself this resistance" (Paul de Man, *The Resistance to Theory*, 19). Theory constantly returns to the particular artwork, to the ungeneralizable, resisting, and troubling the hermeneutic impulse for abstraction and mastery. See J. Hillis Miller, *Others*, 258n32.

35. "Philosophy," writes the Neoplatonist Hierocles of Alexandria, "is a purification and perfection of human life: a purification from our irrational, material nature and the mortal form of the body, a perfection by the recovery of our proper happiness, leading to divine likeness" (*The Commentary of Hierocles the Philosopher on the Pythagorean Verses*, 170). On the importance of distinguishing between Platonism (synonymous with the pursuit of systematic knowledge) and Plato (the author of aporetic/writerly texts), see Harry Berger Jr., *Situated Utterances*, 416; and Paul Allen Miller, "The Platonic Remainder," 321–41.

36. Cf. Faye, *Philosophie et perfection de l'homme*, 212.

37. Seneca, *Epistles*, 72.7. Similarly, Lawrence Kritzman describes Montaigne as a kind of theorist *avant la lettre*: "For Montaigne, philosophy is an impossible engagement since he views thought as a destabilizing agent that is open to constant revision. The essayist doubts the possibility of attaining closure in the act of interpretation.... The consequences of this phenomenon, in the quest for self-knowledge, suggest that Montaigne must theorize the human subject at the limit of the theorizable" (Kritzman, *The Fabulous Imagination*, 2).

38. "The dead must be devoured and digested before new life can ensue: culture is a form of cannibalism" (Cave, *The Cornucopian Text*, 71).

39. Du Bellay, *La Deffense et illustration de la langue françoyse*, 91, my translation.

40. The digestive metaphor originates from Seneca's *Letter 84*: "We should see to it that whatever we have absorbed should not be allowed to remain unchanged, or it will be no part of us. We must digest it; otherwise it will merely enter the memory and not the reasoning power. Let us loyally welcome such foods and *make them our own*" (84.7, emphasis added).

41. On Montaigne's putative rationalism, see Gisèle Mathieu-Castellani, *Montaigne: l'écriture de l'essai*, 222–40.

42. See Nagel, *The View from Nowhere*.

43. Montaigne also objects to the relatives' exploitation of the child's "strangeness" (538) ("estrangeté" [712]) by displaying him for money (the essayist uses the verb "monstrer" [to show], which shares an etymological link with "monster").

44. Levinas, *Time and the Other*, 50.

45. Unlike Pierre Boaistuau and other contemporaries, Montaigne does not dwell on his descriptive account of the child. He is quite resistant to saying anything about the tale: "I leave it to the doctors to discuss it" (538a) ["je laisse aux medecins d'en discourir" [712]). Montaigne merely gives an account of the physical facticity of the child, bracketing an interpretation of his extra limbs, for instance. See Boaistuau's *Histoires prodigieuses*. For well-documented accounts of the monstrous in the early modern period, see Céard, *La Nature et les prodiges*; Platt's edited volume, *Wonders, Marvels, and Monsters in Early Modern Culture*; and Williams, *Monsters and Their Meanings in Early Modern Culture*.

46. Compare with Descartes' observation: "And as I converse only with myself and look more deeply into myself, I will attempt to render myself gradually better known and familiar to myself. I am a thing that thinks." *Meditations on First Philosophy*, 23.

47. See Zahi Zalloua, *Montaigne and the Ethics of Skepticism* (Charlottesville: Rookwood Press, 2005).

48. Descartes, *The Passions of the Soul*, 58. For a rewarding analysis of the incommensurable differences between Montaigne and Descartes, see Hassan Melehy, *Writing Cogito*.

49. Miernowski, *L'Ontologie de la contraction sceptique*, 52.

2. DIDEROT'S *RAMEAU'S NEPHEW*

1. *Rameau's Nephew* was published in French in 1821 as a translation of Goethe's German text, and only first appeared in the original French in 1891. For a detailed account of the publishing history of *Rameau's Nephew* in Germany, see Roland Mortier, *Diderot en Allemagne*, 254–63.

2. For an excellent contextualization of the mind-and-body problem in the eighteenth century, see G. S. Rousseau's edited volume *The Languages of Psyche*.

3. Rabelais, *The Histories of Gargantua and Pantagruel*, 38. Rabelais also insists, however, on the ambiguity of his hermeneutic injunction, warning in the same prologue against the excesses of interpretation, against, precisely, the impulse to allegorize, that is, the impulse to seek a more "serious" meaning at the expense of the bone. Diderot's deployment of allegory is similarly playful and critical of its procedures.

4. As Derek Attridge aptly puts it, "the performance of 'allegoricity,' the pleasure taken in the event of allegorizing, is a literary phenomenon" (Attridge, *The Singularity of Literature*, 86).

5. Ethical critics — particularly of the Neo-Aristotelian and rhetorical tradition — privilege the metaphor of *books as friends*. Literary stories, according to Wayne C. Booth, are "friendship offerings," an invitation to the reader to dialogue with the author. Booth underscores the intimacy of the relation, the familiarity that grows out of the reader's interaction with the literary work. While acknowledging the strangeness of some literary works, Booth argues that what really matters is not aesthetic otherness as such but "what the reader is likely to learn about *ways of dealing with the unfamiliar or the threatening*" (Booth, *The Company We Keep*, 174, 195). Read as an uncanny "friendship offering," *Rameau's Nephew* pushes to the limits Booth's brand of ethical criticism, complicating its pedagogical co-optation at every turn.

6. Diderot, *Rameau's Nephew and Other Works*, trans. Barzun and Bowen, 8, translation modified; *Le Neveu de Rameau*, in *Contes et Romans*, 585. Henceforth all references to these editions are stated parenthetically in the text.

7. Their conversation is occasionally broken by the philosophe's narratorial asides, in which he comments on his exchange with the nephew. And although the reflections of the narrator and spoken words of *Moi* ostensibly spring from the same person, critics have rightfully pointed to modulations in voice that trouble a complete identification between the narrator and *Moi*, resulting in the presence of a "third voice." In Roland Desné's edition (*Le Neveu de Rameau: Le Rêve de d'Alembert*, for instance, such passages are italicized. I will return to the implications of the third voice below.

8. The nephew shares La Mettrie's emphasis on the effects of a good meal on the mind: "What power a meal has! It rekindles joy in a sad heart, and joy flows into the souls of guests who sing glad songs in which the French excel. Only the melancholic is overcome, and the scholar is no longer good for anything" (La Mettrie, *Man a Machine* [1748], 70).

9. Pujol, "L'Espace public du *Neveu de Rameau*," 680.

10. Bernstein, *Bitter Carnival*, 67.

11. Vartanian, "Diderot, or, the Dualist in Spite of Himself," 263.

12. "From the standpoint of Diderot's humanism ... the *Neveu de Rameau* may be read as an allegory of dualism; more precisely, it is a metonymic staging of certain philosophical ideas, in which MOI and LUI personify the two polar forces that constitute the author's psychophysical science" (Vartanian, *Science and Humanism in the French Enlightenment*, 165).

13. Vartanian, "Diderot, or, the Dualist," 265.

14. Vartanian, "Diderot, or, the Dualist," 266.

15. "A certain dignity attaches to the nature of man that nothing must destroy" (21) ["Il faut qu'il y ait une certaine dignité attachée à la nature de l'homme, que rien ne peut étouffer" (598)].

16. In contrast to the philosophe's "simple consciousness," the nephew's "distorted consciousness" has "the feeling that all its defenses have broken down, that every part of its being has been tortured on the rack and every bone broken" (Hegel, *The Phenomenology of Spirit*, 328). For interpretations of *Rameau's Nephew* that engage

Hegel's reading, see Jauss, *The Dialogical and the Dialectical Neveu de Rameau*; Hulbert, "Diderot in the Text of Hegel"; Price, "Hegel's Intertextual Dialectic"; Gearhart, "The Dialectic and Its Aesthetic Other"; and Schmidt, "The Fool's Truth."

17. Lefebvre, *Diderot ou les affirmations fondamentales du matérialisme*, 173, 250.

18. In this respect, the philosophe is more of a sovereign than the king, who still depends on his mistress and God for recognition (83/658).

19. Bernstein, *Bitter Carnival*, 70.

20. Geoffrey Bremner makes a similar remark: "The *Moi* of the *Neveu de Rameau* is not just an individual *philosophe*, or philosopher, he represents the attitude, the stance which the typical philosopher must adopt" (Bremner, *Order and Chance*, 163).

21. "I am far too clumsy to rise so high. I yield to the cranes their foggy realms. I crawl on the earth" (82) ["Je suis trop lourd pour m'élever si haut. J'abandonne aux grues le séjour des brouillards. Je vais terre à terre" (657)].

22. Descartes, *Discourse on the Method for Conducting One's Reason Well*, 1.

23. Derrida, "Cogito and the History of Madness," 41, 38. See Foucault's critical reply to Derrida, "My Body, This Paper, This Fire," originally published in 1972 as an appendix to *History of Madness* (1961), which further underscores the cultural significance of Descartes' silencing and exclusion of madness from philosophical discourse and advocates reading the latter's *Meditations* in terms of their historical and political discursive context, a context that Derridean deconstruction, he alleges, ignores. On the exchange between Foucault and Derrida, see, in particular, Bennington, "Cogito Incognito"; Boyne, *Foucault and Derrida*; Cook, "Madness and the Cogito"; D'Amico, "Text and Context"; Felman, "Madness and Philosophy or Literature's Reason"; Flynn, "Derrida and Foucault"; and Žižek, *Less Than Nothing*, 327–33.

24. Foucault, *History of Madness*, xxxiii (quoted in Derrida, *Writing and Difference*, 37). Foucault omits this formulation of an unadulterated truth about madness from his abridged 1964 preface. Cf. Hacking, "Déraison," 16.

25. Diderot's text makes a powerful appearance later in Foucault's *History of Madness*, suggesting that a dialogue with unreason after Descartes might be thought possible. This possibility is, at times, overwhelmed by Foucault's persisting impulse to see the nephew as a figure of pure transgression, as an "absolute void" (350) in modernity.

26. Early in the dialogue, the nephew takes up the mask of Diogenes (11/588), who was reportedly described by Plato as a "Socrates gone mad," or, we might say, an *unruly* Socrates, while the philosophe embraces Socrates as the *eternal sage*. Later in the text, *Moi* will make his own claim to Diogenes, and reclaim him for the Enlightenment, by endorsing the ancient Cynic's ideal of self-sufficiency [84/658]). See Laertius, *Lives of Eminent Philosophers*, 2:6.54.

27. Derrida, "Cogito and the History of Madness," 56. *Pace* Foucault, Derrida rereads the Cartesian scene as suggesting a more a precarious epistemic subject: "The hyperbolical audacity of the Cartesian Cogito, its mad audacity, which we perhaps no longer perceive as such because, unlike Descartes' contemporary, we are too well assured of ourselves and too well accustomed to the framework of the Cogito,

rather than to the critical experience of it — its mad audacity would consist in the return to an original point which no longer belongs to either a *determined* reason or a *determined* unreason, no longer belongs to them as opposition or alternative" ("Cogito and the History of Madness," 56). As Diderot's image of the philosophe highlights, the Enlightenment's *cogito* is an already all too stable and self-reassuring knowing subject.

28. Talking about his own son's education, the nephew objects as well to an idealist pedagogical regimen, one that would transform his "little savage" into a docile, socially inactive subject. The rational exercise of freedom (the capacity of the will to act in opposition to one's bodily inclinations) does not result in a state of autonomy (as Kant would later argue) but in a state of paralysis, where the self is torn by "two contrary forces" (72) ["deux forces contraires" (647)]. According to Kant, autonomy is the fulfillment of transcendental freedom, involving a free being acting independently of "the natural law of desires and inclinations" (Kant, *Grounding for the Metaphysics of Morals*, 54).

29. *Moi* can be seen as modeling his daughter's pedagogical training after the *Encyclopedia*'s definition of the philosopher: "Other men are determined to act without sensing or knowing the causes that move them, without even thinking that they might exist. By contrast, the *philosophe* sorts out these causes the best he can and sometimes even foresees them and gives himself over to them with full knowledge: he is, so to speak, a clock that sometimes winds itself.... Reason is to the *philosophe* what grace is to the Christian. Grace impels the Christian to act, while reason drives the *philosophe*" (Dumarsais, "Philosophe," in *Encyclopédie ou Dictionnaire raisonné des sciences*, 12:509, my translation). A phantasmatic investment in reason is precisely what *Lui* seeks to unmask as Enlightenment's self-mystification.

30. This expression belongs to the Cartesian François Poullain de la Barre. See his *On the Equality of the Two Sexes* (1673), 49–121.

31. Racevskis, "Michel Foucault, Rameau's Nephew, and the Question of Identity," 25.

32. Rex, *Diderot's Counterpoints*, 273.

33. Unlike Karlis Racevskis, I read the nephew's "fundamental laws of self-interest" with more skepticism (Racevskis, "Michel Foucault, Rameau's Nephew, and the Question of Identity," [26]). I share Kristeva's emphasis on the nephew's resistance to any kind of positive knowledge: "Rameau's Nephew *does not want* to settle down — he is the soul of a game that he does not want to stop, does not want to compromise, but wants only to challenge, displace, invert, shock, contradict" (Kristeva, *Strangers to Ourselves*, 135).

34. Huffer, *Mad for Foucault*, 201. Diderot gives the last words of the dialogue to *Lui*, who enigmatically comments, "he laughs best who laughs last" (87) ["rira bien qui rira le dernier" (661)].

35. The spontaneity of *Lui*'s discourse — "I have never in my life thought before speaking, nor while speaking, nor after speaking" (47) [Je n'ai pensé de ma vie ni avant que de dire, ni en disant, ni après avoir dit" (623)]) — is a mark of frankness.

36. Creech, "*Le Neveu de Rameau*: The 'Diary' of a Reading," 996. Pierre Saint-Amand similarly observes: "By virtue of playing at everyone else, Rameau is literally *nobody*; at the same time, he is the sum of their masks, which he multiplies ad infinitum" (Saint-Amand, *The Pursuit of Laziness*, 80–81).

37. Shea, *The Cynic Enlightenment*, 56.

38. Huffer, *Mad for Foucault*, 205.

39. A notable exception to this tendency is Wilda Anderson, who questions the philosophe's interpretation, reading the laughter provoked by *Lui*'s pantomime as evidence not of his failure but of his success: "It is in fact crucial for the Nephew to make MOI laugh if he wants his persuasion to succeed. Laughter is his tool" (Anderson, *Diderot's Dream*, 245).

40. Diderot, *Paradoxe du comédien*, 314, my translation.

41. Diderot, "Admiration," in *Encyclopédie*, 1:140, my translation.

42. The philosophe describes the nephew as *astonished*: "He stood motionless, dumb, astonished" (68, translation modified) ["il resta immobile, stupide, étonné" (643)].

43. "The philosophy of the enlightenment," as John S. Spink points out, "rehabilitated the passion of pity, till that time disdained and even condemned" (Spink, "Diderot et la réhabilitation de la pitié," in *Colloque international Diderot (1713–84)*, 51). For example, Jaucourt, in his article on pity for the *Encyclopedia*, defines it as a "natural" and "generous" feeling at the sight of another suffering or in a state of misery (Jaucourt, "Pitié," in *Encylopédie*, 12:662).

44. Descartes, *The Passions of the Soul*, 120.

45. As Suzanne Gearhart puts it, "in Diderot's text, these states [of pain, a lack of ease, discomfort], which are potentially those of the reader of the dialogue, are projected into it and exemplified by the *Moi*, who articulates his own conflicting pain and interest for the reader" (Gearhart, "The Dialectic and Its Aesthetic Other," 1060).

3. TRANSLATING MODERNITÉ

1. "Nothing in his work that does not tell of desolation, massacres, fire; everything bears witness against the everlasting and incorrigible barbarity of man" (Baudelaire, *Selected Writings* [sw], 378) ["Tout, dans son œuvre, n'est que désolation, massacres, incendies; tout porte témoignage contre l'éternelle et incorrigible barbarie de l'homme" (*Œuvres complètes* [OC], 2:760)]. Henceforth all references to both editions are stated parenthetically in the text.

2. Baudelaire, *The Flowers of Evil*, 31.

3. In his *Salon of 1846*, Baudelaire addresses his hypothetical bourgeois reader directly: "And so it is to you, bourgeois, that this book is naturally dedicated; for any book that does not appeal to the majority, in numbers and intelligence, is a foolish book" (sw 49, translation modified) ["C'est donc à vous, bourgeois que ce livre est naturellement dédié; car tout livre qui ne s'adresse pas à la majorité, — nombre et intelligence, — est un sot livre," (OC 2:417)]. But, as Nicole Simek points out, "the mocking tone of this piece, coupled with the unflattering portrait of the bourgeoisie's

desire for self-satisfaction seems to reveal that Baudelaire views any attempt to address this class as a constraint, an undesired necessity, even a hopeless cause" (Simek, "Baudelaire and the Problematic of the Reader," 51).

4. Baudelaire defines "beauty" in similar terms: "Beauty is made up, on the one hand, of an element that is eternal and invariable, though to determine how much of it there is is extremely difficult, and, on the other, of a relative circumstantial element, which we may like to call, successively or at one and the same time, contemporaneity, fashion, morality, passion" (392) ["Le beau est fait d'un élément éternel, invariable, dont la quantité est excessivement difficile à déterminer, et d'un élément relatif, circonstanciel, qui sera, si l'on veut, tour à tour ou tout ensemble, l'époque, la mode, la morale, la passion" (OC 2:685)].

5. Benjamin, "On Some Motifs in Baudelaire," 178.

6. Berman, *All That Is Solid Melts into Air*, 133.

7. Bruns, *On the Anarchy of Poetry and Philosophy*, 59.

8. Hiddleston, *Baudelaire and the Art of Modernity*, 223.

9. See Vincent, *Daumier and His World*, 57–60.

10. In *Further Notes on Edgar Poe*, Baudelaire writes: "Poetry cannot, under pain of death or failure, become science or morality" (204, translation modified) ["La poésie ne peut pas, sous peine de mort ou de défaillance, s'assimiler à la science ou à la morale" (OC 2:333)]. Nevertheless, several of Baudelaire's prose poems take as their subject matter the poor (for example, see also "The Bad Glazier," "The Pauper's Toy," "The Eyes of the Poor," "The Counterfeit Coin," "The Rope," and "Windows"), poems that stage ethical scenes with economically marginalized figures without falling prey to didacticism.

11. See Hannoosh, *Baudelaire and Caricature*, 117.

12. On the differences in poetics between *The Flowers of Evil* and *The Spleen of Paris*, see Barbara Johnson's landmark study, *Défigurations du langage poétique*.

13. Hiddleston, *Baudelaire and "Le Spleen de Paris,"* 84. On *The Spleen of Paris* as an unfinished work, see Compagnon, *Baudelaire devant l'innombrable*, 91.

14. Baudelaire, *The Parisian Prowler*, 129. Henceforth all references to this edition are stated parenthetically in the text.

15. Stephens, *Baudelaire's Prose Poems*, 158.

16. Žižek, *Violence*, 4.

17. Kaplan, *Baudelaire's Prose Poems*, 47. On Baudelaire's parodic rewriting of Houssaye's "The Song of the Glazier," see also Murphy, "'Le Mauvais Vitrier' ou la crise du verre"; Burton, "Destruction as Creation"; and Stephens, *Baudelaire's Prose Poems*, 75–78.

18. Scott, *Baudelaire's "Le Spleen de Paris,"* 193.

19. The narrator's last line recalls the language of Baudelaire's "The Counterfeit Coin" ("La Fausse Monnaie"), where that narrator, after discovering his friend's egotistical and self-deluding motives behind his fake act of charity, concludes: "It is never excusable to be mean, but there is some merit in knowing that you are; and the most irreparable of vices is to do evil through stupidity" (70) ["On n'est

jamais excusable d'être méchant, mais il y a quelque mérite à savoir qu'on l'est; et le plus irréparable des vices est de faire le mal par bêtise" (OC 1:324)]. While others, like the complacent glazier, merely accept a readymade mystified social reality, the narrator's mystification is self-generated and, for this reason, less ideological, even (self-delusionally?) subversive.

20. Françoise Meltzer rightly argues for the primacy of this double vision in Baudelaire's writings, in which the poet "records his encounter with modernity as an unintelligible morass of contradictions that he cannot resolve" (Meltzer, *Seeing Double*, 6).

21. While Max Milner sees Baudelaire's sympathies as clearly belonging with the poor working class, emblematized by the glazier (Milner, introduction to *Le Spleen de Paris*, 32), Richard D. E. Burton has suggestively argued that the narrator's violence toward the glazier allegorizes the poet's own frustration with *l'homme du peuple*'s lack of imagination and ineffective mode of resistance to Louis Napoleon's *coup d'état* of December 2, 1851 (the event had left Baudelaire "physically depoliticized" ["physiquement dépoliqué"], as he revealed in a letter of March 1852 [Baudelaire, *Correspondance*, 1:188]) (Burton, "Destruction as Creation," 318–19). By multiplying interpretive registers, however, Baudelaire's text short-circuits the desire for identification as well as erodes any rigid allegorical mapping. For an insightful account of Baudelaire's figuration of the poor in *The Spleen of Paris*, see Patrick Greany, *Untimely Beggar*, 24–45.

22. Similarly, Kaplan locates the poem's irony in its "double polemic directed against contrary standards: complacent didacticism or naive hedonism bereft of sensitivity" (Kaplan, *Baudelaire's Prose Poems*, 47).

23. The first of three versions of the poem was published on February 7, 1862, in *Figaro*; the second on November 1, 1864, in *L'Artiste*, and the third on June 12, 1866, in *L'Événement*. I analyze here the last version of the poem, which is also the one included in *The Spleen of Paris*. In Baudelaire criticism, the distinction between author and narrator is often blurred. The "I" who speaks in the poem shapes the image of Baudelaire, and the image of Baudelaire, who was made famous — or infamous — as a poet of evil with his 1857 work *The Flowers of Evil*, likewise shapes the perception of the poetic "I" in his poetry. This tendency to harmonize the author and the poetic voice is perhaps even stronger in Baudelaire's later prose poems, whose lack of formal structure fosters a sense of authorial self-expression. Take for example Kaplan, who, in his preface to his translation of Baudelaire's *Le Spleen de Paris*, writes: "Baudelaire's contradictory, eccentric personality does unify all fifty pieces of *The Parisian Prowler*" (Baudelaire, *The Parisian Prowler*, viii); "The narrator of Baudelaire's fables seems to typify the author's inner struggles" (Kaplan, *Baudelaire's Prose Poems*, xiii). Maria C. Scott has vigorously sought to dislodge this author-narrator identification: "My argument relies ... on the suspicion that the poet's self-representation in *Le Spleen de Paris* is crucially not to be trusted" (Scott, *Baudelaire's "Le Spleen de Paris,"* 12). While I share Scott's resistance to a conflation between poet and narrator, a categorical

and systematic separation between the two risks homogenizing Baudelaire's narrators, diminishing their complexity and seductive pull. It is perhaps more fruitful to see Baudelaire as skeptically *essaying* his modernist self through his personae or ambivalent narrators.

24. As Benjamin writes: "Empathy is the nature of the intoxication to which the flâneur abandons himself in the world" (Benjamin, "Paris, the Capital of the Nineteenth Century," 85–86).

25. Rob Shields describes the life and world of the *flâneur* as profoundly solipsistic: "This is the life of watching the world go by, not ever exchanging a word acknowledging the presence of an Other. This unethical practice ... reduces the Other to a means" (Shields, "Fancy Footwork," 77).

26. Žižek, *Violence*, 1–2.

27. Žižek, *Violence*, 2.

28. Christopher Prendergast interprets Baudelaire's dedication to Manet as a "declaration of solidarity with a certain aesthetic of *modernité*: the horrors of modern life are to be recorded with apparent indifference, with the matter-of-factness ... of a broken moral vocabulary, the loss of an available scale of 'appropriate' response to what is recorded" (Prendergast, *Paris and the Nineteenth Century*, 153).

29. In an earlier version of the poem, Baudelaire reintroduces the poet-narrator, who ends the story by mocking both the authenticity of the mother's pathos and her state of economic depravity: "My God! — I answered my friend — one meter of a hanged person's rope, at one hundred francs per decimeter, all in all, each paying according to his means, it comes to one thousand francs, a real, an efficient relief for this poor mother" ["Parbleu! — répondis-je à mon ami, — un mètre de corde de pendu, à cent francs le décimètre, l'un dans l'autre, chacun payant selon ses moyens, cela fait mille francs, un réel, un efficace soulagement pour cette pauvre mère" (OC 1:1339)]. The removal of this ending undoubtedly affects our reading of the poem. It is perhaps tempting to see this removal as an instance of hermeneutic generosity, giving more interpretive freedom to the reader. Yet, as Debarati Sanyal demonstrates, Baudelaire's suppression of this ending might also be colored by authorial anxieties, an uncomfortable *rapprochement* between poet and mother, who are both subjected to market forces: "The fate of the noose, the appraisal and circulation of its fragments, resonates with that of poetry and its circulation in the newspapers. As each decimeter of rope is worth one hundred francs, similarly, each line of Baudelaire's prose poems fetched roughly three sous apiece" (Sanyal, *The Violence of Modernity*, 93).

30. Žižek, *The Parallax View*, 354.

31. Similarly, the police inspector's observation, "Something is shady here!" (79) ["Voilà qui est louche" (330)], which is initially read as a kind of cliché to be discarded by the narrator's sympathetic reader, can be reread for its ironic potential.

32. Steve Murphy formulates the painter's suspicious economic arrangement with the child's parents in slightly different terms: "The painter's premise that he can provide a better life for the child, accepted by parents only too aware of the horrors

of poverty, is undercut by his exclusively materialistic vision of the advantages he can offer" (Murphy, "Haunting Memories," 75–76).

33. Žižek, *Violence*, 206.

34. Sanyal, *The Violence of Modernity*, 84.

4. LIVING WITH NAUSEA

1. Sartre, *Nausea*, 1; Sartre, *La Nausée*, in *Œuvres romanesques*, 5. Henceforth all references to these editions are stated parenthetically in the text.

2. Poulet, *Le Point de départ*, 227, my translation.

3. Idt, *La Nausée de Sartre*, 61, my translation. Dominick LaCapra's deconstructive reading of *Nausea* is strikingly similar in its assessment of Roquentin's identity: "The narrator is dismembered and disseminated in the text. The thinking 'I' becomes free-floating" (LaCapra, *Preface to Sartre*, 105).

4. Contat and Rybalka, "*La Nausée*: Notice, Documents, Notes et Variantes," in *Œuvres romanesques*, 1699.

5. Doubrovsky, "Sartre's *La Nausée*," 331.

6. Foucault, "What Is an Author?" in Rabinow, *The Foucault Reader*, 118.

7. "I *was* Roquentin; I used him to show, without complacency, the texture of my life" (Sartre, *The Words*, 251).

8. For Derrida, the logic of signature and countersignature attests to the split scene of interpretation: "There is as it were a duel of singularities, a duel of writing and reading, in the course of which a countersignature comes both to confirm, repeat and respect the signature of the other, of the 'original' work, and to *lead it off* elsewhere, so running the risk of *betraying* it, having to betray it in a certain way so as to respect it, through the invention of another signature just as singular" (Derrida, "This Strange Institution Called Literature," 69).

9. Sartre, *Witness to My Life*, 36.

10. As Christina Howells points out, there is an underlying sameness in all these portraits: "[Roquentin] can imagine convincingly the mentality and speeches of the right-wing *salauds* whose portraits are displayed in the museum of Bouville because they are almost interchangeable and contain no surprises" (Howells, *Sartre: The Necessity of Freedom*, 65).

11. While interpreting *Nausea* primarily in the psychoanalytical register, Andy Leak underscores with good reasons the import of the failed project of biography for Roquentin's identity: "Rollebon was far more than simply *any* project for Roquentin, he had been a paternal guarantor of the latter's identity" (Leak, "Nausea and Desire in Sartre's *La Nausée*," 68).

12. While reading Balzac's nineteenth-century realist novel *Eugénie Grandet* in the Brasserie Vézelise, Roquentin transcribes the conversation of a couple nearby that he overhears. The contrast between both languages could not be greater: Balzac's coherent and seamless narrative (Roquentin opens the novel "at random" [47] ["au hasard" (58)]) jars with the couple's fragmented, crude, and uneventful discourse.

13. Prendergast, "Of Stones and Stories," 57.
14. Sartre, *Being and Nothingness*, 338.
15. Hollier, *The Politics of Prose*, 117.
16. Žižek, *In Defense of Lost Causes*, 203.
17. Doubrovsky, "Phallotexte et gynotexte dans *La Nausée*," 52, my translation.
18. Kritzman, "To Be or Not to Be," 83.
19. Derrida, "The Ends of Man," 115n4, translation modified.
20. Foucault, "What Is Enlightenment?," 43.
21. Prince, "Roquentin et le langage naturel," 104, my translation.

22. "*We put out of action the general positing which belongs to the essence of the natural attitude*; we parenthesize everything which that positing encompasses with respect to being: thus the whole natural world which is continually 'there for us'" (Husserl, *Ideas Pertaining to a Pure Phenomenology*, §32).

23. "Mastery begins ... through the power of naming, of imposing and legitimating appellations" (Derrida, *Monolingualism of the Other*, 39).

24. Bertrand, "L'objet selon Sartre."

25. LaCapra rightly interprets Roquentin's uncanny experience as not so much generated by the experience of radical contingency as by the "vertiginous ambiguity in the interplay of 'opposites' that cannot be definitively stabilized or fixated as pure opposites" (LaCapra, *Preface to Sartre*, 112).

26. Sartre, *Being and Nothingness*, 83.

27. What is at stake here is more than the disciplinary distinctions between literature and philosophy highlighted by Marc Bertrand ("In literature, the inanity of contingency is an effect that one exaggerates and does not control; in philosophy, it is a concept that one uses" [Bertrand, "L'objet selon Sartre," 13]). *Nausea*'s exaggerations of the meaninglessness of contingency are equally instances of hermeneutic defiance. Instrumentalization is not just a concern for philosophy but one it shares with literary criticism.

28. Robbe-Grillet, *For a New Novel*, 53.
29. Robbe-Grillet, *For a New Novel*, 62.
30. Sartre, *The Words*, 32.

31. At times, Roquentin does show himself more hospitable to language's potential to say more. While eating lunch with the Self-Taught Man, for example, Roquentin illustrates the elasticity of the word "heroism" by lifting it from its humanist context (its original semantic field) and putting it in play in a much less "serious" one. He succeeds in linking the Self-Taught Man's assertion that he finds "'an enormous amount of heroism'" ["'une immensité d'héroïsme'"] in Roquentin's attitude toward the human condition, with a dessert order: "'Cheese,' I say heroically" (121) ["'Un fromage,' dis-je avec héroïsme" (143)]. Delighting in his subversion of the Self-Taught Man's authoritative humanist discourse, this Roquentin deviates from the traditional model of the philosopher.

32. Žižek, *How to Read Lacan*, 72.

33. Cf. Prince, "Roquentin et le langage naturel," 109.

34. *Nausea* dramatizes here the antiphenomenological insight that perception is not pure nor primordial, that, in the words of Derrida, "perception does not exist," that "there never was any 'perception'" (Derrida, *Speech and Phenomena*, 45n4, 103).

35. Flaubert, *Selected Letters*, 127–28.

36. Keefe, "The Ending of Sartre's *La Nausée*," 198–99.

37. Keefe, "The Ending of Sartre's *La Nausée*," 184, emphasis added.

38. Manser, *Sartre: A Philosophical Study*, 3. Critics have also dismissed *Nausea*'s ending for its lack of philosophical sophistication, seeing it as "merely sketched in" (Murdoch, *Sartre: Romantic Rationalist*).

39. LaCapra, *Preface to Sartre*, 114.

5. INTOXICATING MEANING

1. Quoted in Robbe-Grillet's "Order and Disorder in Film and Fiction," 3.

2. Robbe-Grillet's main target is Balzac's nineteenth-century brand of realism, which assumes a Godlike narrator: "Who is describing the world in Balzac's novels? Who is that omniscient, omnipresent narrator appearing everywhere at once, simultaneously seeing the outside and the inside of things, following both the movements of a face and the impulses of conscience, knowing the present, the past, and the future of every enterprise? It can only be a God" (Robbe-Grillet, *For a New Novel*, 138–39). For a rewarding contextualization of the *nouveau roman*, see Edmund J. Smyth's "The *Nouveau Roman*: Modernity and Postmodernity."

3. Robbe-Grillet, *For a New Novel*, 33. Robbe-Grillet's language here echoes that of Sartre's in *What is Literature?*, originally published in 1947: "The novels of our elders related the event as having taken place in the past. Chronological order permitted the reader to see the logical and universal relationship, the eternal verities. The slightest change was already understood. A past was delivered to us which had already been thought through" (Sartre, *What Is Literature? and Other Essays*, 185).

4. Robbe-Grillet, *For a New Novel*, 21.

5. Rabinowitz, "Assertion and Assumption," 413.

6. Morrissette, *The Novels of Robbe-Grillet*, 112–13.

7. Jameson, "Modernism and Its Repressed," 169.

8. Leenhardt, *Lecture politique du roman*, 25–26.

9. While the novel's geographical location is never stated, it is reasonable to assume from the description of the climate and vegetation that it most likely takes place in the Caribbean or Africa.

10. Robbe-Grillet, *Jealousy* (1965), 52; *La Jalousie* (1957), 35–36. Henceforth all references to these editions are stated parenthetically in the text.

11. Leenhardt, *Lecture politique du roman*, 55, my translation.

12. Robbe-Grillet has also encouraged the identification between the narrator and the jealous husband in interviews: "In *La Jalousie* we see a narrator, an adult, Caucasian male who tries to maintain order. Moreover, he's a colonial plantation owner,

that is, he belongs to the colonial system. Against him, limiting and destroying his power, we have the blacks, tropical vegetation, and his own wife, who is suspected of maintaining a questionable relationship with the subversive world" (Robbe-Grillet, "Images and Texts: A Dialogue," 43).

13. Blanchot, *The Book to Come*, 261n1.
14. Blanchot, *The Book to Come*, 201.
15. Blanchot, *The Book to Come*, 208.
16. Foucault, "Maurice Blanchot," 11.
17. Foucault, "Maurice Blanchot," 15.
18. Quoted in Oppenheim, *Three Decades of the French New Novel*, 26, emphasis added.
19. *La Jalousie* is in this respect exemplary of Robbe-Grillet's novels, which as Stephen Heath points out, are "to be read at the level of their irretrievability, precisely, that is, at the level at which *reading* is posed as a problem and explored as such" (Heath, *The Nouveau Roman*, 67).
20. Ricardou, *Problèmes du nouveau roman*, 111.
21. Robbe-Grillet, *For a New Novel*, 19, 58.
22. Barthes, *Critical Essays*, 15. This emphasis on objects earned Robbe-Grillet the label of an antihumanist *chosiste* (a champion of things [*choses*]) from Barthes, among others.
23. Robbe-Grillet, *For a New Novel*, 137–39.
24. Jefferson, *The Nouveau Roman and the Poetics of Fiction*, 136.
25. Similarly, Lucien Dällenbach interprets *La Jalousie* as foreclosing any privileged or monolithic approach to the novel: "We do not have to choose here between a phenomenological (realistic) reading and a formal one . . . it would be reductive and anachronistic only to consider one of them" (Dällenbach, *The Mirror in the Text*, 131).
26. Silverman, *The Threshold of the Visible World*, 23, 3.
27. Barthes, *Critical Essays*, 198. Robbe-Grillet advances his own version of *two Robbe-Grillets*: "I never know whether I am Socrates or the Sophist. Or both at once: the one who believes in something and tries to communicate it, and the one who doesn't really believe in it, who manipulates discourse shamelessly in order to make it say one thing and the opposite" (Robbe-Grillet, *Le Voyageur*, 435, my translation).
28. Morrisette, *The Novels of Robbe-Grillet*, 117.
29. Morrisette, *The Novels of Robbe-Grillet*, 117.
30. Blanchot, *The Space of Literature*, 32.
31. Blanchot, *The Space of Literature*, 32.
32. Blanchot, *The Space of Literature*, 33.
33. Blanchot, *The Space of Literature*, 25.
34. Blanchot, *The Space of Literature*, 32.
35. Before Robbe-Grillet, Marcel Proust had recorded the devastating and disrupting effects of jealousy: "It is one of the faculties of jealousy," writes the narrator of *Remembrance of Things Past*, "to reveal to us the extent to which the reality of external

facts and the sentiments of the heart are an unknown element which lends itself to endless suppositions. We suppose that we know exactly what things are and what people think, for the simple reason that we do not care about them. But as soon as we feel the desire to know, which the jealous man feels, then it becomes a dizzy kaleidoscope in which we can no longer make out anything" (Proust, *Remembrance of Things Past*, 747). Jealousy is characterized by its limitlessness: "My jealous curiosity as to what Albertine might have done was unbounded [*infinie*]" (740). In *Jealousy*, however, Robbe-Grillet denies his narrator such reflective or meditative moments where the thematization of his jealous state could take place. Such resistance to psychologization — again dramatized by the absence of an "I" — sets Robbe-Grillet apart from his influential predecessor.

36. Robbe-Grillet, *For a New Novel*, 73.
37. Barthes, *Critical Essays*, 14.
38. Robbe-Grillet comments elsewhere on the New Novelists' affinities with Foucault: "In part, it is our novels that brought about Foucault's reflections on man (and Foucault himself has drawn attention to this). We were almost creating a new philosophy that we ourselves were unaware of, not only as a coherent philosophy, but as any sort of conceptualization of anything" (Robbe-Grillet, "Discussion avec Jean Alter, Renato Barilli, Joseph Duhamel, Françoise Gaillard, G. W. Ireland, Jean Ricardou, Alain Robbe-Grillet, Karlheinz Stierle," 128; my translation).
39. This is a telling example of the ways in which Robbe-Grillet's novel transgresses norms of readability and disrupts ideological complacency. As he says, "*La Jalousie* is an ordered system of extremely high character, extreme complexity, and extreme interest in its opposition to society's view of narrative probability" (Robbe-Grillet, "Order and Disorder in Film and Fiction," 5).
40. For Blanchot, the reader, as "specialist," "interrogates the work in order to know how it was fashioned. He asks it the secrets and the conditions of its creation, and examines it closely to see whether it answers adequately to these conditions, etc. The reader, having become the specialist, becomes an author in reverse" (Blanchot, *Space of Literature*, 203). Barthes similarly describes the reader as searching for secrets. For the specialist, in Barthes's words, "the Robbe Grillet novel is ... [an object] full of secrets; criticism must then begin scrutinizing what is behind this object and around it: it seeks 'keys' (and usually finds them)" (Barthes, *Critical Essays*, 202).
41. Gibson, *Postmodernity, Ethics, and the Novel*, 192.
42. Blanchot, *The Infinite Conversation*, 320.
43. Blanchot, *The Writing of Disaster*, 101.
44. Kearney, "Dialogue with Emmanuel Levinas," 58.
45. Attridge, *The Singularity of Literature*, 130.
46. Robbe-Grillet's "Order and Disorder in Film and Fiction," 12.
47. The novel establishes a certain proximity between A ... and the colonized other: "A ... is humming a dance tune whose words remain unintelligible" (49) ["A ... fredonne un air de danse, dont les paroles demeurent inintelligibles" (29)].

On the relation between A... and the world of the colonized, see Leenhardt, *Lecture politique du roman*, 99; and Lane, "The Stain, the Impotent Gaze, and the Theft of Jouissance," 202.

48. Jefferson, *The Nouveau Roman and the Poetics of Fiction*, 139.
49. Jameson, "Modernism and Its Repressed," 177.
50. "There *is* pure a-grammaticality but as soon as it appears as such, or as it enters a text or a situation, it starts to become grammatical" (Derrida, "Following Theory," 13).
51. Attridge, *The Singularity of Literature*, 49.
52. Robbe-Grillet, "Order and Disorder in Film and Fiction," 18–19.
53. Robbe-Grillet, "Order and Disorder in Film and Fiction," 11.

6. FIDELITY TO SEXUAL DIFFERENCE

1. Levinas, *Time and the Other*, 50.
2. Beauvoir, *The Second Sex*, 6n3.
3. Beauvoir, *The Second Sex*, 6.
4. For a lucid overview of Levinas's reception among feminist critics, see Tina Chanter's edited volume, *Feminist Interpretations of Emmanuel Levinas*; and Chanter, *Time, Death, and the Feminine*.
5. For example, Sonia Sikka "question[s] the notion of alterity, or at least *radical* alterity, as a model for either ethics in general or feminism in particular" (Sikka, "The Delightful Other," 97). See also Sandford, "Levinas, Feminism and the Feminine."
6. Irigaray, *This Sex Which Is Not One*, 74.
7. Irigaray, *This Sex Which Is Not One*, 78. See also Ziarek, "The Ethical Passion of Emmanuel Levinas."
8. Irigaray, *This Sex Which Is Not One*, 78.
9. Irigaray, *This Sex Which Is Not One*, 26.
10. Whitford, *Luce Irigaray*, 45.
11. Sheringham, "Knowledge and Repetition in *Le Ravissement de Lol V. Stein*," 139n8.
12. Leslie Hill attests to the dominance of the psychoanalytic framework in the reception of Duras's novel: "To this day, *Le Ravissement de Lol V. Stein* is the text of Duras's which has given rise to the greatest amount of critical commentary. Much of this, largely in the wake of Lacan, has been framed by issues derived either from psychoanalytic theory or from feminism, if not from both, and questions of desire, sexual difference, and gender identity loom large in discussions of the novel" (Hill, "Lacan with Duras," 147). Levinas's presence in these debates has been largely negligible. Critics of the novel inclined to develop an ethical reading of *The Ravishing of Lol Stein* have pursued the feminist and/or psychoanalytic route. Martin Crowley makes brief but insightful observations about the affinities between Duras and Levinas in relation to the ethical. See Crowley, *Duras, Writing, and the Ethical*.
13. Levinas, *Totality and Infinity*, 84.
14. Irigaray, "What Other Are We Talking About?," 69.
15. Lacan, "Homage to Marguerite Duras, on *Le ravissement de Lol V. Stein*," 17.

16. This affinity between the two Jacques (which extends beyond their shared name to their shared medical training) results from a dubious affective economy. It is suggested that Hold is a psychiatrist: "I'm thirty-six years old, a member of the medical profession. I've been living in South Tahla only for a year. I'm in Peter Beugner's section at the State Hospital" (Duras, *The Ravishing of Lol Stein* [1986], 66) ["Trente-six ans, je fais partie du corps médical. Il n'y a qu'un an que je suis arrivé à S. Tahla. Je suis dans le service de Pierre Beugner à l'Hôpital départemental" (*Le Ravissement de Lol V. Stein* [1964], 75)]. The English edition omits Lol's middle initial, V., from the novel's title. Henceforth all references to these editions are stated parenthetically in the text.

17. Lacan, "Homage to Marguerite Duras," 18.

18. Jardine, *Gynesis*, 175.

19. Lacan's interview with Duras, quoted in Kaivola, "Marguerite Duras and the Subversion of Power," 125.

20. Jardine, *Gynesis*, 176, emphasis added.

21. Jardine, *Gynesis*, 174–75.

22. See Fuss's *Essentially Speaking*, 23–37.

23. Alice Jardine highlights the gender-oriented matter of Duras's works: "[Duras] never fails to emphasize that her texts and films are, above all, *about* women" (175).

24. Evans, *Masks of Tradition*, 125.

25. Evans, *Masks of Tradition*, 138.

26. Edson, "Knowing Lol," 30.

27. Jardine, *Gynesis*, 173.

28. Edson, "Knowing Lol," 19.

29. It should be noted that sexual identification is a necessary but not sufficient condition of Jardine's version of feminism, since she distinguishes between feminist (nonanalyst) readings and psychoanalytical readings produced by women readers who "valorize Lol as character in one way or another" (176).

30. Jardine, *Gynesis*, 176.

31. Martha Noel Evans makes a similar totalizing claim about male discourse: "The author must of necessity seek to replace and destroy the female subject" (141). It is unfortunate that Duras herself contributes to this kind of gender reductionism: "They [men] all live with a nostalgia or longing for violence.... There's a marine in every man" (Duras and Gauthier, *Woman to Woman*, 17).

32. Edson, "Knowing Lol," 20.

33. Edson, "Knowing Lol," 16.

34. Edson, "Knowing Lol," 20.

35. Ricoeur, *Freud and Philosophy*, 33.

36. Ricoeur, *Freud and Philosophy*, 33.

37. To be sure, Jardine's hermeneutic feminist model still relies a bit on a "hermeneutics of faith" to the extent that a restoration of Lol's voice through identification (responding to Duras's Saying, that is, to her invitation to dialogue) remains possible.

Such a faith is not shared by the other feminist camp, who takes the point of the novel to be not to identify with Lol but to criticize Jacques.

38. Levinas, *Otherwise than Being*, 7.

39. As does Evans: "Jacques Hold's narrative embodies the principles and values of male literary tradition, a tradition that includes a territorial, if not proprietary, notion of language, an authoritarian concept of authorship" (Evans, *Masks of Tradition*, 140).

40. Van Noort, "The Dance of the Signifier," 191.

41. Glassman, *Marguerite Duras*, 128n18.

42. One is reminded of Levinas's essay "The Other in Proust," in which Levinas associates mystery with the question of the other ("The mystery in Proust is the mystery of the other" [*Proper Names*, 102]). Here, as in the case of Lol, Albertine embodies a "deep strangeness" that remains unknowable or ungraspable to Marcel (Jacques's male counterpart); it "laughs in the face of knowledge," producing in him "an insatiable curiosity about the alterity of the other, at once empty and inexhaustible" (103).

43. See Laplanche, "Psychoanalysis as Anti-Hermeneutics," 8. While Levinas was usually hostile to the discourse of psychoanalysis, Laplanche's practice strikes me as fruitful for a potential *rapprochement* between Levinas and psychoanalysis.

44. Cf. Ziarek, *An Ethics of Dissensus*, 167.

45. Toward the end of the novel, in the hotel at T. Beach where Lol and Jacques spend the night together after their visit to the casino, the famous site of the ball, Lol troubles her own linguistic designation by referring to herself as both Tatiana and Lol: "There was no longer any difference between her and Tatiana Karl except in her eyes, free of remorse, and in the way she referred to herself... and in the two names she gave herself: Tatiana Karl and Lol Stein" (179) ["Il n'y a plus eu de différence entre elle et Tatiana Karl sauf dans ses yeux exempts de remords et dans la désignation qu'elle faisait d'elle-même... et dans les deux noms qu'elle se donnait: Tatiana Karl et Lol V. Stein" (189)]. Yet unlike Jacques's indexical bewilderment, Lol's implicates an other, opening her to the charge of deploying the same kind of assimilative logic displayed (at times) by her male counterpart. However, Lol's paradoxical identification with Tatiana exceeds a strict exercise of power, since it does not so much buttress Lol's identity — nor expand her ego boundary (her self-*sameness*) at the expense of Tatiana's otherness — as expose its malleability to the maddening point of self-dissolution. Lol's act of name-giving "frees" her from the principle of identity: Lol *is not* Lol, or in Irigarayan terms, Lol "is" both less and more than one.

46. Levinas, "Substitution," 183n44.

47. Suleiman, *Subversive Intent*, 231.

48. According to Lacan, the "subject supposed to know" does not designate the analyst as such but rather denotes his function in the treatment, referring to the analysand's view of the analyst as a figure of absolute certainty, possessing knowledge of the patient's secret meaning or unconscious desire: "He is supposed to know that from which no one can escape, as soon as he formulates it — quite simply, signification"

(Lacan, *The Seminar, Book XI: The Four Fundamental Concepts of Psychoanalysis*, 233). Transference is made possible by the analysand's (mis)identification of the analyst as a "subject supposed to know." In *Ravishing*, Duras complicates this staging of the clinical encounter, as she declines or suspends Jacques's function as a "subject supposed to know," making him, in turn, far more vulnerable to the centrifugal dynamics of transference (cf. Suleiman, *Subversive Intent*, 116; and Russell-Watt, "The Terrors and Pleasure of Analysis," 126).

49. Suleiman, *Subversive Intent*, 116. "We see emerging the possibility of a psychoanalytic discourse that would not be a discourse of mastery but a discourse of mutual entanglement" (117–18).

50. Evans, *Masks of Tradition*, 131.

51. McPherson, *Incriminations*, 71.

52. Levinas, "Reality and Its Shadow," 139.

53. Lacan, "Homage to Marguerite Duras," 20. On the narrative level, the last paragraph of the novel registers Jacques's ambivalent hermeneutics. Waiting for Tatiana in L'Hôtel des Bois, Jacques perceives Lol in the rye field, and comments: "Lol had arrived there ahead of us. She was asleep in the field of rye, worn out, worn out by our trip" (181) ["Lol nous avait précédés. Elle dormait dans le champ de seigle, fatiguée, fatiguée par notre voyage" (191)]. Lacking unequivocal closure — the narrative could go on indefinitely — Jacques Hold's narration sustains and prolongs Lol's enigmaticity, suspending, as it were, his desire to contain or normalize Lol, or to "save" her from her ravishment (Lacan, "Homage to Marguerite Duras," 20). This resistance to a recuperative logic, to a lack of "cathartic potential," as Kristeva describes it, characterizes Duras's art, reflecting the ways her aesthetics sabotages any readerly desire for appropriable meaning (Kristeva, *Black Sun*, 228).

54. "Writing isn't just telling stories. It's exactly the opposite. It's telling everything at once. It's telling of a story, and the absence of the story. It's telling a story through its absence" (Duras, *Practicalities*, 27).

55. Likewise, to Jacques's question, "But what is it you want?" (102) ["Mais qu'est-ce que vous voulez?" (112)], Lol answers unexpectedly, "I want" (102) ["Je veux" (112)], registering her noncompliance with his mode of inquiry. Cf. Cixous, "Castration or Decapitation?," 45.

56. Levinas, *Otherwise than Being*, 167.

CONCLUSION

1. Nussbaum, "Compassion and Terror," 24.
2. Nussbaum, *Love's Knowledge*, 184, emphasis added.
3. Nussbaum, *Love's Knowledge*, 142.
4. Nussbaum, "Compassion and Terror," 26.
5. Nussbaum, *Upheavals of Thought*, 414.
6. Gadamer, "Text and Interpretation," 27.
7. Gadamer, "Text and Interpretation," 41, 27.

8. Gadamer, "Text and Interpretation," 33.

9. "Conversation should seek its partner everywhere," writes Gadamer, "just because this partner is other, and especially if the other is completely different. Whoever . . . insists on difference stands at the beginning of a conversation, not at its end" (Gadamer, "'Destruktion' and Deconstruction," 113).

10. Derrida, "Three Questions to Hans-Georg Gadamer," 52, 53.

11. Derrida, *Aporias*, 16.

12. Derrida, "Autoimmunity," 90.

13. Derrida, "Rams: Uninterrupted Dialogue," 149.

14. Jameson, *Valences of the Dialectic*, 59.

15. Incompleteness — the knowledge that we "will never be completely done with the text," as Gadamer readily admits ("Reply to Jacques Derrida," 57) — cannot simply be conceded, but must be actively practiced, must be pursued in its becoming.

16. See Nobus, "Locating Perversion, Dislocating Psychoanalysis," 5.

17. Barthes, *Critical Essays*, 203.

Works Cited

Abbott, H. Porter. *The Cambridge Introduction to Narrative*. Cambridge: Cambridge University Press, 2002.
Adorno, Theodor. "The Essay as Form." Translated by Bob Hullot-Kentor and Frederic Will. *New German Critique* 32 (1984): 151–71.
———. *Negative Dialectics*. Translated by E. B. Ashton. London: Routledge and Kegan Paul, 1973.
Alter, Robert. *The Pleasures of Reading in an Ideological Age*. New York: Simon and Schuster, 1989.
Anderson, Wilda. *Diderot's Dream*. Baltimore: Johns Hopkins University Press, 1990.
Attridge, Derek. *J. M. Coetzee and the Ethics of Reading: Literature in the Event*. Chicago: University of Chicago Press, 2004.
———. *The Singularity of Literature*. New York: Routledge, 2004.
Badiou, Alain. *Ethics: An Essay on the Understanding of Evil*. Translated by Peter Hallward. New York: Verso, 2001.
———. *Manifesto for Philosophy*. Translated by Norman Madarasz. Albany: SUNY Press, 1999.
———. *Saint Paul: The Foundation of Universalism*. Translated by Ray Brassier. Stanford CA: Stanford University Press, 2003.
———. "Thinking the Event." In Engelmann, *Philosophy in the Present*, 1–48.
Bakhtin, Mikhail. *Art and Answerability: Early Philosophical Essays*. Edited by Michael Holquist and Vadim Liapunov. Translated by Vadim Liapunov. Austin: University of Texas Press, 1990.
———. *Speech Genres and Other Late Essays*. Edited by Caryl Emerson and Michael Holquist. Translated by Vern W. McGee. Austin: University of Texas Press, 1986.
Baldwin, Jon, and Nick Haeffner, eds. "'Fault Lines': Simon Critchley in Discussion on Alain Badiou." *Polygraph* 17 (2005): 295–307.

Barthes, Roland. *Critical Essays*. Translated by Richard Howard. Evanston IL: Northwestern University Press, 1972.

———. *The Neutral: Lecture Course at the Collège de France (1977–1978)*. Translated by Rosalind E. Krauss and Denis Hollier. New York: Columbia University Press, 2005.

———. *The Pleasure of the Text*. Translated by Richard Miller. New York: Noonday Press, 1975.

———. *S/Z*. Translated by Richard Miller. New York: Hill and Wang, 1974.

Bataille, Georges. *On Nietzsche*. Translated by Bruce Boone. London: Continuum, 2004.

Baudelaire, Charles. *Baudelaire: Selected Writings on Art and Literature*. Translated by P. E. Charvet. London: Penguin Books, 1972.

———. *Correspondance*, vol. 1. Edited by Claude Pichois and Jean Ziegler. Bibliothèque de la Pléiade. Gallimard: Paris, 1973.

———. *The Flowers of Evil*. Translated by James McGowan. Oxford: Oxford University Press, 1993.

———. *Œuvres complètes*. Edited by Claude Pichois. 2 vols. Bibliothèque de la Pléiade. Paris: Gallimard, 1975–76.

———. *The Parisian Prowler*. Translated by Edward K. Kaplan. Athens: University of Georgia Press, 1989.

Beauvoir, Simone de. *The Second Sex*. Translated by Constance Borde and Sheila Malovany-Chevallier. New York: Alfred Knopf, 2010.

Beckett, Samuel. *Worstward Ho*. London: Calder, 1983.

Benjamin, Walter. "On Some Motifs in Baudelaire." Translated by Harry Zohn. In Jennings, *The Writer of Modern Life*, 170–210.

———. "Paris, the Capital of the Nineteenth Century." Translated by Harry Zohn. In Jennings, *The Writer of Modern Life*, 30–45.

Bennington, Geoffrey. "Cogito Incognito: Foucault's 'My Body, This Paper, This Fire.'" *Oxford Literary Review* 4, no. 1 (1979): 5–8.

Berger, Harry Jr. *Situated Utterances: Texts, Bodies, and Cultural Representations*. New York: Fordham University Press, 2005.

Berman, Marshall. *All That Is Solid Melts into Air: The Experience of Modernity*. New York: Simon and Schuster, 1982.

Bernstein, Michael. *Bitter Carnival: Ressentiment and the Abject Hero*. Princeton NJ: Princeton University Press, 1992.

Bertrand, Marc. "L'objet selon Sartre: de l'état sauvage à l'humanisation forcée — et retour?" *Etudes Sartriennes* 5 (1985): 7–24.

Blanchot, Maurice. *The Book to Come*. Translated by Charlotte Mandell. Stanford CA: Stanford University Press, 2003.

———. *The Infinite Conversation*. Translated by Susan Hanson. Minneapolis: University of Minnesota Press, 1993.

———. *The Space of Literature*. Translated by Ann Smock. Lincoln: University of Nebraska Press, 1982.

———. *The Writing of the Disaster*. Translated by Ann Smock. Lincoln: University of Nebraska Press, 1995.
Boaistuau, Pierre. *Histoires prodigieuses*. Edited by Gisèle Mathieu-Castellani. Geneva: Slatkine, 1996.
Booth, Wayne. *The Company We Keep: An Ethics of Fiction*. Berkeley: University of California Press, 1988.
Bourdieu, Pierre. *Distinction: A Social Critique of the Judgement of Taste*. Translated by Richard Rice. Cambridge MA: Harvard University Press, 1984.
Boyne, Roy. *Foucault and Derrida: The Other Side of Reason*. London: Unwin Hyman, 1990.
Bremner, Geoffrey. *Order and Chance: The Patterns of Diderot's Thought*. Cambridge: Cambridge University Press, 1983.
Breton, André. *Nadja*. Translated by Richard Howard. New York: Grove Press, 1960.
Bruns, Gerald L. *On the Anarchy of Poetry and Philosophy: A Guide for the Unruly*. New York: Fordham University Press, 2006.
Buell, Lawrence, ed. "Ethics and Literary Study." Special issue, PMLA (January 1999).
Burton, Richard D. E. "Destruction as Creation: 'Le Mauvais Vitrier' and the Poetics and Politics of Violence." *Romanic Review* 83, no. 3 (1992): 297–322.
Cave, Terence. *The Cornucopian Text: Problems of Writing in the French Renaissance*. Oxford: Clarendon Press, 1979.
———. *How to Read Montaigne*. London: Granta Books, 2007.
Céard, Jean. *La Nature et les prodiges: l'Insolite au XVIe siècle, en France*. Geneva: Droz, 1977.
Chanter, Tina, ed. *Feminist Interpretations of Emmanuel Levinas*. University Park: Pennsylvania State University Press, 2001.
———. *Time, Death, and the Feminine: Levinas with Heidegger*. Stanford CA: Stanford University Press, 2001.
Cixous, Hélène. "Castration or Decapitation?" Translated by Annette Kuhn. *Signs* 7, no. 1 (1981): 41–55.
Compagnon, Antoine. *Baudelaire devant l'innombrable*. Paris: Presses Universitaires de la Sorbonne, 2003.
———. *Chat en poche*. Paris: Éditions du Seuil, 1993.
Conley, Tom. "Mapping Montaigne: The 'Apologie' as Diagram and Discourse." *Montaigne Studies* 6, nos. 1–2 (1994): 63–85.
Contat, Michel, and Michel Rybalka, eds. *Œuvres romanesques*, by Jean-Paul Sartre. Bibliothèque de la Pléiade. Paris: Gallimard, 1981.
Cook, Deborah. "Madness and the Cogito: Derrida's Critique of *Folie et Déraison*." *Journal of the British Society for Phenomenology* 21, no. 2 (1990): 164–74.
Creech, James. "*Le Neveu de Rameau*: The 'Diary' of a Reading." *Modern Language Notes* 95, no. 4 (1980): 995–1004.
Critchley, Simon. *Infinitely Demanding: Ethics of Commitment, Politics of Resistance*. New York: Verso, 2007.
Crowley, Martin. *Duras, Writing, and the Ethical: Making the Broken Whole*. Oxford: Clarendon Press, 2000.

Dällenbach, Lucien. *The Mirror in the Text*. Translated by Jeremy Whiteley and Emma Hughes. Chicago: University of Chicago Press, 1989.

D'Amico, Robert. "Text and Context: Derrida and Foucault on Descartes." In *The Structural Allegory: Reconstructive Encounters with the New French Thought*, edited by John Fekete, 164–82. Minneapolis: University of Minnesota Press, 1984.

Davis, Colin. *Critical Excess: Overreading in Derrida, Deleuze, Levinas, Žižek, and Cavell*. Stanford CA: Stanford University Press, 2010.

Davis, Todd, and Kenneth Womack, eds. *Mapping the Ethical Turn: A Reader in Ethics, Culture, and Literary Theory*. Charlottesville: University Press of Virginia, 2001.

Dean, Tim. "Art as Symptom: Žižek and the Ethics of Psychoanalytic Criticism." *Diacritics* 32, no. 2 (2002): 20–41.

Deleuze, Gilles. *Difference and Repetition*. Translated by Paul Patton. New York: Columbia University Press, 1994.

de Man, Paul. *The Resistance to Theory*. Minneapolis: University of Minnesota Press, 1986.

Derrida, Jacques. *Adieu to Emmanuel Levinas*. Translated by Pascale-Anne Brault and Michael Naas. Stanford CA: Stanford University Press, 1999.

———. *Aporias*. Translated by Thomas Dutoit. Stanford CA: Stanford University Press, 1993.

———. *Archive Fever: A Freudian Impression*. Translated by Eric Prenowitz. Chicago: University of Chicago Press, 1995.

———. "Autoimmunity: Real and Symbolic Suicides: A Dialogue with Jacques Derrida." In *Philosophy in a Time of Terror: Dialogues with Jürgen Habermas and Jacques Derrida*, edited by Giovanna Borradori, 85–136. Chicago: University of Chicago Press, 2003.

———. "Cogito and the History of Madness." In *Writing and Difference*, translated by Alan Bass, 31–63. Chicago: University of Chicago Press, 1978.

———. "'Eating Well,' or the Calculation of the Subject: An Interview with Jacques Derrida." In *Who Comes after the Subject?*, edited by Eduardo Cadava, Peter Connor, and Jean-Luc Nancy, 96–119. New York: Routledge, 1991.

———. "The Ends of Man." In *Margins of Philosophy*, translated by Alan Bass, 109–36. Chicago: University of Chicago Press, 1982.

———. "Following Theory." In *life.after.theory*, edited by Michael Payne and John Schad, 1–51. New York: Continuum, 2003.

———. "Force of Law: The 'Mystical Foundation of Authority.'" In *Acts of Religion*, edited by Gil Anidjar, 230–300. New York: Routledge, 2002.

———. *The Gift of Death*. Translated by David Wills. Chicago: University of Chicago Press, 1995.

———. *Of Grammatology*. Translated by Gayatri Chakravorty Spivak. Baltimore: Johns Hopkins University Press, 1976.

———. *Monolingualism of the Other; or, The Prosthesis of Origin*. Translated by Patrick Mensah. Stanford CA: Stanford University Press, 1998.

———. *Psyche: Inventions of the Other*, vol. 1. Edited by Peggy Kamuf and Elizabeth Rottenberg. Stanford CA: Stanford University Press, 2007.

———. "Rams: Uninterrupted Dialogue — Between Two Infinities, the Poem." In *Sovereignties in Question: The Poetics of Paul Celan*, edited by Thomas Dutoit and Outi Pasanen, 135–63. New York: Fordham University Press, 2005.

———. *Rogues: Two Essays on Reason*. Translated by Pascale-Anne Brault and Michael Naas. Stanford CA: Stanford University Press, 2005.

———. *Speech and Phenomena and Other Essays on Husserl's Theory of Signs*. Translated by David B. Allison. Evanston IL: Northwestern University Press, 1973.

———. "Structure, Sign, and Play in the Discourse of the Human Sciences." In *Writing and Difference*, 278–93. Translated by Alan Bass. Chicago: University of Chicago Press, 1978.

———. "This Strange Institution Called Literature." In *Acts of Literature*, edited by Derek Attridge, 33–75. New York: Routledge, 1992.

———. "Three Questions to Hans-Georg Gadamer." Translated by Diane P. Michelfelder and Richard Palmer. In Michelfelder and Palmer, *Dialogue and Deconstruction*, 52–54.

———. "'To Do Justice to Freud': The History of Madness in the Age of Psychoanalysis." Translated by Pascale-Anne Brault and Michael Naas. *Critical Inquiry* 20, no. 2 (1994): 227–66.

———. "Violence and Metaphysics." In *Writing and Difference*. Translated by Alan Bass, 79–153. Chicago: University of Chicago Press, 1978.

———. *The Work of Mourning*. Edited by Pascale-Anne Brault and Michael Naas. Chicago: University of Chicago Press, 2001.

Descartes, René. *Discourse on the Method for Conducting One's Reason Well and Seeking Truth in the Sciences*. Translated by Donald A. Cress. Indianapolis: Hackett Publishing Company, 1998.

———. *Meditations on First Philosophy*. Translated by Donald A. Cress. Indianapolis: Hackett Publishing Company, 1979.

———. *The Passions of the Soul*. Translated by Stephen Voss. Indianapolis: Hackett Publishing Company, 1989.

Diderot, Denis. "Admiration." In Diderot and d'Alembert, *Encyclopédie*, 1:140–41.

———. *Le Neveu de Rameau*. In *Contes et Romans*. Edited by Michel Delon. Bibliothèque de la Pléiade. Paris: Gallimard, 2004.

———. *Le Neveu de Rameau: Le Rêve de d'Alembert*. Edited by Roland Desné. Paris: Messidor/Éditions sociales, 1984.

———. *Paradoxe du comédien*. In *Œuvres esthétiques*. Edited by Paul Vernière. Paris: Classiques Garnier, 1968.

———. *Rameau's Nephew and Other Works*. Translated by Jacques Barzun and Ralph H. Bowen. Indianapolis: Hackett Publishing Company, 2001.

Diderot, Denis, and Jean le Rond d'Alembert, eds. *Encyclopédie ou Dictionnaire raisonné des sciences, des arts et des métiers, par une Société de Gens de lettres*. University of

Chicago: ARTFL Encylopédie Project (Spring 2011 Edition). Edited by Robert Morrissey. http://encyclopedie.uchicago.edu/.

Dolar, Mladen. "'I Shall Be with You on Your Wedding-Night': Lacan and the Uncanny." *October* 58 (1991): 5–23.

Doubrovsky, Serge. "Phallotexte et gynotexte dans *La Nausée:* 'Feuillet sans date.'" In Issacharoff and Vilquin, *Sartre et la mise en signe*, 31–55.

———. "Sartre's *La Nausée*: Fragment of an Analytic Reading." Translated by Marilyn Schuster. In *Homosexualities and French Literature: Cultural Contexts/Critical Texts*, edited by George Stambolian and Elaine Marks, 330–40. Ithaca NY: Cornell University Press, 1979.

Du Bellay, Joachim. *La Deffense et illustration de la langue françoyse*. Geneva: Droz, 2001.

Dumarsais, César Chesneau. "Philosophe." In Diderot and d'Alembert, *Encyclopédie*, 12:509–11.

Duras, Marguerite. *Practicalities*. Translated by Barbara Bray. New York: Grove Press, 1987.

———. *The Ravishing of Lol Stein*. Translated by Richard Seaver. New York: Pantheon, 1986.

———. *Le Ravissement de Lol V. Stein*. Paris: Gallimard, 1964.

Duras, Marguerite, and Xavière Gauthier. *Woman to Woman*. Translated by Katherine A. Jensen. Lincoln: University of Nebraska Press, 1987.

Eaglestone, Robert. *Ethical Criticism: Reading after Levinas*. Edinburgh: Edinburgh University Press, 1997.

Eagleton, Terry. *Figures of Dissent: Critical Essays on Fish, Spivak, Žižek and Others*. New York: Verso, 2003.

Edson, Laurie. "Knowing Lol: Duras, Epistemology, and Gendered Mediation." *SubStance* 68 (1992): 17–31.

Engelmann, Peter, ed. *Philosophy in the Present*. Translated by Peter Thomas and Alberto Toscano. Cambridge: Polity, 2009.

Eskin, Michael. "Introduction: The Double 'Turn' to Ethics and Literature?" *Poetics Today* 25, no. 4 (2004): 557–72.

Evans, Martha Noel. *Masks of Tradition*. Ithaca NY: Cornell University Press, 1987.

Faye, Emmanuel. *Philosophie et perfection de l'homme: De la Renaissance à Descartes*. Paris: Vrin, 1998.

Felman, Shoshana. "Madness and Philosophy or Literature's Reason." *Yale French Studies* 52 (1975): 206–28.

Fish, Stanley. *Doing What Comes Naturally: Change, Rhetoric, and the Practice of Theory in Literary and Legal Studies*. Durham: Duke University Press, 1989.

Flaubert, Gustave. *The Selected Letters of Gustave Flaubert*. Translated by Francis Steegmuller. Freeport NY: Libraries Press, 1953.

Flynn, Bernard. "Derrida and Foucault: Madness and Writing." In *Derrida and Deconstruction*, edited by Hugh Silverman, 201–18. New York: Routledge, 1989.

Foucault, Michel. *History of Madness*. Translated by Jonathan Murphy and Jean Khalfa. New York: Routledge, 2006.

———. "The Masked Philosopher." In *Politics, Philosophy, Culture: Interviews and Other Writings, 1977–1984*, edited by Lawrence D. Kritzman, 323–30. New York: Routledge, 1988.

———. "Maurice Blanchot: The Thought from Outside." In *Foucault/Blanchot*. Translated by Brian Massumi, 1–58. New York: Zone, 1987.

———. "My Body, This Paper, This Fire." Translated by Geoffrey Bennington. *Oxford Literary Review* 4, no. 1 (1979): 9–28.

———. *Power/Knowledge: Selected Interviews and Other Writings, 1972–1977*. Edited by Colin Gordon. New York: Pantheon Books, 1980.

———. *The Use of Pleasure*. Translated by Robert Hurley. New York: Vintage Books, 1985.

———. "What Is an Author?" In Rabinow, *The Foucault Reader*, 101–20.

———. "What Is Enlightenment?" In Rabinow, *The Foucault Reader*, 32–50.

Fuss, Diana. *Essentially Speaking: Feminism, Nature, and Difference*. New York: Routledge, 1989.

Gadamer, Hans-Georg. "'Destruktion' and Deconstruction." Translated by Geoff Waite and Richard Palmer. In Michelfelder and Palmer, *Dialogue and Deconstruction*, 102–13.

———. "Reply to Jacques Derrida." Translated by Diane P. Michelfelder and Richard Palmer. In Michelfelder and Palmer, *Dialogue and Deconstruction*, 55–57.

———. "Text and Interpretation." Translated by Dennis J. Schmidt and Richard Palmer. In Michelfelder and Palmer, *Dialogue and Deconstruction*, 21–51.

Garber, Marjorie, Beatrice Hanssen, and Rebecca L. Walkowitz, eds. *The Turn to Ethics*. New York: Routledge, 2000.

Gearhart, Suzanne. "The Dialectic and Its Aesthetic Other: Hegel and Diderot." *Modern Language Notes* 101, no. 5 (1986): 1042–66.

Gibson, Andrew. *Postmodernity, Ethics, and the Novel: From Leavis to Levinas*. New York: Routledge, 1999.

Glassman, Deborah N. *Marguerite Duras: Fascinating Vision and Narrative Cure*. London: Associated University Press, 1991.

Gontier, Thierry. "Charron face à Montaigne: Stratégies du scepticisme." In *Montaigne et la question de l'homme*, edited by Marie-Luce Demonet, 103–43. Paris: PUF, 1999.

Graff, Gerald. *Beyond the Culture Wars: How Teaching the Conflicts Can Revitalize American Education*. New York: Norton, 1992.

———. "Why How We Read Trumps What We Read." *Profession* 9 (2009): 66–74.

Greany, Patrick. *Untimely Beggar: Poverty and Power from Baudelaire to Benjamin*. Minneapolis: University of Minnesota Press, 2008.

Hacking, Ian. "Déraison." *History of the Human Sciences* 24, no. 4 (2011): 13–23.

Hand, Seán, ed. *The Levinas Reader*. Oxford: Blackwell, 1992.

Hannoosh, Michèle. *Baudelaire and Caricature: From the Comic to an Art of Modernity*. University Park: Pennsylvania State University Press, 1992.

Harpham, Geoffrey Galt. *Shadows of Ethics: Criticism and the Just Society*. Durham NC: Duke University Press, 1999.

Hartle, Ann. *Michel de Montaigne: Accidental Philosopher*. Cambridge: Cambridge University Press, 2003.

Heath, Stephen. *The Nouveau Roman: A Study in the Practice of Writing*. Philadelphia: Temple University Press, 1973.

Hegel, G.W.F. *The Phenomenology of Spirit*. Translated by A. V. Miller. Oxford: Clarendon Press, 1977.

Hiddleston, J. A. *Baudelaire and the Art of Modernity*. Oxford: Clarendon Press, 1999.

———. *Baudelaire and "Le Spleen de Paris."* Oxford: Clarendon, 1987.

Hierocles. *The Commentary of Hierocles the Philosopher on the Pythagorean Verses*. Translated and edited by Hermann S. Schibli. In *Hierocles of Alexandria*. Oxford: Oxford University Press, 2002.

Hill, Leslie. "Lacan with Duras." In *Writing and Psychoanalysis: A Reader*, edited by John Lechte, 143–66. New York: Arnold, 1996.

Hoffmann, George. "From Amateur to Gentleman to Gentleman Amateur." In Zalloua, *Montaigne After Theory, Theory After Montaigne*, 19–38.

Hollier, Denis. *The Politics of Prose: Essay on Sartre*. Translated by Jeffrey Mehlman. Minneapolis: University of Minnesota Press, 1986.

Howells, Christina. *Sartre: The Necessity of Freedom*. Cambridge: Cambridge University Press, 1988.

Huffer, Lynne. *Mad for Foucault: Rethinking the Foundations of Queer Theory*. New York: Columbia University Press, 2010.

Hulbert, James. "Diderot in the Text of Hegel: A Question of Intertextuality." *Studies in Romanticism* 22 (1983): 267–91.

Husserl, Edmund. *Ideas Pertaining to a Pure Phenomenology and to a Phenomenological Philosophy, First Book: General Introduction to a Pure Phenomenology*. Translated by F. Kersten. The Hague: Martinus Nijhoff, 1982.

Idt, Geneviève. *La Nausée de Sartre*. Paris: Hatier, 1971.

Irigaray, Luce. *This Sex Which Is Not One*. Translated by Catherine Porter. Ithaca NY: Cornell University Press, 1985.

———. "What Other Are We Talking About?" In *Encounters with Levinas*, edited by Thomas Trezise. *Yale French Studies* 104 (2004): 67–81.

Iser, Wolfgang. *The Implied Reader: Patterns of Communication in Prose Fiction from Bunyan to Beckett*. Baltimore: Johns Hopkins University Press, 1974.

Issacharoff, Michael, and Jean-Claude Vilquin, eds. *Sartre et la mise en signe*. Lexington KY: French Forum, 1982.

Jakobson, Roman. "Closing Statement: Linguistics and Poetics." In *Style in Language: Conference on Style, Indiana University, 1958*, edited by Thomas A. Sebeok, 350–77. Bloomington: Indiana University Press, 1960.

Jameson, Fredric. "Modernism and Its Repressed; or, Robbe-Grillet as Anti-Colonist." In *The Ideologies of Theory: Essays, 1971–1986*, 1:167–80. Minneapolis: University of Minnesota Press, 1988.

———. *Valences of the Dialectic*. New York: Verso, 2009.

Jardine, Alice. *Gynesis: Configurations of Woman and Modernity*. Ithaca NY: Cornell University Press, 1985.
Jaucourt, Chevalier Louis de. "Pitié." In Diderot and d'Alembert, *Encyclopédie*, 12:662–63.
Jauss, Hans Robert. *The Dialogical and the Dialectical Neveu de Rameau: How Diderot Adopted Socrates and Hegel Adopted Diderot*. Berkeley: Center for Hermeneutical Studies in Hellenistic and Modern Culture, 1983.
Jefferson, Ann. *The Nouveau Roman and the Poetics of Fiction*. Cambridge: Cambridge University Press, 1980.
Jennings, Michael W., ed. *The Writer of Modern Life: Essays on Charles Baudelaire*. Cambridge MA: Harvard University Press, 2006.
Johnson, Barbara. *Défigurations du langage poétique: la seconde révolution baudelairienne*. Paris: Flammarion, 1979.
Kaivola, Karen. "Marguerite Duras and the Subversion of Power." In Knapp, *Critical Essays on Marguerite Duras*, 94–127.
Kant, Immanuel. *Grounding for the Metaphysics of Morals*. Translated by James W. Ellington. Indianapolis: Hackett Publishing Company, 1993.
Kaplan, Edward K. *Baudelaire's Prose Poems: The Esthetic, the Ethical, and the Religious in "The Parisian Prowler."* Athens: University of Georgia Press, 1990.
Kearney, Richard, ed. "Dialogue with Emmanuel Levinas." In *Dialogues with Contemporary Continental Thinkers Paul Ricoeur, Emmanuel Levinas, Herbert Marcuse, Stanislas Breton, Jacques Derrida: The Phenomenological Heritage*, 47–69. Manchester: Manchester University Press, 1984.
Keefe, Terence. "The Ending of Sartre's *La Nausée*." In *Critical Essays on Jean-Paul Sartre*, edited by Robert Wilcocks, 82–201. Boston: G. K. Hall, 1988.
Kermode, Frank. "Literary Criticism: Old and New Styles." *Essays in Criticism* 51, no. 2 (2001): 191–207.
———. *Pleasure and Change: The Aesthetics of Canon*. Oxford: Oxford University Press, 2004.
Knapp, Bettina L., ed. *Critical Essays on Marguerite Duras*. New York: G. K. Hall, 1998.
Kristeva, Julia. *Black Sun: Depression and Melancholia*. Translated by Leon S. Roudiez. New York: Columbia University Press, 1989.
———. *Strangers to Ourselves*. Translated by Leon S. Roudiez. New York: Columbia University Press, 1991.
Kritzman, Lawrence. *The Fabulous Imagination: On Montaigne's Essays*. New York: Columbia University Press, 2009.
———. "To Be or Not to Be: Sexual Ambivalence in Sartre's *La Nausée*." *L'Esprit Créateur* 43, no. 3 (2003): 79–86.
Lacan, Jacques. "The Agency of the Letter in the Unconscious, or Reason since Freud." In *Écrits: A Selection*, translated by Alan Sheridan, 146–78. London: Tavistock, 1977.
———. "Homage to Marguerite Duras, on *Le ravissement de Lol V. Stein*." Translated by Peter Connor. In Knapp, *Critical Essays on Marguerite Duras*, 16–22.

―――. *The Seminar, Book XI: The Four Fundamental Concepts of Psychoanalysis.* Translated by Alan Sheridan. London: Hogarth Press and Institute of Psycho-Analysis, 1977.
LaCapra, Dominick. *Preface to Sartre.* Ithaca NY: Cornell University Press, 1978.
Laertius, Diogenes. *Lives of Eminent Philosophers.* Vol. 2. Translated by Robert D. Hicks. Cambridge MA: Harvard University Press, 2005.
La Mettrie, Julien Offray de. *Man a Machine.* Translated by Richard A. Watson and Maya Rybalka. Indianapolis: Hackett Publishing Company, 1994 [1748].
Lane, Jeremy F. "The Stain, the Impotent Gaze, and the Theft of Jouissance: Towards a Žižekian Reading of Robbe-Grillet's *La Jalousie.*" *French Studies* 56, no. 2 (2002): 193–206.
Laplanche, Jean. "Psychoanalysis as Anti-Hermeneutics." *Radical Philosophy* 79 (1996): 7–12.
Leak, Andy. "Nausea and Desire in Sartre's *La Nausée.*" *French Studies* 43, no. 1 (1989): 61–72.
Leenhardt, Jacques. *Lecture politique du roman: La Jalousie d'Alain Robbe-Grillet.* Paris: Éditions de Minuit, 1973.
Lefebvre, Henri. *Diderot ou les affirmations fondamentales du matérialisme.* Paris: L'Arche éditeur, 1983.
Levinas, Emmanuel. *Autrement qu'être ou au-delà de l'essence.* The Hague: Martinus Nijhoff, 1974.
―――. "Dialogue with Emmanuel Levinas." In *Dialogues with Contemporary Continental Thinkers: The Phenomenological Heritage: Paul Ricoeur, Emmanuel Levinas, Herbert Marcuse, Stanislas Breton, Jacques Derrida*, edited by Richard Kearney, 47–69. Manchester: Manchester University Press, 1984.
―――. *Ethics and Infinity.* Translated by Richard A. Cohen. Pittsburgh: Duquesne University Press, 1985.
―――. *On Escape.* Translated by Bettina Bergo. Stanford CA: Stanford University Press, 2003.
―――. "The Other in Proust." In *Proper Names*, translated by Michael B. Smith, 99–105. Stanford CA: Stanford University Press, 1996.
―――. *Otherwise than Being, or, Beyond Essence.* Translated by Alphonso Lingis. The Hague: Martinus Nijhoff, 1981.
―――. "Reality and Its Shadow." Translated by Alphonso Lingis. In Hand, *The Levinas Reader*, 129–43.
―――. "Substitution." In *Basic Philosophical Writings*, translated by Adriaan T. Peperzak and Simon Critchley, edited by Adriaan T. Peperzak, Simon Critchley, and Robert Bernasconi, 79–96. Bloomington: Indiana University Press, 1996.
―――. *Time and the Other.* Translated by Richard A. Cohen. In Hand, *The Levinas Reader*, 37–58.
―――. *Totality and Infinity: An Essay on Exteriority.* Translated by Alphonso Lingis. Pittsburgh: Duquesne University Press, 1969.
Manser, Anthony. *Sartre: A Philosophical Study.* London: Athlone Press, 1966.

Mathieu-Castellani, Gisèle. *Montaigne: l'écriture de l'essai*. Paris: PUF, 1988.
McPherson, Karen. *Incriminations: Guilty Women/Telling Stories*. Princeton NJ: Princeton University Press, 1994.
Melehy, Hassan. *Writing Cogito: Montaigne, Descartes, and the Institution of the Modern Subject*. Albany: SUNY Press, 1997.
Meltzer, Françoise. *Seeing Double: Baudelaire's Modernity*. Chicago: University of Chicago Press, 2011.
Michelfelder, Diane P., and Richard E. Palmer, eds. *Dialogue and Deconstruction: The Gadamer-Derrida Encounter*. Albany: SUNY Press, 1989.
Miernowski, Jan. *L'Ontologie de la contraction sceptique: Pour l'étude de la métaphysique des Essais*. Paris: Champion, 1998.
Miller, Hillis J. *The Ethics of Reading*. New York: Columbia University Press, 1987.
———. *Others*. Princeton NJ: Princeton University Press, 2001.
———. *Versions of Pygmalion*. Cambridge MA: Harvard University Press, 1990.
Miller, Paul Allen. "The Platonic Remainder: Derrida's *Khôra* and the *Corpus Platonicum*." In *Derrida and Antiquity*, edited by Miriam Leonard, 321–41. Oxford: Oxford University Press, 2010.
Milner, Max. Introduction to *Le Spleen de Paris: Petits Poèmes en prose*, edited by Max Milner, 9–47. Paris: Imprimerie nationale, 1979.
Montaigne, Michel de. *The Complete Works of Montaigne*. Translated by Donald Frame. Stanford CA: Stanford University Press, 1957.
———. *Essais*. Translated and edited by André Lanly. Paris: Champion, 1989.
———. *Les Essais de Michel de Montaigne*. Edited by Pierre Villey and V. L. Saulnier. Paris: Presses Universitaire de France, 1965.
———. *The Essayes of Michael lord of Montaigne*. Translated and edited by John Florio. London: G. Richards, 1908.
———. *The Essays of Michel de Montaigne*. Translated by M. A. Screech. New York: Penguin Books, 1991.
Morrissette, Bruce. *The Novels of Robbe-Grillet*. Ithaca NY: Cornell University Press, 1975.
Mortier, Roland. *Diderot en Allemagne (1750–1850)*. Paris: Presses Universitaire de France, 1954.
Murdoch, Iris. *Sartre: Romantic Rationalist*. New Haven CT: Yale University Press, 1959.
Murphy, Steve. "Haunting Memories: Inquest and Exorcism in Baudelaire's 'La corde.'" *Dalhousie French Studies* 30 (1995): 65–91.
———. "'Le Mauvais Vitrier' ou la crise du verre." *Romanic Review* 82, no. 3 (1990): 339–49.
Nagel, Thomas. *The View From Nowhere*. Oxford: Oxford University Press, 1986.
Neto, José R. Maia. "*Epoche* as Perfection: Montaigne's View of Ancient Skepticism." In *Skepticism in Renaissance and Post-Renaissance Thought: New Interpretations*, edited by José R. Maia Neto and Richard H. Popkin, 13–42. Amherst NY: Prometheus Books, 2004.
Newton, Adam Zachary. *Narrative Ethics*. Cambridge MA: Harvard University Press, 1995.

Nietzsche, Friedrich. *On the Genealogy of Morals*. Translated by Walter Kaufmann. New York: Vintage, 1989.

———. *Twilight of the Idols/The Anti-Christ*. Translated by R. J. Hollingdale. New York: Penguin Books, 1990.

Nobus, Dany. "Locating Perversion, Dislocating Psychoanalysis." In *Perversion: Psychoanalytic Perspectives/Perspectives on Psychoanalysis*, edited by Dany Nobus and Lisa Downing, 3–18. New York: Karnac Books, 2006.

Nussbaum, Martha C. "Compassion and Terror." *Daedalus* 132, no. 1 (2003): 10–26.

———. *Love's Knowledge: Essays on Philosophy and Literature*. New York: Oxford University Press, 1990.

———. *Upheavals of Thought: The Intelligence of Emotions*. Cambridge: Cambridge University Press, 2001.

Oppenheim, Lois, ed. *Three Decades of the French New Novel*. Chicago: University of Illinois Press, 1986.

Panichi, Nicola. "Nietzsche et le 'gai scepticisme' de Montaigne." *Noesis* 10 (2006): 93–114.

Phelan, James. *Living to Tell about It*. Ithaca NY: Cornell University Press, 2005.

Pico della Mirandola, Giovanni. *Oration on the Dignity of Man*. Translated by Elizabeth Livermore Forbes. In *The Renaissance Philosophy of Man*, edited by Ernst Cassirer, Paul Oskar Kristeller, and John Herman Randall Jr., 223–54. Chicago: University of Chicago Press, 1948.

Pippin, Robert B. *Nietzsche, Psychology, and First Philosophy*. Chicago: University of Chicago Press, 2010.

Platt, Peter G, ed. *Wonders, Marvels, and Monsters in Early Modern Culture*. Newark: University of Delaware Press, 1999.

Poulet, Georges. *Le Point de départ*. Paris: Plon, 1964.

Poullain de la Barre, François. *On the Equality of the Two Sexes*. In *Three Cartesian Feminist Treatises*, translated by Vivien Bosley, 49–121. Chicago: University of Chicago Press, 2002.

Prendergast, Christopher. "Of Stones and Stories: Sartre's *La Nausée*." In *Teaching the Text*, edited by Susanne Kappeler and Norman Bryson, 56–72. Boston: Routledge and Kegan Paul, 1983.

———. *Paris and the Nineteenth Century*. Cambridge: Blackwell, 1992.

Price, David W. "Hegel's Intertextual Dialectic: Diderot's *Le Neveu de Rameau* in the *Phenomenology of Spirit*." *Clio* 20 (1991): 223–33.

Prince, Gerald. "Roquentin et le langage naturel." In Issacharoff and Vilquin, *Sartre et la mise en signe*, 103–13.

Proust, Marcel. *Remembrance of Things Past*. Translated by C. K. Scott Moncrieff. New York: Random House, 1934.

Pujol, Stéphane. "L'Espace public du *Neveu de Rameau*." *Revue d'histoire littéraire de la France* 93, no. 5 (1993): 669–84.

Rabelais, François. *The Histories of Gargantua and Pantagruel*. Translated by J. M. Cohen. New York: Penguin Books, 1955.

Rabinow, Paul, ed. *The Foucault Reader*. New York: Pantheon Books, 1984.
Rabinowitz, Peter J. "Assertion and Assumption: Fictional Patterns and the External World." PMLA 96, no. 3 (1981): 408–19.
Racevskis, Karlis. "Michel Foucault, Rameau's Nephew, and the Question of Identity." In *The Final Foucault*, edited by James Bernauer and David Rasmussen, 21–33. Cambridge MA: MIT Press, 1994.
Rancière, Jacques. *The Philosopher and His Poor*. Translated by John Drury, Corinne Oster, and Andrew Parker. Durham NC: Duke University Press, 2004.
Regosin, Richard. "'Mettre la theorique avant la practique': Montaigne and the Practice of Theory." In Zalloua, *Montaigne After Theory, Theory After Montaigne*, 264–80.
———. *Montaigne's Unruly Brood: Textual Engendering and the Challenge to Paternal Authority*. Berkeley: University of California Press, 1996.
Rex, Walter E. *Diderot's Counterpoints: The Dynamics of Contrariety in His Major Works*. Oxford: Voltaire Foundation, 1998.
Ricardou, Jean. *Problèmes du nouveau roman*. Paris: Éditions du Seuil, 1967.
Ricoeur, Paul. *Freud and Philosophy: An Essay on Interpretation*. Translated by Denis Savage. New Haven CT: Yale University Press, 1970.
Rigolot, François. "Interpréter Rabelais aujourd'hui: anachronies et catachronies." *Poétique* 103 (1995): 269–83.
Robbe-Grillet, Alain. "Discussion avec Jean Alter, Renato Barilli, Joseph Duhamel, Françoise Gaillard, G. W. Ireland, Jean Ricardou, Alain Robbe-Grillet, Karlheinz Stierle." In *Nouveau Roman: hier aujourd'hui*, edited by Jean Ricardou, 118–30. Paris: Union générale d'éditions, 1972.
———. *For a New Novel: Essays on Fiction*. Translated by Richard Howard. New York: Grove Press, 1966.
———. "Images and Texts: A Dialogue." Translated by Karlis Racevskis. In *Generative Literature and Generative Art*, edited by David Leach, 38–47. Fredericton NB: York Press, 1983.
———. *La Jalousie*. Paris: Éditions de Minuit, 1957.
———. *Jealousy*. Translated by Richard Howard. New York: Grove Press, 1965.
———. "Order and Disorder in Film and Fiction." Translated by Bruce Morrissette. *Critical Inquiry* 4, no. 1 (1977): 1–20.
———. *Pour un nouveau roman*. Paris: Éditions de Minuit, 1963.
———. *Le Voyageur: Textes, causeries et entretiens [1947–2001]*. Edited by Olivier Corpet with Emmanuelle Lambert. Paris: Christian Bourgois, 2001.
Rousseau, G. S, ed. *The Languages of Psyche: Mind and Body in Enlightenment Thought*. Berkeley: University of California Press, 1990.
Russell-Watt, Lynsey. "The Terrors and Pleasure of Analysis: *Le Ravissement de Lol V. Stein*." *Nottingham French Studies* 46, no. 3 (2007): 121–33.
Saint-Amand, Pierre. *The Pursuit of Laziness: An Idle Interpretation of the Enlightenment*. Translated by Jennifer Curtiss Gage. Princeton NJ: Princeton University Press, 2011.

Sandford, Stella. "Levinas, Feminism and the Feminine." *The Cambridge Companion to Levinas*, edited by Simon Critchley and Robert Bernasconi, 39–60. Cambridge: Cambridge University Press, 2002.

Sanyal, Debarati. *The Violence of Modernity: Baudelaire, Irony, and the Politics of Form*. Baltimore: Johns Hopkins University Press, 2006.

Sartre, Jean-Paul. *Being and Nothingness: An Essay on Phenomenological Ontology*. Translated by Hazel E. Barnes. New York: Philosophical Library, 1956.

———. *Nausea*. Translated by Lloyd Alexander. New York: New Directions, 1964.

———. *La Nausée*. In *Œuvres romanesques*. Edited by Michel Contat and Michael Rybalka. Bibliothèque de la Pléiade. Paris: Gallimard, 1981.

———. *What Is Literature? and Other Essays*. Translated by Bernard Frechtman. Cambridge MA: Harvard University Press, 1988.

———. *Witness to My Life: The Letters of Jean-Paul Sartre to Simone de Beauvoir, 1926–1939*. Edited by Simone de Beauvoir. Translated by Lee Fahnestock and Norman MacAfee. New York: Scribner's Sons, 1992.

———. *The Words: The Autobiography of Jean-Paul Sartre*. Translated by Bernard Frechtman. New York: George Braziller, 1964.

Schmidt, James. "The Fool's Truth: Diderot, Goethe, and Hegel." *Journal of the History of Ideas* 57, no. 4 (1996): 625–44.

Schrift, Alan D. *Nietzsche and the Question of Interpretation: Between Hermeneutics and Deconstruction*. New York: Routledge, 1990.

Scott, Maria C. *Baudelaire's "Le Spleen de Paris": Shifting Perspectives*. Aldershot: Ashgate, 2005.

Seneca. *Epistles*. Loeb Classical Library. Translated by Richard M. Gummere. Cambridge MA: Harvard University Press, 1996.

Shankman, Steven. *Other Others: Levinas, Literature, Transcultural Studies*. Albany: SUNY Press, 2010.

Shea, Louisa. *The Cynic Enlightenment: Diogenes in the Salon*. Baltimore: Johns Hopkins University Press, 2010.

Sheringham, Michael. "Knowledge and Repetition in *Le Ravissement de Lol V. Stein*." *Romance Studies* 2 (1983): 124–40.

Shields, Rob. "Fancy Footwork: Walter Benjamin's Notes on *Flânerie*." In *The Flâneur*, edited by Keith Tester, 61–80. London: Routledge, 1994.

Sikka, Sonia. "The Delightful Other: Portraits of the Feminine in Kierkegaard, Nietzsche, and Levinas." In Chanter, *Feminist Interpretations of Emmanuel Levinas*, 96–118.

Silverman, Kaja. *The Threshold of the Visible World*. New York: Routledge, 1996.

Simek, Nicole. "Baudelaire and the Problematic of the Reader in *Les Fleurs du mal*." *Pacific Coast Philology* 37 (2002): 43–57.

Smyth, Edmund J. "The *Nouveau Roman*: Modernity and Postmodernity." In *Postmodernism and Contemporary Fiction*, edited by Edmund J. Smyth, 54–73. London: Batsford, 1991.

Spink, John S. "Diderot et la réhabilitation de la pitié." In *Colloque international Diderot (1713–84)*, edited by Anne-Marie Chouillet, 51–60. Paris: Aux amateurs de livres, 1985.

Spivak, Gayatri Chakravorty. *An Aesthetic Education in the Era of Globalization*. Cambridge MA: Harvard University Press, 2012.

———. *Outside in the Teaching Machine*. New York: Routledge, 1993.

Stephens, Sonya. *Baudelaire's Prose Poems: The Practice and Politics of Irony*. Oxford: Oxford University Press, 1999.

Suleiman, Susan Rubin. *Subversive Intent: Gender, Politics, and the Avant-Garde*. Cambridge MA: Harvard University Press, 1990.

Todorov, Tzvetan. *Imperfect Garden: The Legacy of Humanism*. Translated by Carol Cosman. Princeton NJ: Princeton University Press, 2002.

———. *Le Jardin imparfait: La pensée humaniste en France*. Paris: Bernard Grasset, 1998.

Trezise, Thomas. "Unspeakable." *Yale Journal of Criticism* 14, no. 1 (2001): 39–66.

van Noort, Kimberly Philpot. "The Dance of the Signifier: Jacques Lacan and Marguerite Duras's *Le Ravissement de Lol V. Stein*." *Symposium* 51, no. 3 (1997): 186–201.

Vartanian, Aram. "Diderot, or, the Dualist in Spite of Himself." In *Diderot Digression and Dispersion: A Bicentennial Tribute*, edited by Jack Undank and Herbert Josephs, 250–68. Lexington KY: French Forum, 1984.

———. *Science and Humanism in the French Enlightenment*. Charlottesville VA: Rookwood Press, 1999.

Vincent, Howard P. *Daumier and His World*. Evanston IL: Northwestern University Press, 1968.

Whitford, Margaret. *Luce Irigaray: Philosophy in the Feminine*. New York: Routledge, 1991.

Williams, Wes. *Monsters and Their Meanings in Early Modern Culture: Mighty Magic*. Oxford: Oxford University Press, 2011.

Wolff, Janet. *The Aesthetics of Uncertainty*. New York: Columbia University Press, 2008.

Zalloua, Zahi. "(Im)Perfecting the Self: Montaigne's Pedagogical Ideal." Edited by Anne L. Birberick. *EMF: Studies in Early Modern France* 12 (2008): 111–26.

———, ed. *Montaigne After Theory, Theory After Montaigne*. Seattle: University of Washington Press, in association with Whitman College, 2009.

———. *Montaigne and the Ethics of Skepticism*. EMF: Critiques. Charlottesville VA: Rookwood Press, 2005.

Ziarek, Ewa Plonowska. "The Ethical Passion of Emmanuel Levinas." In Chanter, *Feminist Interpretations of Emmanuel Levinas*, 78–95.

———. *An Ethics of Dissensus: Postmodernity, Feminism, and the Politics of Radical Democracy*. Stanford CA: Stanford University Press, 2001.

Žižek, Slavoj. *For They Know Not What They Do: Enjoyment as a Political Factor*. New York: Verso, 1991.

———. *How to Read Lacan*. New York: Norton, 2006.

———. *In Defense of Lost Causes*. New York: Verso, 2008.

———. *Less Than Nothing: Hegel and the Shadow of Dialectical Materialism*. New York: Verso, 2012.

———. *Organs without Bodies: On Deleuze and Consequences*. New York: Routledge, 2004.

———. *The Parallax View*. Cambridge MA: MIT Press, 2006.

———. "'Philosophy Is Not a Dialogue.'" In Engelmann, *Philosophy in the Present*, 49–72.

———. *The Plague of Fantasies*. New York: Verso, 1997.

———. "A Plea for a Return to *Différance* (with a Minor *Pro Domo Sua*)." In *Adieu Derrida*, edited by Costas Douzinas, 109–33. Basingstoke: Palgrave Macmillan, 2007.

———. *Violence: Six Sideways Reflections*. New York: Picador, 2008.

Index

Abbot, H. Porter, 156n7
absurdities: aesthetics and, 108; existentialism and, 17, 88–89, 92, 96–98; experiences of, 104–5; imperfections as, 32; perceptions of, 116, 120
admiration, 61–63
"Admiration" (Diderot), 62–63
Adorno, Theodor, 24, 149
adultery, 119–22, 125–26
aesthetics: hunger for, 76; literature and, 1, 3; modernity and, 16–17, 65–66, 68–73, 82, 85, 173n28; and objects, 108, 126; strangeness of, 70–71. *See also* beauty; pleasure
The Aesthetics of Uncertainty (Wolff), 156n6
allegories: about children and monsters, 35–38, 166n43; about colonialism, 113–14; dialogues and, 44–45; about male domination, 133; dualism and, 167n12; about husbands and narrators, 112, 114, 117–22, 124–25, 126, 127, 176–77n12; interpretations for, 44–45, 166n3, 172n21; of irresolution, 122, 123–24, 127; mind-and-body problem as, 15–16, 43–64; paradoxes in, 36, 38; pleasure in, 44–45, 166n4

Alter, Robert, 155–56n5
alterity: ethics of otherness and, 7, 32–34, 126–28, 149–53, 173n25, 179n5; feminist criticism and, 130–31, 179n5; of God, 40; hospitality toward, 61, 63; through interpretations, 19, 36–38, 126–28; literary criticism and, 6–7; of Lol Stein and Jacques Hold, 143–45; models for otherness and, 35–36, 39–40, 179n5; narcissism and, 31–33, 143–42; of the Other, 79, 143–44; of the Said, 39–40; skepticism and, 15, 32–34; translations and, 65. *See also* difference; otherness
An Aesthetic Education in the Era of Globalization (Spivak), 9
anachronisms, 25–26
analogies, 9–10, 159n43
analysts, 142–43, 145, 181–82n48
Anderson, Wilda, 170n39
anthropomorphism, 104–5, 119–20
"Apology for Raymond Sebond" (Montaigne), 21–22, 29, 40, 163n5
aporias, 26, 59
Art and Answerability (Bakhtin), 160n47
artwork, 16, 66–73, 85, 106–9, 116, 126
astonishment, 38–41, 63, 71, 81, 170n42

INDEX

Attridge, Derek, 2–3, 123, 127, 160n46, 162n74, 166n4
authors: Antoine Roquentin as, 92–94, 99, 109; artwork of, 116; functions of, 89, 157n22; hands of, 119; as implied authors, 156n7; Jacques Hold as, 136–37, 138–47, 181n39; and relationships with readers, 17
autonomy, 6, 16–17, 38, 118, 126, 169n28

"The Bad Glazier" (Baudelaire), 73–74, 75–77
Badiou, Alain, 7–8, 11–12, 158n29, 158nn31–32 161n53, 161n56
Badiou, Alain, works of: *Ethics*, 7–8, 11–12, 158n29; *Manifesto for Philosophy*, 158n32; *Saint Paul*, 13; "Thinking the Event," 161n56
Bakhtin, Mikhail, 160n47
Balzac, Honoré de, 94, 174n12
Barthes, Roland: and acts of reading and rereading, 3–4, 159–60n44; regarding ethics and literature, 153; regarding pleasure from literature, 4–5; concerning Robbe-Grillet, 116, 117, 120, 177n22, 177n27, 178n40; and specificity of literature, 160n48
Barthes, Roland, works of: *Critical Essays*, 116–17, 120, 153, 160n48, 178n40; *The Neutral*, 34; *The Pleasure of the Text*, 4–5; *S/Z*, 159–60n44
Bataille, Georges, 111
Baudelaire, Charles, 16–17, 65–66, 68–73, 85, 171n10, 172nn20–21, 173n28. See also modernity
Baudelaire, Charles, works of: "The Bad Glazier," 73–74, 75–77; "The Counterfeit Coin," 171–72n19; "Crowds," 78–79; *The Flowers of Evil*, 72, 171n12; *Further Notes on Edgar Poe*, 171n10; *The Painter of Modern Life*, 69–70, 78; "The Rope," 77–84; *Salon of 1846*, 66–67, 170–71n3; *Some French Caricaturists*, 71; *The Spleen of Paris*, 16–17, 72–85, 171nn12–13, 172–73n23; *The Universal Exposition of 1855*, 67
beasts. See monsters
beauty, 67–68, 71, 171n4. See also aesthetics
Beauvoir, Simone de, 89, 129–30
Beckett, Samuel, 160n45
behaviors, 46–48, 51–53, 73–74, 76–77, 83–84, 122
Being and Nothingness (Sartre), 96, 106
Benjamin, Walter, 70, 173n24
Berger, Harry, Jr., 165n35
Berman, Marshall, 70
Bernstein, Michael, 52–53
Bertrand, Marc, 104, 175n27
Beyond the Culture Wars (Graff), 160n51
biographies, 92–94, 99, 174n11
bizarrerie. See strangeness
Blanchot, Maurice, 6, 115, 118–19, 123, 159n39, 178n40
Blanchot, Maurice, works of: *The Book to Come*, 114; *The Infinite Conversation*, 11, 123, 159n39; *The Space of Literature*, 118–19; *The Writing of the Disaster*, 6, 9, 123, 157n25
bliss. See aesthetics; pleasure
Boaistuau, Pierre, 166n45
bodies, 59–62, 96–98, 99–100, 119, 170n39. See also mind-and-body problem
books: as artwork, 106–9; dedications within, 72, 82, 170–71n3, 173n28; friendships with, 15, 43, 167n5; relationships with, 22, 115, 163n2
The Book to Come (Blanchot), 114
Booth, Wayne C., 2, 156n7, 167n5
Bordeaux Copy (Montaigne), 35–36. See also Montaigne, Michel de, works of, *Essays*
Bourdieu, Pierre, 14, 162n71
bourgeoisie: artwork about, 71–72; ideologies of, 50–53, 90–92, 95–96,

INDEX

98; morality of, 80–82; as readers, 67–69, 170–71n3
Bouville, 89–92, 95–96, 98, 174n10
breakdowns. *See* madness
Bremner, Geoffrey, 168n20
Breton, André, 130–31
Bruns, Gerald L., 70
Burton, Richard D. E., 172n21

cannibalism, 34–35, 40, 150, 165n38
capitalism, 84, 113
caricatures, 71–72
Cartesianism, 15, 49, 54, 88, 168–69n27, 169n30. *See also* Descartes, René; dualism
Cave, Terence, 24–25, 26
centipedes, 119–20
Chanter, Tina, 179n4
charity, 75, 171–72n19, 173–74n32
Charron, Pierre, 164n31
children, 35–41, 55–56, 79–84, 166n43, 166n45, 169n28
The Child with Cherries (Manet), 82
chronologies, 112, 118, 176n3
classes, 2, 49–53, 90–92, 162n71, 170–71n3, 172n21. *See also* bourgeoisie; capitalism
cogito, 54, 55, 61, 88, 168–69n27
"Cogito and History of Madness" (Derrida), 54–55
colonialism, 113–14, 176–77n12
commentaries, 3–4, 13, 37, 83
communication. *See* language
Compagnon, Antoine, 171n13
The Company We Keep (Booth), 2
"Compassion and Terror" (Nussbaum), 149–51
comprehension. *See* interpretations; knowledge
Conley, Tom, 163n5
consciousness: and contradictions of nephew, 50–53, 167n16; and identity of Antoine Roquentin, 88, 90–92, 94–100, 174n3, 174n11; jealousy and, 119; of readers, 160n47
contingencies: in acts of essaying and writing, 23, 97–98; in existence and reality, 97–98, 105–6, 107–8, 116, 158n32, 175n25, 175n27; historicism and, 77, 93; in literature and philosophy, 105, 175n27; and modernity, 16, 70–71
contradictions. *See* paradoxes
conversations. *See* dialogues
"The Counterfeit Coin" (Baudelaire), 171–72n19
Critchley, Simon, 158n31, 159n32
"Crowds" (Baudelaire), 78–79
Crowley, Martin, 179n12
curiosity, 12–13, 37, 82, 124, 177–78n35, 181n42
cynicism, 168

Dällenbach, Lucien, 177n25
Daumier, Honoré, 71–72
Davis, Colin, 158n27
Dean, Tim, 156n15
"death of the author," 1, 17
deaths, 30–31, 80, 82–84, 94, 99, 113, 120–22, 141, 157n22, 171n10
debates, 15, 49, 54–55, 131–32, 168n23, 179n12
dedications, 72, 82, 170–71n3, 173n28
La Deffense et illustration de la langue françoyse (Du Bellay), 34–35
Delacroix, Eugène, 66–69, 71
De la sagesse (Charron), 164n31
de Man, Paul, 165n34
demystification, 4, 28, 36, 40, 80–81, 85
Derrida, Jacques: regarding *cogito*, 168–69n27; and double meanings, 18, 162n79; regarding Emmanel Levinas, 129; concerning ethics, 8–9, 151–52, 161–62n64; regarding humanism, 101; concerning interpretations and perceptions, 159n36, 176n34;

203

Derrida, Jacques (*continued*)
  regarding justice, 160n49; concerning madness, 54–55; and metaphor of "eating well," 10, 160n45, 160n47; and reader-response criticism, 13, 157n23; and "relation without relation" (*rapport sans rapport*), 9, 12, 152; regarding signature and countersignature, 162n76, 174n8
Derrida, Jacques, works of: *Aporias*, 8, 152, 162n79; *Archive Fever*, 162n72; "Autoimmunity," 152; "Cogito and the History of Madness," 54–55, 168–69n27; "'Eating Well,' or the Calculation of the Subject," 10; "The Ends of Man," 101; "Following Theory," 161–62n64, 179n50; "Force of Law," 13; *The Gift of Death*, 9, 18, 35, 162n79; *Of Grammatology*, 12; *Monolingualism of the Other*, 175n23; *Psyche: Inventions of the Other*, 161–62n64; "Rams: Uninterrupted Dialogue," 152; *Rogues*, 9; *Speech and Phenomena*, 176n34; "This Strange Institution Called Literature," 162n76, 174n8; "Structure, Sign, and Play in the Discourse of the Human Sciences," 159n36 ; "'To Do Justice to Freud,'" 160n49; "Three Questions to Hans-Georg Gadamer," 151–52; "Violence and Metaphysics," 8, 55, 129; *The Work of Mourning*, 160n45
Descartes, René, 39, 43–44, 54, 88, 166n46. *See also* Cartesianism; dualism
Descartes, René, works of: *Discourse on Methods and Meditations*, 43–44, 54, 88; *Meditations on First Philosophy*, 166n46; *The Passions of the Soul*, 39
desires, 28, 113, 119–20, 145–46. *See also* fascination
Desné, Roland, 167n7
dialectic, 11–12, 83–84, 127, 146, 151

dialogisms, 160n47
dialogues: allegories and, 44–45; language in conversational discourse and, 59–62, 115, 144, 145–47, 151, 174n12, 183n9; between *Moi* and *Lui*, 15–16, 43, 47–64, 167n7, 168nn25–26; as monologue, 45–47, 59–61; questions as, 29, 34, 182n55; with readers, 137, 151, 157n23, 167n5, 170n45; with Self-Taught Man, 100–101, 175n31
diaries, 87–88, 94–96, 97
Diderot, Denis: allegory usage by, 166n3; dialogue usage by, 15–16, 43, 45, 48, 64, 168n25, 169n34, 170n45; regarding humanism, 49, 167n12; regarding self-mastery, 61–62
Diderot, Denis, works of: "Admiration," 62–63; *Paradox on the Comedian*, 61; *Rameau's Nephew*, 15–16, 43–64, 166n1, 167n12, 167–68n16
difference: ethics of, 7–14, 32–33, 35–38, 63, 130, 158n29; hospitality toward, 46–47; regarding sexuality, 125–26, 129–31, 136–37, 145–47. *See also* alterity; otherness
Diogenes Laertius. *See* Laertius, Diogenes
discourses. *See* dialogues
disidentifications, 98–99
Distinction (Bourdieu), 14, 162n71
Dolar, Mladen, 160–61n52
Donnadieu, Marguerite. *See* Duras, Marguerite
double binds, 3, 12, 85, 153, 156n9
double meanings, 18, 31, 74–75, 117, 150–51, 162n79
double turns, 155n2
double visions, 77, 172n20
Doubrovsky, Serge, 89
dualism, 44, 49, 70, 167n12. *See also* Cartesianism; Descartes, René
Du Bellay, Joachim, 34–35

Duras, Marguerite, 18, 130–47, 179n12, 180n16, 180n37, 181n45, 182n53, 182n54
Duras, Marguerite, works of: *The Ravishing of Lol Stein*, 18, 130–47, 179n12, 180n16, 180n37, 181n45, 182n53; *Practicalities*, 182n54

Eaglestone, Robert, 34
Eagleton, Terry, 159n34
"'Eating Well,' or the Calculation of the Subject" (Derrida), 10
Edson, Laurie, 133–35, 136–37
egocentrism, 57–58, 144–45. *See also* narcissism
empathy, 79, 173n24
encounters. *See* events; experience
Encyclopédie (Diderot and d'Alembert), 62–63, 170n43
endings: for *Jealousy*, 122; for *Nausea*, 108–9, 176n38; for prose poems, 75, 76–77, 80–84, 173n29; for *The Ravishing of Lol Stein*, 146–47, 182n53
enigmas. *See* mystification; Stein, Lol
enjoyment. *See* pleasure
the Enlightenment, 16, 30, 56, 62–63, 101, 168–69nn26–27, 170n43
epiphanies, 103–5, 141–42, 143–44, 145–46
epistemology, 11, 35–36, 43–44, 63–64, 87–88, 123–24, 133–34
Eskin, Michael, 155n2
essaying, acts of, 15, 21–24, 23, 27–28, 38, 97–98, 173n23
essays, 15, 24–34, 38
The Essays (Montaigne), 21–41, 163n1, 163n5, 163–64nn12–14, 164n29, 166n45
ethical criticism, 1–3, 7–14, 130, 150, 153
ethics: regarding acts of reading and interpretations, 1–15, 123, 126–28, 149–53, 161–62n64; concerning alterity, differences, and otherness, 7, 32–38, 63, 125–31, 144–53, 158n29, 173n25, 179n5; of madness, 53–59; and ontology, 8–11, 162n66; pure ethics as, 8–9, 35; regarding translations, 65–66, 111–12. *See also* morality
Ethics (Badiou), 7–8, 11–12, 158n29
Eugénie Grandet (Balzac), 174n12
Evans, Martha Noel, 133, 134–35, 136–37, 180n31, 181n39
events: acts of reading and interpretation as, 13–14, 111–15, 122–23, 125–26, 162n72; chronologies of, 112, 118, 176n3; contingencies and truths regarding, 7–8, 11–12, 93–94, 158–59nn31–32, 161n53; existence and experiences as, 95–96, 138–39, 152; of love, 161n56; reality as, 102–6, 116–22
evil geniuses, 44, 54
Exemplaire de Bordeaux (Montaigne). *See* Montaigne, Michel de, works of, *Essays*
existence, 97–98, 105–8, 116, 158n32, 175n25, 175n27, 176n34. *See also* experience
existentialism, 17, 88–89, 92, 96–98
experience, 92, 95–96, 103–5, 136–39, 142, 152. *See also* existence

fantaisies, 5, 15, 27–28, 45, 157n22
fantasies, 5–6, 15, 45, 64, 99–100, 119–22
fascination, 79, 118–22. *See also* desires
fathers, 80, 83–84
Faye, Emmanuel, 29
feminism. *See* feminist criticism; feminists
feminist criticism, 18, 56, 129–37, 147, 179nn4–5, 179n12, 180n37
feminists, 132–37, 147
Femmes d'Alger (Delacroix), 67
flâneur. See strollers
Flaubert, Gustave, 107
The Flowers of Evil (Baudelaire), 72, 171n12

food. *See* cannibalism; hunger; meals
For a New Novel (Robbe-Grillet), 111, 116, 176n2
Foucault, Michel: concerning the Enlightenment, 101; regarding functions of authors, 89; regarding knowledge, 12–13; concerning language, 115, 158–59n32; regarding madness and philosophy, 54–55, 168n24; regarding men and death, 120, 178n38; regarding pleasure, 5
Foucault, Michel, works of: *History of Madness*, 168nn23–25; "The Masked Philosopher," 13; "Maurice Blanchot," 115; "My Body, This Paper, This Fire," 168n23; *Power/Knowledge*, 158n31; *The Use of Pleasure*, 5, 12, 24; "What Is an Author?" 89; "What Is Enlightenment?" 13, 101
freedom, 92, 104, 169n28
Freud, Sigmund, 142, 155
friendships, 15–16, 43, 45–47, 79–80, 81–82, 84, 167n5. *See also* relationships
Further Notes on Edgar Poe (Baudelaire), 171n10

Gadamer, Hans-Georg, 151, 183n9
Gearhart, Suzanne, 170n45
generosity, 41, 145, 164n29, 173n29
genres, 24, 27, 72, 111
Glassman, Deborah N., 142
glaziers, 73–77, 172n19
God, 7, 9, 28, 35–37, 40, 176n2. *See also* spirituality
Gontier, Thierry, 164n31
Graff, Gerald, 160n51
grammar, 124, 127, 131, 179n50
Greany, Patrick, 172n21
Gynesis (Jardine), 132–33

Hallward, Peter, 158–59n32
Hand, Sean, 158n27

hands, 96–98, 119
Hartle, Ann, 165n33
Heath, Stephen, 177n19
hedonism. *See* aesthetics; pleasure
Hegel, G.W.F., 50, 167–68n16
hermeneutics: of faith and suspicion, 4, 135–36, 155n5, 180–81n37; models for, 33, 156n15, 180–81n37; unruly literature and, 2, 10–11, 14–15, 18, 44–45, 64, 151–53. *See also* interpretations; perspectives
Hiddleston, J.A., 71
Hierocles, 165n35
Hill, Leslie, 179n12
Histoires prodigieuses (Boaistuau), 166n45
historicism, 24–27, 70–71, 77, 93–94
The Histories of Gargantua and Pantagruel (Rabelais), 44
historiographies, 93–94
History of Madness (Foucault), 168nn23–25
Hobbes, Thomas, 57
Hoffmann, George, 24, 27
Hold, Jacques: as analyst, 142–43, 145, 181–82n48; as author, 136–37, 138–47, 181n39; epiphany of, 143–44, 145–46; identifications with, 132–35, 136, 180n16; knowledge of Lol Stein by, 141, 143, 145–47; narcissism of, 140, 143–44; as narrator, 131–47, 182n53; paradoxes about, 134–35, 143–44, 145–46; profession of, 142, 180n16; ravishment of, 144–45; the Said of, 132–37; the Saying of, 138–47; as subject, 135–36, 141
Hollier, Denis, 97–98
"Homage to Marguerite Duras" (Lacan), 132
hospitality, 46–47, 61, 63, 152–53, 175n31
Houssaye, Arsène, 72–73, 74–76
Howells, Christina, 174n10
How to Read Montaigne (Cave), 24–25

Huffer, Lynne, 61
humanism: Denis Diderot regarding, 49, 167n12; as ideology, 34–35, 54–56; Michel de Montaigne and, 24–25, 28, 30–31, 34–35, 164n15; resistance to, 34–35, 100–101
humanity: behaviors and compulsions of, 73–74, 76–77; dignity of, 50, 167n15; interpretations and perspectives regarding, 35–38, 53–54, 66–67, 88–89, 115–18; sufferings of, 66–69, 71, 149; and women as subjects, 67–71, 133–34, 165n37
hunger, 48–50, 57, 75, 76. *See also* meals
husbands, 112–14, 117–22, 124–25, 126, 127, 176–77n12
Husserl, Edmund, 102
hysterics. *See* madness

identifications: with husbands, 117–18; with Jacques Hold, 132–35, 136, 180n16; with Lol Stein, 132–33, 136, 181n45; with readers, 81, 117–18; regarding sexuality, 99–100, 134, 136–37, 180n29; with Tatiana Karl, 144, 181n45; of voices, 114, 134, 136, 167n7, 172n23, 176n12, 180–81n37
identities: and consciousness of Antoine Roquentin, 88, 90–92, 94–100, 174n3, 174n11; of Lol Stein, 138–39, 181n45; of nephew, 49–50, 54, 59; regarding sexuality, 99–100
ideologies: regarding authors, 157n22; of colonialism, 113–14; regarding enjoyment and pleasure, 157n20; humanism as, 34–35, 54–56; irony regarding, 52–53, 83, 85, 162n71; of literature, 94; concerning realism and verisimilitude, 97–98; theories and, 21, 155–56n5; regarding violence, 66, 83–85
idlers. *See* strollers
Idt, Geneviève, 88

imparfait. *See* imperfections
imperfections, 29–32, 37
imperialism. *See* colonialism
implied authors, 156n7
The Implied Reader (Iser), 157n.23
impulses, 33, 164n29, 166n3
interests, 56–59, 169n33
interpellations, 3, 5, 13, 137
interpretations: of allegories, 44–45, 166n3, 172n21; alterity through, 19, 36–38, 126–28; anachronisms and, 25–26; of essays, 163–64n14; ethical decisions and, 13, 161–62n64; historicism and, 24–26; of humanity and world, 37–38, 66–67, 88–89, 115–18; irony concerning perceptions and, 82–84, 108–9, 120, 157n23; logic regarding, 157n23, 159n36; models for, 123–28, 152–53, 156n15, 160–61n52; of monstrosities, 36–38; multiplicity of, 8, 159n36; by narrators, 60–61, 62, 63, 170n39, 170n45; by nephew, 56–57; by readers, 3–6, 10–15, 25–26, 64, 122–28, 147, 160–61n52, 163n12; regarding signatures and countersignatures, 89, 174n8; and Theory, 156n5; translations and, 65–66, 82, 111–13. *See also* hermeneutics; perspectives
Irigaray, Luce, 130
irony: concerning behaviors and violence, 76–77, 83–85, 122; through dialogue, 59, 62; regarding ideologies, 52–53, 83, 85, 162n71; concerning interpretations and perceptions, 82–84, 108–9, 120, 157n23; concerning madness, 54–55; regarding perfection, 28
irresolutions, 122, 123–24, 127
Iser, Wolfgang, 157n23

Jakobson, Roman, 159n43
jalousie. *See* jealousy

INDEX

Jameson, Fredric, 21, 113, 126
Jardine, Alice, 132–33, 134, 136, 180–81n37, 180n23, 180n29
Le Jardin imparfait (*Imperfect Garden*, Todorov), 30–31
Jaucourt, Chevalier Louis de, 170n43
jealousy, 113–14, 117, 118, 119–22, 177–78n35
Jealousy (Robbe-Grillet), 17, 111–28, 176–77n12, 177n19, 177n25, 178n35, 178n39
Jefferson, Ann, 126
Johnson, Barbara, 171n12
jouissance. *See* aesthetics; pleasure; sublimation

Kant, Immanuel, 169n28
Kaplan, Edward K., 172nn22–23
Karl, Tatiana, 138–40, 144, 181n45
Keefe, Terence, 108
Kermode, Frank, 1
knowledge: epiphanies regarding, 103–5, 143–44, 145–46; of Lol Stein, 141, 143, 145–47; objects of, 13, 33, 34–36, 39–40, 143; and understanding of self, 12–13, 21, 29, 31, 38, 56, 101, 150–51; of world, 43–44
Kristeva, Julia, 169n33
Kritzman, Lawrence, 32, 100, 165n37

Lacan, Jacques, 132, 146, 180n16, 181–82n48
LaCapra, Dominick, 108, 174n3, 175n25
Laertius, Diogenes, 168n26
La Mettrie, Julien Offray de, 167n8
Lane, Jeremy F., 179n47
language: in dialogue and discourse, 59–62, 114–15, 144, 145–47, 151, 174n12, 183n9; epiphanies and visions regarding, 103–5, 141–42; ethics and, 131, 150–51; fascination and, 119; hospitality toward, 175n31;

logos and, 55, 101–2, 105, 115, 157n25; of metaphors, 94–95, 102–6; of ontology, 9; paradoxes concerning, 9–10; perceptions through, 106–7, 120; of skepticism, 33–34; of women, 130
Laplanche, Jean, 143, 181n43
Leak, Andy, 174n11
Lecture politique du roman (Leenhardt), 112–14
Leenhardt, Jacques, 112–14, 179n47
Lefebvre, Henri, 50
Levinas, Emmanuel: and acts of *unsaying and resaying*, 123, 147; regarding ethics, 6–7, 123, 146, 158n27, 158n29, 162n66; feminist criticism and, 129–31, 179n4, 179n12; regarding the Other and otherness, 6–7, 157n25, 158n27; regarding persecution and ravishment, 144–45
Levinas, Emmanuel, works of: "Dialogue with Emmanuel Levinas," 123; *Ethics and Infinity*, 162n66; *On Escape*, 87; "The Other in Proust," 181n42; *Otherwise than Being*, 9, 131, 157n25; "Reality and Its Shadow," 146, 158n27; "Substitution," 144–45; *Time and the Other*, 36, 129; *Totality and Infinity*, 6–7, 131, 157n25, 159n39
liberation. *See* freedom
linguistics. *See* language
literary criticism, 1, 6–7, 123, 150, 155–56nn4–5
literature: aesthetics of and pleasure from, 1–6, 126; as artwork, 66–67; canons and narratives of, 6, 14, 126, 146, 158n27, 162n74; contingencies in books and, 105, 107–8, 175n27; functions of authors in, 89, 157n22; language in, 94–95, 114–15, 174n12; singularity and specificity of, 2, 10–11, 13, 18–19, 160n46, 160n48;

208

unruliness of hermenuetics for, 2, 10–11, 14–15, 18, 44–45, 64, 151–53; unthought of, 4, 156n14
lithographs, 71–72
logic: of humanism, 100–101; illogic of, 26, 100; regarding interpretations, 157n23, 159n36; of men, 134–35, 147, 181n45; regarding the Other, 8–9, 33, 160n46; resistance to, 101, 182n53; of signatures and countersignatures, 174n8
logocentrism. See *logos*
logos, 53, 55, 101–2, 106
love, 57–58, 63, 78, 80, 81, 84, 161n56
Love's Knowledge (Nussbaum), 150, 156n5
Lui ("He"), 15–16, 43, 47–48, 49–52, 53–59, 63–64, 169nn34–35. See also nephews

madness, 53–59, 60–62, 74, 76, 130–31, 138–39, 168n23, 168–69nn25–27
Manet, Édouard, 82, 173n28
mastery, 6, 27–28, 45, 61–62, 64, 102, 119–20
Mathieu-Castellani, Gisèle, 166n41
meals, 46, 47–48, 49–50, 57, 167n8. See also hunger
Melehy, Hassan, 166n48
Meltzer, François, 172n20
men, 18, 120, 129–37, 145–47, 180n31, 181n39, 181n45. See also Hold, Jacques; husbands; nephews
metaphors: acts of short-circuiting as, 4, 105, 156n15; about digestion and cannibalism, 34–35, 40, 165n40; ducks vs. rabbits as, 25, 26; language of, 94–95, 102–8; about literature and prose poems, 14, 73, 162n72; about the Said and "eating well," 10, 160n45, 160n47; seats vs. donkeys as, 102–3, 104–5; serpents as, 73, 104; about translations, 66–67

Miller, Paul Allen, 165n35
Milner, Max, 172n21
mind-and-body problem, 15–16, 43–64, 166n2
models: for acts of reading, 2–7, 123–28, 152–53, 161n52; regarding alterity and otherness, 35–36, 39–40, 179n5; for colonialism, 113–14; for ethics of difference, 7–14, 130; for hermeneutics, 33, 156n15, 180–81n37; for humanism, 100–101, 175n31; for interpretation, 123–28, 152–53, 156n15, 160–61n52; of violence, 80–81, 83–85
modernism. See Baudelaire, Charles; modernity
"Modernism and Its Repressed" (Jameson), 113, 126
modernité. See modernity
modernity, 16–17, 65–66, 68–73, 82, 85, 111, 168n25, 173n28. See also Baudelaire, Charles; unruliness
Moi ("I"): dialogues with, 15–16, 43, 49–52, 53–59, 63–64, 167n7; monologues and self-dialogues by, 45–47, 59–61; as narrator and philosopher, 46–47, 52, 168n20, 169n29; perspectives and views of, 53–54, 61; sovereignty of, 52, 168n18; voice of, 59, 167n7
monologues, 45–47, 59–61
monsters, 27–28, 35–38, 45, 49, 166n43
monstrosities, 35–38, 166n45
Montaigne, Michel de: acts of essaying by, 15, 21–24, 27–28, 38; regarding acts of reading, 18, 163n13; acts of short-circuiting by, 32; humanism and, 24, 28, 30–31, 34–35, 164n15; imperfection and skepticism of, 15, 29–34, 165n33; regarding interpretations, 163–64n14; as philosopher, 31–34, 165n33, 165n37; rationalism and, 35–36; as reader, 163n12; and relationships with books, 22, 163n2

Montaigne, Michel de, works of: *The Essays*, 15, 21–41, 163n1, 163n5, 163–64nn12–14, 164n29, 166n45
morality, 56–57, 63, 74–77, 80–82, 83. *See also* ethics
Morrissette, Bruce, 112, 117–18
Mortier, Roland, 166n1
mothers, 78, 80, 81, 84, 173n29
Mudville. *See* Bouville
Murphy, Steve, 173–74n32
music. *See* songs
mutilation, 97
mysteries, 129–30, 181n42
mystification, 74, 157n22, 169n29, 172n19

Nadja (Breton), 130–31
Nagel, Thomas, 36
narcissism, 5–6, 31–33, 45, 82, 140, 143–44. *See also* egocentrism
narratives: implied authors in, 156n7; as literature, 6, 126, 146, 158n27; by men, 18, 130–31, 133–34, 136–37, 145, 181n39; resistance to, 94–96, 121–22; voices in, 114, 123. *See also* Baudelaire, Charles; Duras, Marguerite; Robbe-Grillet, Alain; Sartre, Jean-Paul
narrators: regarding charity, 75, 171–72n19; and *cogito*, 54, 55; dialogues and monologues with, 45–49, 60–61, 167n7; and glaziers, 73–77, 172n19; husbands as, 112, 114, 117–22, 124–25, 126, 127, 176–77n12; identities of, 114, 174n3, 176n12; interpretations by, 60–61, 62, 63, 170n39, 170n45; Jacques Hold as, 131–47, 182n53; morality of, 74–76, 81–82, 83; painters as, 78–84; poets as, 77–78, 83, 172–73n23, 173n29; realism and, 111, 176n2; relationships between readers and, 117–18, 137, 138, 140–41; voices of, 59, 114, 167n7, 172n23. *See also Moi* ("I")

naturalism, 37–41
nausea, 90, 97, 106, 120
Nausea (Sartre), 17, 87–109, 120–21, 174n3, 174n11, 175n27, 176n34, 176n38
Negative Dialectics (Adorno), 149
Neoplatonism, 34, 165n35
nephews: acts of short-circuiting by, 52, 58; animality and morality of, 48, 56–57; appearance and behaviors of, 46–48, 51–53; consciousness and contradictions of, 50–53, 167n16; as evil genius, 54, 58–59; friendships and relationships with, 45, 46–47, 49; hunger and meals of, 46, 47–48, 49–50, 57, 167n8; identity of, 49–50, 54, 59; interpretations by, 56–57; madness and skepticism of, 54–57, 60–62, 168n26; modernity and, 168n25; pantomimes of, 59–62, 170n39; self-interests of, 56–59, 169n33. *See also Lui* ("He")
Neto, José R. Maia, 29
new novels, 17–18, 111–12, 114–18, 120, 126, 176n3. *See also* Duras, Marguerite; Robbe-Grillet, Alain
Newton, Adam Zachary, 156n9
Nietzsche, Friedrich, 28, 32
nouveau roman. See new novels
The Novels of Robbe-Grillet (Morrissette), 112
Nussbaum, Martha C., 149–51, 156n5
Nussbaum, Martha C., works of: "Compassion and Terror," 149–51; *Love's Knowledge*, 150, 156n5; *Upheavals of Thought*, 151

objects: admiration and pity toward, 62–63; aesthetics and, 108, 126; anthropomorphism of, 104–5, 119–20; bodies as, 99–100; caricatures of, 71–72; desire and fascination for, 79, 119–21, 141; imitations and mimicries concerning, 29, 115–16, 134; interpretations and parallax gap concerning, 11–12, 160n52; of knowledge, 13, 33, 34–36, 39–40, 143; perceptions and visions regarding, 87, 90–91, 106–7, 116, 118–21; violence toward, 76, 80–81, 84–85, 99–100; women as, 129–30. *See also* children; nephews; Stein, Lol

obsessions. *See* jealousy

"Of a Monstrous Child" (Montaigne), 35–41

"Of Cato the Younger" (Montaigne), 32–33

"Of Cripples" (Montaigne), 38–41

"Of Idleness" (Montaigne), 27, 45

"Of Repentance" (Montaigne), 27

"Of the Power of the Imagination" (Montaigne), 27–28

On the Equality of the Two Sexes (Poullain), 169n30

On the Genealogy of Morals (Nietzsche), 28

On Nietzsche (Bataille), 111

ontology, 8–11, 27–28, 39–40, 71, 105–6, 123, 148, 162n66

Oration and Dignity of Man (Pico della Mirandola), 28

"Order and Disorder in Film and Fiction" (Robbe-Grillet), 111, 124, 127, 179n39

the Other: aesthetics and pleasure regarding, 78–79; alterity of, 79, 143–44, 181n42; as events, 152; Lol Stein as, 131, 138–39; narrators and, 45–49, 61, 63; otherness and, 6–9, 33, 35, 61, 63, 149–53, 160n46; and relationship with self, 150–51; the Saying of, 6, 157n25; women as, 130. *See also* otherness

otherness, 6–9, 33, 35, 61–63, 65, 91–92, 127–28, 146, 149–53. *See also* alterity; difference; the Other

Otherwise than Being (Levinas), 9, 131, 157n25

Outside in the Teaching Machine (Spivak), 65

pain. *See* sufferings

The Painter of Modern Life (Baudelaire), 69–70, 78

painters, 66–69, 71, 78–84

paintings, 66–69, 71, 91

Panichi, Nicola, 164n27

pantomimes, 59–62, 170n39

paradoxes: in allegories, 36, 38; and contradictions, 50–53; concerning ethics, 65; hermeneutics and, 33, 152; concerning human sufferings, 69; about knowledge and logic, 33, 101, 134–35, 143–44, 145–46; concerning language and metaphors, 9–10, 95; in novels, 108–9, 132–33; regarding readers, 147

parallaxes, 11–12, 16, 26–34, 38, 64, 70–71, 152, 161n57

The Parallax View (Žižek), 4, 11–12, 156n14

paralysis, 19, 39, 63, 151, 169n28

parents, 173–74n32. *See also* fathers; mothers

parodies, 75–77, 88, 171n17

Parrottin, Rémy, 91–92

pathos. *See* pity; sympathies

perceptions, 87, 90–91, 106–7, 116, 118–21, 176n34

perfection, 28–32, 34, 165n35

persecution, 144–45

perspectives, 26–27, 35–36, 53–54, 61, 73, 163–64n14. *See also* hermeneutics; interpretations

phallocentrism. *See* feminist criticism

Phelan, James, 156n7

phenomenology, 17, 96–98, 116, 120, 176n34, 177n25

The Phenomenology of Spirit (Hegel), 50, 167–68n16
philosophe. See *Moi* ("I"); narrators
The Philosopher and His Poor (Rancière), 162n71
philosophers: Giovanni Pico della Mirandola as, 28; Hierocles as, 165n35; Michel de Montaigne as, 31–34, 165n33, 165n37; narrators and *Moi* as, 46–47, 52, 168n20, 169n29; Seneca as, 34, 165n40; Socrates as, 29, 34, 168n26, 177n27
philosophies: contingencies in, 105, 175n27; dialogues and, 43; of the Enlightenment, 16, 30, 62–63, 101, 168–69nn26–27, 169n29, 170n43; essays as, 24; existentialism as, 17, 88–89, 92, 96–98; madness and, 54–55, 168n23; naturalism as, 37–41; Neoplatonism as, 34, 165n35; phenomenology as, 17, 96–98, 116, 120, 176n34, 177n25; Pyrrhonianism as, 33–34; realism and verisimilitude as, 17, 97–98, 111–18, 120, 126, 133, 176n2; unruliness of, 15–16. See also theories
Pico della Mirandola, Giovanni, 28
Pippin, Robert, 164n27
"Pitié" (Jaucourt), 170n43
pity, 62–63, 170n43, 173n29
The Plague of Fantasies (Žižek), 1, 8
plantations, 113, 176–77n12
pleasure, 4–6, 44–45, 78–79, 157n20, 166n4. See also aesthetics
The Pleasure of the Text (Barthes), 4–5
poems. See prose poems; songs
poets, 77–79, 83, 172–73n23, 173n29
politics, 52–53, 172n21
the poor, 72, 73–84, 171n10, 171–72n19, 172n21, 173–74n32
portraits. See paintings
possession. See power
Poulet, Georges, 88

Poullain de la Barre, François, 169n30
poverty. See the poor
power: and control by husbands, 113, 118–22, 177n12; through identifications, 99–100; knowledge as, 12–13, 21, 33; through language and *logos*, 100–102, 105–6; of men, 130, 134–35; of minds, 164n29; and possession of the other, 62–64, 146; within societies, 52, 72, 98
Prendergast, Christopher, 95, 173n28
Prince, Gerald, 101
pronouns: "I" as, 44, 45, 61, 88, 99, 121, 144, 172n23, 174n3; "one" as, 150–51. See also *Moi* ("I"); nephews; voices
prose poems, 16, 68–69, 72, 73–85, 171n10, 171–72n19, 172n23, 173n29
Proust, Marcel, 177–78n35
psychoanalysis, 27–28, 132–37, 142–43, 179n12
"Psychoanalysis as Anti-Hermeneutics" (Laplanche), 143
psychophysics, 49, 167n12
Pujol, Stéphane, 48
pure ethics, 8–9, 35
Pyrrhonianism, 33–34

questions, 29, 34, 182n55

Rabelais, François, 44, 166n3
Rabinowitz, Peter J., 112
Racevskis, Karlis, 169n33
Rameau, Jean-François. See nephews
Rameau's Nephew (Diderot), 15–16, 43–64, 166n1, 167n12, 167–68n16
Rancière, Jacques, 162n71
raping, acts of, 99–100. See also ravishment
rapprochement, 8, 173n29, 181n43
rationalism, 35–36, 101
The Ravishing of Lol Stein (Duras), 18, 130–47, 179n12, 180n16, 181n45, 182n53
ravishment, 138, 141–42, 144–45. See also raping, acts of

reader-response criticism, 10–11, 157n23, 160n47. *See also* readers, interpretations by

readers: admiration by, 62–63; bourgeoisie as, 67–69, 170–71n3; consciousness of, 160n47; dedications to, 170–71n3; dialogues with, 137, 151, 157n23, 167n5, 170n45; double binds and, 3, 85, 153, 156n9; double visions and, 77, 172n20; *fantaisies* of, 5, 157n22; feminists and women as, 132–33, 147, 180n29; identifications with, 81, 117–18; interpellations by, 3, 5, 13, 137; interpretations by and perspectives of, 3–6, 10–15, 25–27, 64, 82–83, 108–9, 122–28, 160–61n52, 163n12; men as, 133–34; relationships with, 17, 117–18, 137, 138, 140; as specialists, 178n40; sympathies of, 16. *See also* reader-response criticism

reading, acts of: anachronisms and, 25–26; autonomy in, 6, 16–17; concerns for, 132, 160n51; as dialectic, 11–12, 83–84, 127, 151; double binds and, 3, 85, 153, 156n9; ethics regarding, 1–15, 123, 126–28, 149–53, 161–62n64; by feminists and psychoanalysts, 132–37, 147; ideologies concerning, 4, 11, 84–85, 127–28, 159–60n44, 178n39; interpretations and translations regarding, 13–14, 111–18, 122–23, 125–26, 147, 162n72, 177n25; models for, 2–7, 123–28, 152–53; the Other and, 35, 160n46; parallaxes and, 11–12, 26–27, 70–71, 152; as problem, 177n19; rereading and, 3–4, 159–60n44; unruliness in, 2–6, 10–15, 111–12, 115, 117, 149–53

realism, 17, 97–98, 111–18, 120, 126, 133, 176n2

reality, 97–98, 102–8, 116–17, 120–22, 158n32, 175n25, 175n27

"Reality and Its Shadow" (Levinas), 146, 158n27

the Real of Being, 8, 11–12, 105–6, 114–15, 120, 121. *See also* self

refutations. *See* debates

Regosin, Richard, 163n2

relationships: through acts of reading, 115–16, 117; with books, 22, 115, 163n2; between Jacques Hold and Lol Stein, 137, 143; through language, 105–6, 120; regarding mind-and-body problem, 15–16, 43–64, 166n2; with readers, 17, 117–18, 137, 138, 140–41; relation without relation as, 9, 12, 18, 33, 40–41, 117, 143, 152, 159n39, 161n56; between self and the Other, 150–51; singularity of literature and, 2, 18–19, 160n46; with world, 179. *See also* friendships

Remembrance of Things Past (Proust), 177–78n35

resistance, acts of, 32, 34–35, 94–101, 121–25, 146, 165n34, 182n53

Resistance to Theory (de Man), 165n34

The Rhetoric of Fiction (Booth), 156n7

Ricardou, Jean, 115–16

Ricoeur, Paul, 135–36

Rigolot, François, 25

Robbe-Grillet, Alain: regarding acts of reading, 115, 127, 178n39; acts of short-circuiting by, 122; concerning events, 176n3; concerning metaphors, 105; regarding new novels, 111–12, 176n3; realism and, 116–17, 176n2; Roland Barthes concerning, 116, 117, 120, 177n22, 177n27, 178n40

Robbe-Grillet, Alain, works of: *Jealousy*, 17, 111–28, 176–77n12, 177n19, 177n25, 178n35, 178n39; *For a New Novel*, 17, 111, 116, 176n2; "Order and Disorder in Film and Fiction," 111, 124, 127, 179n39, *Le Voyageur*, 177n27

Rollebon, Marquis de. *See* biographies
"The Rope" (Baudelaire), 77–84
ropes, 80, 173n29
Roquentin, Antoine: acts of resistance by, 94–101; as author, 92–94, 99, 109; consciousness and identity of, 88, 90–92, 94–100, 174n3, 174n11; diary of, 87–88, 94–96, 97; hypocrisies and paradoxes of, 95–96, 108; nausea of, 90, 97, 102, 106, 120; usage of language and metaphors by, 102–8, 175n31
Rousseau, G. S., 166n2
Rue Transnonain (Daumier), 71–72

the Said, 9–10, 39–40, 123–24, 131, 132–37, 147, 161n53
Saint-Amand, Pierre, 170n36
Saint Paul (Badiou), 13
Salon of 1846 (Baudelaire), 66–67, 170–71n3
the Same, 7, 90–92, 115, 130, 174n10
sameness. *See* the Same
Sanyal, Debarati, 173n29
Sartre, Jean-Paul, 17, 88–89
Sartre, Jean-Paul, works of: *Being and Nothingness*, 96, 106; *Nausea*, 17, 87–109, 120–21, 176n38; *What is Literature?*, 176n3; *Witness to My Life*, 89; *The Words*, 17, 89, 108
satire, 71–72
the Saying: analogies about, 9–10, 159n43; and acts of *unsaying and resaying*, 9–10, 123–24, 131, 136, 147, 161n53; of Jacques Hold, 138–47; of Lol Stein, 132–37, 180–81n37; of Marguerite Duras, 132–37, 180n37; of the Other, 6, 157n25
Schrift, Alan D., 159n36
Scott, Maria C., 76, 172–73n23
The Second Sex (Beauvoir), 129–30
self: aesthetics and pleasure regarding, 78–79, 108; dialogues with, 45–47, 59–61; interests of, 56–59, 169n33;

knowledge and understanding of, 12–13, 21, 29, 31, 38, 56, 101, 150–51; love of, 57–58, 63; mastery of, 6, 27–28, 45, 61–62; perfection of, 28–32, 34, 165n35; reinvention of, 99–100; and relationship with the Other, 150–51. *See also* the Real of Being
Self-Taught Man, 100–101, 175n31
Seneca, 34, 165n40
sexuality: differences regarding, 125–26, 129–31, 136–37, 145–47; identifications and identities regarding, 99–100, 134, 180n29; jealousy regarding, 119–20; unruliness of, 27–28, 45, 130
Shea, Louisa, 59
Shields, Rob, 173n25
short-circuiting, acts of: acts of reading and, 4, 152; by Alain Robbe-Grillet, 122; through dialogues, 64; as metaphors, 4, 105, 156n15; by Michel de Montaigne, 32; by nephew, 52, 58; in new novels, 122; of the Said, 131
signatures and countersignatures, 89, 174n8
Sikka, Sonia, 179n5
Silverman, Kaja, 117
Simek, Nicole, 170–71n3
The Singularity of Literature (Attridge), 2–3, 123, 127, 160n46, 166n4
skepticism, 15, 32–34, 54–57, 60–62, 152–53, 155n5, 168n26
Smock, Ann, 157n25
Smyth, Edmund J., 176n2
societies, 47, 49–53, 72, 89–92, 95–96, 98–99, 162n71, 170–71n3. *See also* allegories, about children and monsters
Socrates, 29, 34, 168n26, 177n27
Some French Caricaturists (Baudelaire), 71
"The Song of the Glazier" (Houssaye), 74–76
songs, 106, 124–27, 178n47

The Space of Literature (Blanchot), 118–19
This Sex Which Is Not One (Irigaray), 130
speech. *See* language
Spink, John S., 170n43
spirituality, 76–77. *See also* God
Spivak, Gayatri Chakravorty, 9, 65
The Spleen of Paris (Baudelaire), 16–17, 72–85, 171nn12–13, 172–73n23
status. *See* classes
Stein, Lol: abandonment and ravishment of, 138, 141–42, 145; breakdown and madness of, 138–39; death and silence of, 141–42; as enigma, 143–45, 182n53; identifications with and identities of, 132–33, 136, 138–39, 181n45; knowledge of, 141, 143, 145–47; as the Other, 131, 138–39; as the Saying, 132–37, 180–81n37; as subject, 132–35
strangeness, 67–68, 70–71
strollers, 78–79, 173nn24–25
subjects: bourgeoisie as, 71, 91–92, 96; *cogito* and, 168–69n27; desires and fascinations of, 113, 118–22; in events, 7–8, 11–13, 158–59n32; humanity and women as, 67–71, 133–34, 165n37; husbands and men as, 113, 129, 130, 180n31; Jacques Hold as, 135–36, 141; language and *logos* regarding, 101–2, 115, 157n25; Lol Stein as, 132–35; paradoxes about, 132–33; and relation without relation, 9, 40–41, 143, 161n56; resistance concerning, 98–101. *See also* nephews
subject supposed to know, 145, 181–82n48
sublimation, 59–64
"Substitution" (Levinas), 144–45
sufferings, 66–69, 71, 76, 149
suicides. *See* deaths
Suleiman, Susan Rubin, 145
superego, 157n20
Symbolic Order, 8, 10–11, 130
sympathies, 16

synecdoches, 48
S/Z (Barthes), 159–60n44

"Text and Interpretation" (Gadamer), 151
theism. *See* God; spirituality
theories: feminist criticism as, 18, 56, 129–37, 147, 179n12, 179nn4–5, 180n37; historicism as, 24–27, 70–71, 77, 93–94; ideologies and unruliness concerning, 18, 21, 152–53, 155–56n5; psychoanalysis as, 27–28, 132–37, 142–43, 179n12; reader-response criticism as, 10–11, 157n23, 160n47; resistance to, 32, 165n34. *See also* philosophies
Todorov, Tzvetan, 30–31
Totality and Infinity (Levinas), 6–7, 131, 157n25, 159n39
translations: for artwork, 16, 66–69, 73, 82, 85; double meanings for, 18, 30–31, 162n79; and interpretations, 65–66, 82, 111–13; *Rameau's Nephew* as, 43, 166n1
trends. *See* turns
Trezise, Thomas, 159n43
truth, 7–8, 11–12, 47, 93–94, 150, 153, 158n31, 161n53; events of, 7–8, 11–12, 93–94, 158n31, 161n53; about societies, 47
tunes. *See* songs
turns, 1–2, 155n2
Twilight of the Idols (Nietzsche), 32

understanding. *See* knowledge
The Universal Exposition of 1855 (Baudelaire), 67
unreason. *See* madness
unruliness: in acts of reading, 2–6, 10–15, 111–12, 115, 117, 149–53; of admiration, 62–63; essays and, 15, 23–24, 27–28, 31, 38, 40; of fantasies, 5–6, 15, 45; feminist criticism and, 18, 130–31, 147; hermeneutics and, 2, 10–11, 14–15, 18, 44–45, 64, 151–53; of metaphors, 105; of new novels, 17–18, 111–12, 114–18;

unruliness (*cont.*)
    of philosophies, 15–16; of prose poems, 82–83; of sexuality, 27–28, 45, 130. *See also* modernity
The Use of Pleasure (Foucault), 5, 12, 24

Valences of the Dialectic (Jameson), 21, 152
values. *See* ethics; morality
vanity. *See* self, love of
Vartanian, Aram, 48–49
verisimilitude. *See* realism
The View From Nowhere (Nagel), 36
violence: rape as act of, 99–100; irony concerning behaviors and, 76–77, 83–85, 122; models of, 80–81, 83–85; mutilation as act of, 97; in prose poems, 73–85; ravishment as act of, 144–45; and self-perfection, 28
Violence (Žižek), 73, 80–81, 84
"Violence and Metaphysics" (Derrida), 8, 55, 129
visions. *See* double visions; experience; perceptions
visual arts. *See* artwork
voices, 114, 134, 136, 167n7, 172n23, 176n12, 180–81n37. *See also* pronouns

What Is Literature? (Sartre), 176n3
"Why How We Read Trumps What We Read" (Graff), 160n51

Wills, David, 162n79
Wolff, Janet, 156n6
women, 67–71, 129–30, 133–34, 136–37, 165n37, 180n29
wonder. *See* astonishment
words. *See* language
The Words (Sartre), 17, 89, 108
world, 35–38, 43–44, 53–54, 88–89, 102, 115–19, 175n22, 179
The Writing of the Disaster (Blanchot), 6, 9, 123, 157n25

Zalloua, Zahi, 164n15
Žižek, Slavoj: concerning ideological disidentifications, 98; interpretive agency and, 4, 156n15; parallax gap and, 11–12, 161n57; short-circuiting metaphor and, 4, 156n15; concerning truth-events, 8; regarding violence, 73, 80–81, 83, 84
Žižek, Slavoj, works of: *For They Know Not What They Do*, 157n20; *In Defense of Lost Causes*, 98; *How to Read Lacan*, 106; *Less Than Nothing*, 168n23; *Organs without Bodies*, 8; *The Parallax View*, 4, 11–12, 156n14; "'Philosophy Is Not a Dialogue,'" 43; *The Plague of Fantasies*, 1, 8; "A Plea for a Return to *Différance*," 161n57; *Violence*, 73, 80–81, 84

IN THE SYMPLOKĒ STUDIES IN
CONTEMPORARY THEORY SERIES

Enjoying What We Don't Have:
The Political Project of Psychoanalysis
Todd McGowan

Tragically Speaking: On the
Use and Abuse of Theory for Life
Kalliopi Nikolopoulou

Reading Unruly: Interpretation
and Its Ethical Demands
Zahi Zalloua

To order or obtain more information on
these or other University of Nebraska Press
titles, visit www.nebraskapress.unl.edu.

www.ingramcontent.com/pod-product-compliance
Lightning Source LLC
Chambersburg PA
CBHW030621230426
43661CB00053B/2096